OUTDOOR EDUCATION

Methods and Strategies

Ken Gilbertson

Timothy Bates

Terry McLaughlin

Alan Ewert

HUMAN
KINETICS

Library of Congress Cataloging-in-Publication Data

Outdoor education : methods and strategies / Ken Gilbertson . . . [et al.].
   p. cm.
 Includes bibliographical references and index.
 ISBN 0-7360-4709-3 (hard cover)
 1. Outdoor education. I. Gilbertson, Ken, 1954-
 LB1047.O985 2006
 371.38'4--dc22

                            2005012480

ISBN: 0-7360-4709-3

The Web addresses cited in this text were current as of May 2005, unless otherwise noted.

Acquisitions Editor: Gayle Kassing, PhD; **Developmental Editor:** Ray Vallese; **Assistant Editor:** Derek Campbell; **Copyeditor:** Alisha Jeddeloh; **Proofreader:** Joanna Hatzopoulos Portman; **Indexer:** Bobbi Swanson; **Permission Manager:** Dalene Reeder; **Graphic Designer:** Nancy Rasmus; **Graphic Artist:** Denise Lowry; **Photo Managers:** Dan Wendt and Sarah Ritz; **Cover Designer:** Keith Blomberg; **Photographer (cover):** H. Willson/Robertstock.com; **Photographer (interior):** © Eyewire/Photodisc/Getty Images (pp. 3, 43, 107, and 127), © Ira Estin (p. 15), © Wolf Ridge ELC (p. 27), © Photodisc Royalty-Free (pp. 59, 75, 85, 117, and 175), © University of Minnesota Duluth Outdoor Program (p. 137); **Art Manager:** Kelly Hendren; **Illustrator:** Mic Greenberg; **Printer:** Sheridan Books

We thank Wolf Ridge Environmental Learning Center for the use of photos on pages 27, 80, 113, and 155. Wolf Ridge Environmental Learning Center, 6282 Cranberry Road, Finland, MN 55603, 218-353-7414, www.wolf-ridge.org.

Printed in the United States of America   10 9 8 7 6 5 4 3 2 1

Human Kinetics
Web site: www.HumanKinetics.com

United States: Human Kinetics, P.O. Box 5076, Champaign, IL 61825-5076
800-747-4457
e-mail: humank@hkusa.com

Canada: Human Kinetics, 475 Devonshire Road Unit 100, Windsor, ON N8Y 2L5
800-465-7301 (in Canada only)
e-mail: orders@hkcanada.com

Europe: Human Kinetics, Stanningley, Leeds LS28 6AT, United Kingdom
+44 (0) 113 255 5665
e-mail: hk@hkeurope.com

Australia: Human Kinetics, 57A Price Avenue, Lower Mitcham, South Australia 5062
08 8277 1555
e-mail: liaw@hkaustralia.com

New Zealand: Human Kinetics, Division of Sports Distributors NZ Ltd., P.O. Box 300 226 Albany, North Shore City, Auckland
0064 9 448 1207
e-mail: info@humankinetics.co.nz

This book is dedicated to all the past, present, and future outdoor education instructors, for their diligence, efforts, and belief that what they are doing makes a difference in our world.

CONTENTS

Part III Methods and Delivery of Outdoor Education

PREFACE

In an expanding population that is growing ever more urbanized and technological, the call for effective educators who teach in and about the outdoors is steadily increasing. Accordingly, there is a need for educators who know *how* to teach in and about the outdoors. College students learning to be future outdoor educators as well as instructors in schools, parks, and nature centers have to be able to choose appropriate methods in a proper progression to meet a variety of student outcomes. Training in these skills is valuable to all who use the outdoors to teach.

When teaching courses in outdoor education methods we have worked with many different audiences. Invariably, we have found that there is a need for clear instruction on methods of delivery for teaching people with different expectations and skills. Most training programs and texts focus on methods and techniques that are primarily used indoors in a traditional classroom. This book focuses on methods and techniques that are unique to teaching in an outdoor setting. Teaching methods used outdoors are different. For example, logistics, weather conditions, physical comfort in the outdoors, and finding examples of the topic such as a plant or bird species are less controlled. Thus, using the best methodology to reach the audience is a valuable skill for any professional educator.

The Purpose of This Book

We have designed this book to help all educators who use the outdoors as a learning setting. The book presents clearly defined teaching methods for people who teach in a variety of organizations including schools, nature centers, adventure centers, camps, environmental learning centers, government agencies, and universities. These methods apply to many subject areas such as physical education, science education, environmental studies, and rec-

reation. You will be guided toward applying the correct method in the appropriate sequence at the developmental ability of the learner. This book will benefit any educator, new or veteran, in becoming more deliberate in provoking students' awareness, appreciation, and knowledge of the outdoors. Ultimately, we hope to advance your ability to increase people's enjoyment of the outdoors and their understanding of the environment.

Through this book, outdoor educators will learn how to establish optimal learning opportunities, how to design effective lessons, and how to identify and use the best methods for the place and the participants. This book will help you become an effective educator when teaching in, about, and for the outdoors. However, it is useful for any teacher in any setting. It is our hope that, no matter where you teach, you will become a more capable educator in the outdoors.

This book covers definitions of outdoor education, fundamental learning theories, professional expectations of the outdoor educator, how to structure a lesson, and an extensive set of educational methods and their best application to foster optimal learning. In addition, each chapter includes learning objectives, activities, and stories that will help you understand how to best apply the material.

Features

Features of this book include the following:

- Methods and strategies that have been tested in several different outdoor education settings, including residential environmental learning centers, university undergraduate and graduate courses, outdoor programs, nature centers, public schools, and park systems. They have been tested by the authors, who have over 90 years of combined outdoor education experience.

- Chapter objectives that focus what you will learn and summaries of the chapter's major topics.
- Sample lesson plans that will aid you in designing your own lessons by providing a model of effective instructional planning.

In addition, we have designed several tools to help you easily apply the knowledge and skills to your individual needs and educational setting:

- Case studies (Stories From Real Life)
- Thought-provoking questions (Explore Your World)
- Interactive exercises for applying concepts (Discover Outdoor Education)
- Ideas for refining your teaching methods (Tips and Techniques)

Organization

Outdoor Education: Methods and Strategies is divided into three parts. Part I covers the foundations of outdoor education. Chapter 1 focuses on defining outdoor education. You will discover that outdoor education is a blend of different disciplines and is supported by many theoretical foundations. From this underpinning, chapter 2 explains the components for professional practice in outdoor education and explores the associated responsibilities of professional conduct. Chapter 3 covers the theories that are the foundation of outdoor educational practice, including how people learn and the stages of learning.

Part II emphasizes the preparation that is necessary to teach an outdoor lesson. Chapter 4 focuses on understanding the audience complexities that influence learning in an outdoor setting. Chapter 5 helps you understand how to establish a learning environment and manage student behavior. You will be able to explore different options for what you can do when working with a group of students. This chapter is extensive and includes case studies to illustrate how student management works. Chapter 6 describes how to establish a productive learning environment, including details on site selection,

setup, learning barriers, and unique conditions. Chapter 7 discusses guidelines for designing and evaluating a lesson and providing materials that make the lesson more effective.

Part III provides detailed instructional methods and examples for delivering outdoor lessons. Categorizing methods into three discreet approaches is difficult and simplistic, and each lesson typically uses a variety of methods. Still, in our efforts to cover the range of methods, we have decided to use three primary categories or instructional approaches: hands, head, and heart (physical, cognitive, and emotional). With that understanding, we have arranged Part III in the following manner. Chapters 8 through 10 elaborate on specific methods of instruction. Each focuses on a different instructional approach, including using physical activity, imparting knowledge, and enhancing learning through emotion. Chapter 11 presents exemplary lesson plans that illustrate the methods presented in this book. Chapter 12, the epilogue, summarizes the concepts presented throughout this book. In addition, it presents a final model of the complete learning process in outdoor education.

The text is supported by two appendixes. Appendix A lists professional organizations, magazines, and Internet resources, and appendix B contains sample forms that you can adapt to meet your needs.

The Art and Science of Outdoor Education

Teaching in the outdoors is both an art and a science. It is an art because creativity and flexibility are needed to develop interesting and exciting activities in settings that can quickly change from clear and sunny to cold and rainy. It is a science because the best lessons and associated activities are well planned, are based on solid theory, use an assortment of methods, and have clearly determined outcomes. We hope that this book serves as a useful guide to help educators provide optimal learning for their students through nature.

ACKNOWLEDGMENTS

As in any major project, success is dependent upon the contributions, cooperation, and support by many people—some personal and some professional. We wish to acknowledge the following people in the process of writing this book:

First, and foremost, our spouses, who are patient in our absence, late nights, and many weekends working as outdoor educators and/or authors. Katie, Julie, Vern, and Alison—you are all tremendous! We also wish to acknowledge Gayle Kassing of Human Kinetics, who so patiently and skillfully guided this project into the other editors' hands. Gayle, as a front-line person and fellow educator, you are first-rate in seeing a project bloom and grow. To Ray Vallese, who is exceptionally talented at asking innocent questions. To Chase Hastings, for his cheerful administrative support. Finally, to each of our colleagues who are so fine to work with. Your miles of experience, talent as educators, and knowledge of our field in all its aspects have made this opportunity one of those rare gifts of why we do what we do.

PART I

Foundations of Outdoor Education

"My conclusion is that outdoor education is truly a powerful teaching tool; it holds much potential. Through 'doing', facing challenges, and stepping outside your comfort zone, learning certainly takes on a new dimension. More specifically, there are valuable (nearly priceless) lessons to be learned through facing challenges, stepping outside your comfort zone, assuming ownership, and working as or with leaders. With that in mind, outdoor education is an ideal catalyst for learning about these notions."

—Anna Schmidt

CHAPTER 1

Defining Outdoor Education

CHAPTER OBJECTIVES

By the end of the chapter, you should be able to do the following:

- Explain the role of outdoor education in learning about and through the outdoors.

- Describe characteristics of outdoor educators.

- Define outdoor education.

- Describe the history of outdoor education.

- Apply one of the models of outdoor education to your experience.

Whether people are discovering something new about nature, developing a skill, or simply learning how to be comfortable in the outdoors, they often experience a wide range of emotions. People experiencing the outdoors may feel everything from a sense of awe to a surge of exhilaration to a desire to protect a special place. Whether they have years of training or are experiencing the outdoors for the first time, many individuals come back from the outdoor environment rejuvenated in ways difficult to duplicate in other environments or situations (Kaplan and Kaplan 1989).

Sigurd Olson, renowned wilderness writer, often wrote of the human need to explore and experience natural places. According to Olson, as modern pressures such as technological advances increase, we become even further removed from the earth. He believed that the need for risk, adventure, and self-sufficiency are increasingly sought after because they are basic human needs that the outdoors provides (1984).

As interest in the outdoors continues to grow, in part due to the stress people experience in everyday life, so too grows the demand for instructors who are highly trained and competent in the outdoors. Professional training in a variety of dimensions is essential in order to provide a deliberate experience that is appropriate for the audience's needs and expectations.

All **outdoor education** requires a distinct set of skills and experiences that help define what kinds of professional expectations the instructor must prepare for. Students expect to receive a certain quality of experience, and they look to the instructor to provide that experience in a safe manner. It is this expectation of professional instruction that has helped determine what makes a professional outdoor educator.

Why the Outdoors?

Of all the characteristics that distinguish outdoor education from other types of education, the physical setting is often the most readily apparent. The very term *outdoor education* connotes a location distinctive from most educational settings. Using the outdoor environment as an educational location not only facilitates diverse learning opportunities, it also implies the use of specialized knowledge and skills. This chapter provides an overview of the historical use of the outdoors for education, development of physical skills, pedagogical manipulation of the physical environment, specific activities and theatrics, and initiative activities. The primary

goal of this chapter is to provide you with an idea of why the outdoors can be a highly effective place for learning and what skills and activities can help enhance that effectiveness.

Not surprisingly, the skill and art of teaching people about the outdoors has evolved into several different professions. Students can learn about the outdoors through a variety of methods or approaches. For example, a person visiting a state park learning about wildflower identification and natural history would be learning from an interpreter. A person visiting an environmental learning center to learn about the natural world and associated human influences would be receiving **environmental education.** A person learning how to become a rock climber would be participating in an **adventure education** program and be under the supervision of an adventure educator. All these approaches to learning about the outdoors are part of outdoor education (Hammerman, Hammerman, and Hammerman 2001; Priest 1986).

Over time, outdoor education has broadened from camping programs to include comprehensive delivery of knowledge and skills about the outdoors. For example, Priest (1986) described outdoor education as an umbrella that includes all forms of education about the outdoors. The umbrella of outdoor education covers adventure education and environmental education. Priest also recognized that student expectations for learning vary from seeking interpersonal growth to building social relationships. In addition, outdoor education includes building relationships with the earth through understanding the natural world and the place of humans within the natural world. For Priest, outdoor education is comprised of six primary points (1986, 13):

1. It is a method for learning.
2. It is experiential.
3. It takes place primarily outdoors.
4. It requires the use of all senses (it is holistic).
5. It is based upon interdisciplinary curricula.
6. It is about relationships involving people and natural resources.

Thus, within this context, outdoor education encompasses everything from scaling a major Himalayan peak, to taking school children outside the classroom for their learning, to bird watching out the bedroom window. Outdoor education has been described as a place (natural environment), a subject (ecological processes), and a reason (resource stewardship) for learning. It has been called a method

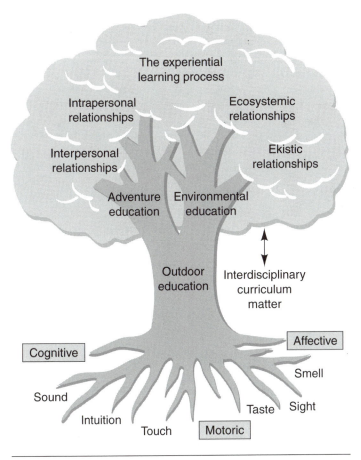

Priest's model of outdoor education.

Reprinted from S. Priest, 1988, "The ladder of environmental learning," *Journal of Adventure Education and Outdoor Leadership* 5(2): 23-25. By permission of the publisher and author.

(experiential), a process (sensory), and a topic (relationships) of learning (Priest 1990, 113).

From another perspective, outdoor education is a method of teaching and learning that emphasizes direct, multisensory experiences; takes place in the outdoor environment; and uses an integrated approach to learning by involving the natural, community, and individual environments. Through the use of the outdoors, outdoor education programs strive to elevate the physical, emotional, cognitive, social, and spiritual levels of the individual.

It is therefore the combination of learning in and through the natural world that defines outdoor education. Feeling the sun, wind, and rain, or seeing wild creatures, or filling one's senses with novel sounds and smells are new experiences for many people in today's urban society. While the outdoors provides for many sensory experiences, it is also a setting where a higher quality of learning can take place. Seeing a bison in a zoo will evoke different feelings from seeing a herd of bison grazing in a prairie with no fence between

you and them. Learning how to canoe in an indoor swimming pool is considerably different from learning how to canoe on a lake. Why? Because the outdoors allows people to experience nature while learning with others who have similar interests. In short, it provides a more complete learning experience.

Model of Outdoor Education

Outdoor education often focuses on three primary subject areas: ecological relationships, developing physical skills, and interpersonal relationships.

Ecological Relationships

It is valuable to understand at least a few concepts about the interactions of plants and animals, or the relationships that comprise ecology. Although learning about nature may not be the students' primary goal, learning some ecological concepts can enhance their overall experience.

The material covered will depend on the purpose of the class. For example, people who are kayaking on a river might simply learn how geological features affect the behavior of the river, while a person backpacking in the North Dakota Badlands who wants to learn which grass species are more nutritious at certain times of the year and how that influences bison grazing requires a greater depth of knowledge about prairie ecology.

Physical Skills Development

Outdoor education involves the development of a wide range of physical skills such as canoeing, hiking, camping, or horseback riding. For example, students who learn the basics of how to stay comfortable in the outdoors are better able to learn because their personal comfort has been addressed. On the other end of the spectrum, students may seek in-depth instruction to gain advanced skills in an activity such as white-water canoeing or ice climbing.

In addition, physical skills development involves much more than the obvious activities

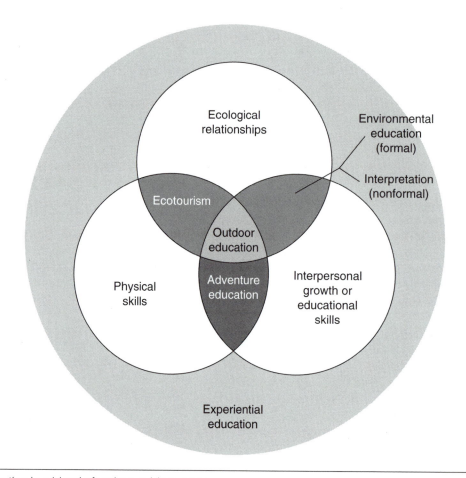

Outdoor education is a blend of various subject areas.

of canoeing, rock climbing, backpacking, or sea kayaking. It also includes learning how to use equipment. For example, students in a birding class must first learn how to operate the binoculars. If this basic skill is overlooked, the new birders will become frustrated because they miss out on sighting a passing bird. As they fumble with the binoculars they may simply give up trying to see any birds at all.

Interpersonal Growth

People pursuing outdoor education are not necessarily interested in learning about ecology or refining certain physical skills. Instead, they may be seeking to learn more about themselves and how they interact with those around them. This increase in self-awareness and insight is referred to as **interpersonal growth.**

The skills that an outdoor educator uses to foster interpersonal growth are similar to those that any educator uses. Consider the skills required to educate a group of people who don't know each other

and who will soon spend an extended period of time together learning about a certain subject. The outdoor educator has to challenge individual and group learning, build group cohesion, and achieve the goal of the lesson, all of which require specific skills in human relations. Thus, education skills and skills to teach interpersonal growth are very similar.

For many students and teachers, the preferred method of delivering outdoor education is direct experience. Direct experience is most often referred to as **experiential education.** In outdoor education, learning about the outdoors by being outdoors and experiencing the topic at hand is preferable to being indoors simply talking about the topic.

Environmental Education

Environmental education as a field developed quite abruptly. Over the years, many people such as author Henry David Thoreau, Sierra Club founder John Muir, and wildlife ecologist Aldo Leopold spoke of the need to protect the natural environment, but it was Wisconsin senator Gaylord Nelson who started the environmental education movement through the introduction of Earth Day on April 22, 1970.

At that time there was also a movement by educators throughout the United States who were beginning to define the concept of environmental education. William Stapp, a professor at the University of Wisconsin, and Robert Roth, a professor at Ohio State University, presented similar definitions of environmental education in 1969. Stapp's definition focuses more on environmental issues and the prevention or resolution of those issues, while Roth's definition emphasizes the need to appreciate nature and understand certain ecological principles.

Stapp's version continues to serve as the foundational definition of environmental education: "*Environmental education* is aimed at producing a citizenry that is *knowledgeable* concerning the biophysical environment and its associated problems, aware of *how* to help solve these problems, and *motivated* to work toward their solution" (Stapp 1969, 30). Roth (1969, 195) expanded on this definition in his doctoral dissertation: "Environmental education is the education about ecological concepts and their effects on humankind. Its purpose is to increase an understanding and appreciation toward the interaction of man and the natural environment."

Results from Roth's doctoral research led to five primary concepts to guide environmental education delivery toward an outcome of an **environmentally literate citizen:**

1. Living things are interdependent with one another and their environment.
2. Human beings have affected plant and animal succession and environmental processes.
3. The management of natural resources to meet the needs of successive generations demands long-range planning.
4. Safe waste disposal, including the reduction of harmful and cumulative effects of various solids, liquids, gases, radioactive wastes, and heat, is important if the well-being of human beings and the environment is to be preserved.
5. Environmental management involves the application of knowledge from many different disciplines.

Today there are several different definitions of environmental education. Hines, Hungerford, and Tomera (1986/87) define environmental education as learning that produces an **environmentally responsible citizenry.** While the predominant trend is to define environmental education as a means to prevent and solve environmental problems, other perspectives include environmental education as learning that increases awareness and appreciation of the natural world. In Europe this perspective is viewed as a "green" approach to environmental education, while the environmental problem perspective is viewed as a "gray" approach. Other concepts of environmental education include conservation education, which is a simplified form of science education, and environmental activism.

The National Environmental Education Advisory Council (NEEAC), which advises the Environmental Protection Agency (EPA), defines environmental education as the following: "Environmental education is a learning process that increases people's knowledge and awareness about the environment and associated challenges, develops the necessary skills and expertise to address these challenges, and fosters attitudes, motivations, and commitments to make informed decisions and take responsible action" (UNESCO 1978).

The different definitions of environmental education can seem confusing. However, there are some common themes that help guide the delivery of environmental education:

1. The outcome of environmental education is to increase awareness and appreciation of the natural world through increasing one's knowledge of the natural world.
2. Environmental education tends to focus more on environmental problem solving, and it is taught most often to formal school groups, grades kindergarten through 12.
3. It is not a form of science education, but it uses scientific concepts to teach about the natural world, preferably while being outdoors.

Because of the outdoor setting, environmental education tends to present sequential topics over a longer period of time, often measured in days or weeks. Environmental education is also presented in a manner that enhances critical-thinking skills. Students develop problem-solving skills that allow them to recognize and resolve environmental problems. A primary outcome of this approach is to build students' abilities to make informed decisions about their behavior toward the environment.

A common set of goals for environmental education is to build

- ecological awareness,
- environmental issues awareness,
- the ability to investigate and evaluate environmental issues, and
- action skills to help students become environmentally literate citizens.

Interpretation

Interpretation is the transference of natural or cultural history, obtained from technical researchers such as ecological scientists or historians, through an educational presentation to the general public. It is typically presented in a short time period (1/2 to 3 hours). While interpretation includes environmental education, it focuses more on awareness, appreciation, and knowledge of the natural environment or historical sites.

Freeman Tilden, author of several well-known works about national parks, explained the idea of interpretation. In *Interpreting Our Heritage* (1957), he defines interpretation as, "An educational activity which aims to reveal meanings and relationships through the use of original objects, by firsthand experience, and by illustrative media, rather than simply to communicate factual information" (8). Following are his six principles of interpretation:

1. If it doesn't relate, it is sterile.
2. Information is not interpretation (it is revelation based on information).
3. Interpretation is an art (any art is teachable).
4. The chief aim is provocation (not instruction).
5. It should present a whole concept.
6. It should be age appropriate (not a dilution of adult material).

Adventure Education

Adventure education is education that is conducted in a wilderness-like setting or through nature and physical skills development to promote interpersonal growth or enhance physical skills in outdoor pursuits. The agency most associated with adventure education is Outward Bound. While adventure education programs existed earlier, the establishment of the first Outward Bound school in Colorado in 1964 is considered to be the start of adventure education

Overcoming physical challenges in a wilderness setting can promote growth.

in the United States. Outward Bound's purpose is to teach self-awareness and self-confidence and to strengthen one's sense of community by facing physical challenges in a **wilderness setting.** By developing skills such as camping, canoeing, rock climbing, and navigation, individuals can enhance their interpersonal and intrapersonal skills.

Adventure education can be defined as, "A variety of self-initiated activities utilizing an interaction with the natural environment, that contain elements of real or apparent danger, in which the outcome, while uncertain, can be influenced by the participant and the circumstance" (Ewert 1989, 6). When students participate in a structured program that uses perceived risk to enhance and influence learning, they are participating in more than just an adventure experience, they are participating in adventure education.

Adventure education is used in many cases to teach physical skills that enable a person to travel through the natural environment. It is also used to promote personal growth.

Experiential Education

Experiential education is a method, a profession, and a philosophy, but in this book we will refer to it as a method. In *Experience and Education* (1938), philosopher and educational reformer John Dewey delineated the use of direct experience in education, or experiential education. Experiential learning is learning that occurs through an authentic experience. According to Dewey, it requires a great deal of planning, organization, and structure by the teacher. Experiential education is not merely having an experience in the outdoors, it is challenging and must follow rigorous scientific principles. The role of the teacher in experiential education is to ensure that the student is having an educational opportunity rather than a noneducative (having no effect on learning) or miseducative (learning incorrectly) learning experience. Since Dewey's writings, experiential education has become a field of study with an international following.

The Association for Experiential Education (AEE) is the international professional organization that guides experiential education. They define experiential education as "a philosophy and methodology in which educators purposefully engage with learners in direct experience and focused reflection in order to increase knowledge, develop skills, and clarify values."

Building on their definition, AEE further supports the practice of experiential education through 12 principles (the priority or order in which each professional places these principles may vary). They are:

- Experiential learning occurs when carefully chosen experiences are supported by reflection, critical analysis, and synthesis.

- Experiences are structured to require the learner to take initiative, make decisions, and be accountable for the results.

- Throughout the experiential learning process, the learner is actively engaged in posing questions, investigating, experimenting, being curious, solving problems, assuming responsibility, being creative, and constructing meaning.

- Learners are engaged intellectually, emotionally, socially, soulfully, and/or physically. This involvement produces a perception that the learning task is authentic.

- The results of the learning are personal and form the basis for future experience and learning.

- Relationships are developed and nurtured: learner to self, learner to others, and learner to the world at large.

- The educator and learner may experience success, failure, adventure, risk-taking, and uncertainty, since the outcomes of experience cannot be totally predicted.

- Opportunities are nurtured for learners and educators to explore and examine their own values.

- The educator's primary roles include setting suitable experiences, posing problems, setting boundaries, supporting learners, insuring physical and emotional safety, and facilitating the learning process.

- The educator recognizes and encourages spontaneous opportunities for learning.

- Educators strive to be aware of their biases, judgments, and pre-conceptions and how they influence the learner.

- The design of the learning experience includes the possibility to learn from natural consequences, mistakes, and successes.

Note: There is no single term that encompasses all the roles of the participant or of the professional within experiential education. Therefore, the term "learner" is meant to include student, client, trainee, participant, etc., and the term "educator" is meant to include therapist, facilitator, teacher, trainer, practitioner, counselor, etc.

As defined by the Association for Experiential Education (AEE). To participate in the ongoing conversation about what defines experiential education or for more information, log on to www.aee.org.

While none of the definitions of experiential education imply that the outdoors is necessary for experiential learning, it is often assumed that outdoor education and direct experience go hand in hand. This is a significant shift because the Association of Experiential Education began with a focus on the outdoors.

Education Structure

The structure of an education experience is often determined by the setting where the instruction takes place. The structure is quite important because it influences the purpose of the instruction, which influences audience type as well as intended outcomes. In this context, there are three predominant structures of outdoor education: nonformal, formal, and informal.

Nonformal Education

Nonformal education is structured, but the physical setting is outside of a formal school building, usually in a nature-based area such as a nature center, environmental learning center, state park, or wilderness area. Participation is typically voluntary (except in cases such as mandated alternative programs for adjudicated clients, or clients ordered to attend by a judge). The instructor presents a structured, sequential program and may or may not conduct an evaluation. When an evaluation occurs, it is rarely a requirement to proceed to another level unless the student is seeking some type of certification, such as wilderness first aid certification or canoe instructor certification. In these cases the student must meet a standard in order to attain the certification.

The quality of instruction in nonformal education is no less than that of any other setting. The primary differences are the setting and lack of evaluation.

Nonformal education is planned and structured, but the length of time students spend with their instructor is usually measured in days, rarely in weeks. The instructor can present a moderate depth of knowledge and skills and can follow a limited sequence of multiple topics. In addition, students have considerable choice in whether they wish to continue the lesson.

Formal Education

Formal education occurs within an organized school system. Most often this refers to the education that occurs in preschool through 12th grade. However, higher education certainly occurs in a formal education setting as well. The most significant aspect of formal education is that students must meet certain requirements before they can proceed to the next level. For example, students often have to pass an exam in order to complete a course or grade level. The physical setting of most formal education is a school building. This is the most structured educational setting, and it also involves the longest periods of time, commonly weeks or months. This is the setting where teachers can develop the strongest learning relationship with their students.

Informal Education

Informal education is entirely determined and controlled by the student. Students essentially teach themselves. For example, consider an individual who wants to refresh her rock-climbing skills. She goes to the local rock-climbing gym to practice her skills. She

© University of Minnesota Duluth Outdoor Program

Students can test their skills informally.

does not ask for any instruction, although a climbing instructor is available to provide advice if asked. The climber may be practicing some techniques that limit her success, but she is not aware of her limitations. Informal outdoor education often takes place in clubs and when friends learn from friends.

Informal learning can result in higher retention (Tamir 1990). It is believed that learning retention can be higher because of the extent of practice through trial and error. However, it can also result in poor technique or misinformation, and it can be difficult for an instructor to correct incorrect habits. Examples of informal education include following a self-guided nature trail and practicing kayaking skills during an open pool time.

Development of Outdoor Education

Although outdoor education is a relatively new kind of learning within formal education, it has a long and rich history. Its roots lie in a variety of academic traditions. For example, educational reformer John Amos Comenius (1592-1670) believed that children learned best through the use of their senses, and where better to experience this holistic learning than the outdoors? Likewise, philosopher Jean-Jacques Rousseau (1712-1778) and educational reformer Johann Heinrich Pestalozzi (1746-1827) both believed in the efficacy of direct experience.

One of the first outdoor education programs began in 1861, when Frederick William Gunn established the first organized camp, the Gunnery Camp for Boys. Mr. Gunn is the first teacher on record to provide outdoor camping experiences for children in the United States and is recognized as the father of organized camping. In 1880, the Reverend George L. Hinckley started the first church camp in the United States, where campers participated in activities such as boating, swimming, and fishing. Sumner F. Dudley established the first Young Men's Christian Association (YMCA) Camp in 1885. And in 1889, Dr. and Mrs. Luther Gulick developed the first organized camp for girls, and Dr. Gulick became the first president of the Camp Fire Girls in 1912.

One of the first advocates for outdoor education as we know it today was L.B. Sharp (1947), who stated, "That which ought and can best be taught inside the schoolrooms should there be taught, and that which can best be learned through experience dealing directly with native materials and life situations outside the school should there be learned." Rillo (1980) suggests that this statement represents Sharp's greatest contribution to the development of outdoor education—that knowledge that logically is best taught in an outdoor setting should be taught there.

Another notable advocate of using the outdoors as an educational setting was Julian Smith. For Smith, outdoor education included the complementing views of education *in* and *for* the outdoors (Carlson 1980). For advocates of this perspective, the outdoors is both a learning setting as well as an environment where a broad array of skills and knowledge can be taught and used. Brannan (2003) provides an excellent illustration of this approach. In this illustration, outdoor education activities can

Stories From Real Life: Adapting to Student Expectations

A group of middle-aged adults came to my canoe workshop more to learn about nature than how to do technically correct strokes, while I was excited to teach them how to snap the canoe into an eddy. They were expecting to gain a sense of wonder and knowledge of nature on calm water, while I was set to warm them up on an easy rapid. I wanted to teach the adventure of moving-water canoeing skills while they expected to have the lake shoreline interpreted to them. This discrepancy in expectations for outdoor education influenced both the techniques and methods I used while leading toward two distinct outcomes of learning. To teach the skills of an eddy turn, I needed a rapid with a large eddy. I had to focus on teaching distinct steps of the skill and techniques to focus on individual river features. On the other hand, to teach nature observation on calm water, I needed to use a different setting and teach skills of observation such as watching for movement or listening to certain sounds. You can see how each general outcome required different ways to teach with different kinds of learning results.

be useful methods for students to learn about the characteristics of water. Such activities include the following:

- Throwing objects such as stones across the stream or lake (topic: surface tension)
- Heating water over a campfire or backpacking stove (topic: thermal absorption qualities of water)
- Purifying water before drinking (topic: pathogens and water-borne illnesses)
- Evidence of dew on objects such as tents and cooking gear (topic: dew point and weather-related phenomena)

The idea of the outdoors as a place to learn, whether through direct experience, specific activities, or formal curricula, carries with it a long history of scholarship, reflection, and practice. In the next section, we explore how specific needs can be met through outdoor education.

Rationale for Teaching Outdoors

From a pedagogical perspective, any educational philosophy or method must meet the needs of a particular curriculum, whether it is part of an organized school system, private business, or not-for-profit organization. In other words, the setting and method of instruction must work in concert to fulfill the organization's educational mission.

The outdoors can be an effective venue for learners to develop an understanding of basic concepts. These basic concepts extend far beyond the acquisition of simple facts by including relationship building, values formation, and increasing sensitivity and awareness of the environment surrounding the individual.

Not surprisingly, compared to the traditional classroom approach there are a number of unique considerations associated with teaching in an outdoor setting. Some of these factors include the following:

- Taking students into the outdoors exposes them to potential hazards, such as risks associated with transportation and inclement weather or medical-related events.
- Teaching in the outdoors often requires certain skills on the part of the teacher. For example, field-based instructors need expertise in the subject they are teaching as well as in risk management, student assessment, and emergency response.
- Outdoor education often requires specialized equipment and materials.
- Outdoor teaching typically involves longer periods of time than is normally afforded in the typical classroom setting as well as externalities such as transportation expenses. Hence, there is often a need for extra time, effort, and expense in offering these types of opportunities.

Despite these concerns, outdoor education is particularly effective at addressing a number of educational needs (Hammerman, Hammerman, and Hammerman 2001). These needs include providing effective learning environments, understanding basic concepts, instilling real-life examples in the learning process, and developing student appreciation of and sensitivity to the natural environment.

Effective Learning Environments

Several authors point to the effectiveness of outdoor settings as locations for learning in the cognitive, factual, emotional, and spiritual domains. Some authors suggest that this effectiveness is enhanced because the learning is a transactive process in which the learners' interaction with the setting greatly facilitates learning and teaching (Beard and Wilson 2002). For example, observing a beaver fell a tree to build its dam is far more instructive than merely talking about how beavers build dams.

Others, such as Gair (1997), point out that education in natural settings encourages relationship

Explore Your World

Consider outdoor education and its different forms, such as adventure education, interpretation, or environmental education. Why are you teaching your topic to that particular audience in that particular setting? Are your expectations and preparation the same as theirs?

building; the development of new interests, skills, and personal abilities; and an understanding of the connection between theoretical and practical knowledge, attributes that are often overlooked in many traditional curricula. In addition, outdoor education provides for application and practice. For example, hiking in the desert enhances understanding of dehydration much better than a simple lecture in a temperature-controlled environment like a classroom.

Understanding Basic Concepts

Concepts present students with a road map to help them make sense of the world. In outdoor settings theoretical concepts can be matched with real-life examples. For example, the water cycle takes on more relevance if students have to follow a lightning drill in an afternoon thunderstorm or if they follow progressively larger streams as they flow into rivers. The outdoors is not only a venue in which students can learn facts about the natural environment, it is a venue in which students can investigate knowledge such as communication skills, personal responsibility, and ethical behavior.

Instilling Real-Life Examples

Raffan (1995) notes that direct experience through interaction with a natural landscape can provide a powerful set of learning connections: toponymic, narrative, experiential, and numinous. **Toponymic connections** result in understanding real-life settings from learning about the names of places and topographical features. For example, numerous peaks, rivers, and other features are named after a person or historical event. As a result, many of these features have an interesting story behind their name. This **narrative connection,** which may consist of stories and oral histories, often connects the students with the real-life example. Relative to the real world, the place becomes part of the physical understanding held by the learner through the stories about that place. In the **experiential connection,** students further their understanding of the real-life example by living it. They know it because they were actually there. This sense of place often creates a mystic or **numinous connection** that links the person with that particular place through the development of a spiritual bond.

Because of these four learning connections, knowledge learned through outdoor settings can often be far deeper and more personally meaningful than knowledge that is learned in a traditional classroom setting.

Appreciating the Natural Environment

It is widely understood that exposure to the outdoors helps foster an intrinsic interest in nature and an appreciation of the natural environment (Brannan 2003). Likewise, there can be little doubt that people place many different values on outdoor settings. Roston (1985) and Ewert (1990) posit that these values take on a broad array of meanings and ramifications. Such values include the following:

- Life-support—The natural environment provides human beings with basic and irreplaceable life-support systems such as water purification, oxygen production, and temperature control.

The outdoors helps people feel restored.

- Economic—Many people focus on the harvesting and commercialization of various components of the environment, such as timber harvesting, fishing, and mining.

- Recreational—Natural environments are valued for the multitude of recreational settings and opportunities they provide. The setting and the activity together often provide individuals with a powerful, personally meaningful recreational experience.

- Scientific—Wilderness settings have been valued by the scientific community because they represent baseline locations, or areas that have been less affected by humans, and as such can provide a standard from which to measure change in other locations. More recently, outdoor settings have provided training sites for a host of educational endeavors ranging from forestry to group processing of shared experiences. In addition, the outdoors and natural environment also provide a genetic pool of plants and animals that is useful both for scientific study and for its resiliency as a biodiverse area.

- Aesthetical and spiritual—Few would deny the aesthetic and spiritually uplifting qualities of the outdoors. Kaplan and Kaplan (1989) extend this notion by suggesting that the outdoor environment can also be a place where humans experience catharsis and restoration. In one sense, this reconnection with one's inner self resulting in a sense of restoration is perhaps the most valuable quality outdoor locations provide to contemporary society.

In 1968, Donaldson and Donaldson wrote, "Outdoor education is education *in, about,* and *for* the outdoors. Its *raison d' etre* is that 20th-century people have removed themselves from the land—and both they and the land are worse off for it!" (7).

Summary

Some people consider outdoor education subservient to environmental education. Others feel that it is nothing more than a school camping program. Rather than debate the hierarchy of the definitions of outdoor education, they should all be considered as tools to use at certain times with certain audiences to help them best learn about, in, and for the outdoors. A common theme of all the definitions is that through direct structured experience in the outdoors, people learn about nature, themselves, and their place in their community.

This chapter described the different aspects of outdoor education: environmental education, adventure education, interpretation, and experiential education. It also discussed outdoor education settings, including nonformal settings, or programs occurring outside of a school room; formal settings, or settings associated with school systems; and informal settings, or settings where people learn entirely on their own without structured guidance by an instructor.

Explore Your World

1. What type of outdoor education are you going to be providing?
   - Environmental education
   - Adventure education
   - Interpretation
   - Experiential education

2. What do your students expect from you?
   - Instruction to a single skill or brief topic
   - An in-depth course to learn a comprehensive skill
   - A full course to gain some type of license or certification

3. What setting are the students seeking?
   - Nonformal
   - Formal
   - Informal

Once you have considered these questions, you are ready to jump into lesson planning and the best methods for teaching outdoor education.

CHAPTER 2

Describing the Outdoor Educator

CHAPTER OBJECTIVES

By the end of the chapter, you should be able to do the following:

- Describe professionalism in outdoor education.

- Explain how to become a professional outdoor educator.

- Explain how to build your skills and knowledge.

- Describe your professional responsibilities in providing outdoor instruction.

A profession is an area of knowledge and skills that is unique. Outdoor education is considered a distinct profession because of its setting, audience types, and breadth of knowledge and skills required for instructors. Most professional outdoor educators start with a foundation of skills and knowledge in the subject matter. They develop and use effective techniques based on the needs of the audience and the setting, and they organize their time and plan their teaching appropriately. The quality of their lessons combined with the manner in which they present the lessons requires a high degree of skill and experience, or **professionalism.** Outdoor education professionals are innovative, hard working, and respected members of the community who promote exploration of the outdoors in a safe, educational manner.

One major aspect of outdoor education that sets it apart from other teaching professions is the setting in which it occurs. The outdoor classroom is often inconsistent and varies due to changes in weather conditions and changes in the site, and it offers many distractions to learners because there are so many things to look at. The professional instructor should be prepared to deal with whatever situation may arise. To be successful in any situation, good instructors must have training ranging from first aid to leadership to lesson planning. This chapter will explore the characteristics of a successful outdoor education professional, and it will discuss how to achieve the level of success that you desire.

Professionalism

What does it mean to be a professional? How is an outdoor education professional different from a professional in any other field? These are tough questions, and the road to professionalism takes time, thought, and perseverance. Where do you start on this path? Most people start by learning the subject or skill that they are going to teach in an outdoor setting.

Know Your Topic

An old adage is that if you want to learn something, teach it. That is not to say that you learn only through the actual act of teaching; you also learn through the preparation for teaching. It is crucial that the instructor of a given topic, whether it be the natural history of the white pine or basic rock climbing, have a full understanding of and background in the topic. What do a full understanding and background entail? Let's look at an example from cross-country skiing. If your task is to teach a group of high school students an introductory lesson on classic cross-country skiing, you will need an understanding of related terminology, the ability to perform the necessary skills at a level beyond the students, and the skill of analyzing students' skiing techniques and explaining to them what they are doing correctly and what they need to improve.

Your depth of knowledge on a specific topic may be determined by the students' needs. Advanced students need an instructor who has advanced skills and knowledge. Conversely, students who are looking for introductory skills or information do not need an advanced instructor. You need to match knowledge and skill with the level of the audience you are teaching.

Often the organization you work for will have guidelines or policies for the skills and knowledge they require for each type of instruction. These guidelines are often based on national standards and an accreditation process by a national or international organization. For example, wilderness first response certification is typically required by outdoor educa-

Stories From Real Life: Rookie Instructor Has an Effect

It was one of my first lessons teaching canoeing skills to adults. Boy, was I nervous! How could I, a college kid, teach these 30- and 40-year-olds? Maybe they had more life experience than I, but I had spent a fair amount of time developing the lesson, paddling on the river, and getting my canoeing instructor certification. And my supervisor boosted my confidence, telling me, "You will always have something to offer that will help them build their skills, even if they are expert paddlers already (which they aren't, or they wouldn't have signed up for the course)." When the lesson was over I had a whole new perspective. The participants learned a lot and gave great evaluations. They improved their skills and I learned that I can teach people who are older but less experienced than me.

Discover Outdoor Education

Go to appendix A and look up three different organizations that set standards for outdoor education. Describe their expectations for skills and knowledge of outdoor educators. Are they similar or different?

tion organizations for outdoor educators who lead groups into remote wilderness areas.

In general, you should be well prepared and have a solid understanding of what you are teaching. The type of program, lesson objectives, student expectations, and organization determine the depth of understanding you need.

Have the Skills

Just because you know how to do something doesn't mean you can do it. Outdoor education involves more than imparting knowledge through effective techniques, it involves helping others develop skills. To teach a skill, you need to be able perform the skill. Don't get caught in the trap that managers often unknowingly set by asking you to teach a skill you just learned. Teaching a skill is a science and an art that is based on experience in the skill. Experience is not the only aspect of teaching skills effectively, however. The competent instructor takes the time and energy to break the skill down into its components and determine how each component is performed. This helps you determine a proper sequence of skill

development, and it also helps you better coach the student toward skill understanding. Both skill and ability in the topic you are teaching are important, but teaching skills are also essential.

Over time, associations and large organizations develop industry standards. These industry standards are a recognized level of what amount of practice is necessary for teaching specific skills. For example, the National Park Service (NPS) has developed interpretive modules that help define effective interpretation in the parks. The American Canoe Association (ACA) has developed curricula that describe and define proper progressions of skills in several paddling disciplines (www.acanet.org). These are just two of the many organizations in outdoor education that help define industry standards. Standards are based on input from many seasoned instructors over time. Wise outdoor educators will participate in training provided by leading organizations in the industry to strengthen their skills and learn from the experience of others. See appendix A for more information on organizations that establish standards.

Students develop specific skills while cross-country skiing.

Stories From Real Life:

Experience Doesn't Equal Ability to Teach

The program was set for the instructor certification course in coastal kayaking. One participant was particularly vocal about how much he had paddled and how much he knew. As the instructor trainer, I actually was a bit intimidated. He surely had paddled a lot more than I and had explored all over the world. But once the course began, it was clear that he had not taken the time to break down each skill into understandable parts so that he could teach them in a clear progression to beginner paddlers. He left the course with a whole new world opened to him beyond just performing the skill.

Camp Realizes What They're Missing

A colleague happened to see the same camp staff training year after year on the river. The wilderness camp operated river trips to remote regions all over northern Canada. Yet they always seemed to be teaching outdated skills and techniques for safety and maneuvering in the river. Their attitude seemed to be, "It worked for us in the past, so it will work for us in the future."

My colleague, who was an instructor trainer in canoeing and had spent many summers traveling northern rivers, offered to conduct the next year's training. After a bit of cajoling and explanation of what would be taught, the camp agreed. The camp soon realized what they were missing. They had not been exposed to current techniques and methods for boat handling and safety techniques for river travel. Needless to say, the camp continues to this day to hire certified instructor trainers who are current in their knowledge and skill.

How do you develop the skills and knowledge to be an effective outdoor educator? Take classes, find a mentor, or learn on your own. Your learning style and ability to motivate yourself will determine which option is best for you. Many outdoor educators have developed most of their skills on their own. However, this is typically less efficient and more difficult than participating in programs like courses, workshops, or classes sponsored by qualified organizations.

Formal Instruction

Where you go depends on a number of factors. Remember industry standards? These should be the key criteria that you look for when seeking opportunities to build your skills and knowledge. Organizations should be following industry standards for training instructors. Universities, nature centers, extension services, outdoor centers, and so on all offer training opportunities that can help you learn about a specific topic. To find who is following industry standards, seek out national associations (see appendix A) and connect with member organizations.

Informal Instruction

Learning on your own falls into the category of informal learning. To build your skills and knowledge, certain resources are essential. Currently, the quickest and easiest resource is the Internet, although if you work at a remote camp, it may not be available or download rates may be very slow. Two pitfalls may await you when using the Internet. The first is the time it takes to actually find what you are looking for—sometimes if you are looking for obscure information, searching the Internet takes longer than picking up a book or asking an experienced person. The second pitfall is inaccurate information. Anyone can make a Web site stating their own opinions on the proper way to do things, so you need to make sure the information is from a reliable source.

Books and videos are also great resources. Libraries are a gold mine of information. Often the effort that goes into publishing a book or developing a video increases the likelihood that it is accurate, though not always. A good way to determine usefulness of resources is to see if they are referred to or endorsed by national organizations.

An effective educator knows to assess an activity's safety before plunging in.

When learning on your own, one of the most useful resources is people. People are the quickest and most effective resource in your quest to develop skills and knowledge. Most communities, no matter how small, have people with expertise in a variety of skills and knowledge. Use documented information to support what you learn from experienced individuals.

The trap that often occurs with informal learning, particularly when learning a skill, is that you learn the skill wrong. This means your technique is wrong, and if you go on to teach that skill, you end up teaching the skill wrong. Get sound information from reliable sources so your skills and knowledge are accurate.

Another necessity along the path to becoming a professional outdoor educator is access to ideas and lesson plans that will help you create your own lesson plans. It is likely that if you have an idea for a lesson, someone has already done some variation of that lesson already. With a few phone calls or Internet searches, you may find what you are looking for.

Discover Outdoor Education

Think of an area of outdoor education that you are particularly interested in, such as canoeing, bird watching, or rock climbing. Maybe you have already taught something in that area. Consider what you might teach a group of beginners. In what sequence, or progression, would you teach that topic? Now, look in appendix A for an organization that correlates with that area of outdoor education. Try to find a **lesson plan** developed by that organization for people with entry-level skills. Does your progression coincide with theirs? Where are the differences? At this point you may not understand why there is a difference, but remember that their progression is based on input from many individuals over time.

Explore Your World

You already have skills and knowledge about certain outdoor topics. Where did you learn them? Was your learning based on some type of industry standard?

You can learn a lot about people by observing. To understand the behaviors and abilities of people from different ages and backgrounds, seek out opportunities to observe other educators' lessons with different groups. Seek out teachers who will allow you to observe their classes. Find after-school recreation programs that will allow you to sit in. Observe adult and senior groups at a local nature center. The more opportunities you take advantage of, the more you will understand different groups and the more prepared you will be to teach them.

The North American Association for Environmental Education (NAAEE) has developed criteria for determining the usefulness and validity of written curricula and Internet-based information. Go to http://naaee.org for details.

Know Your Participants

Preparation for teaching must also include learning about the people you will be teaching. You will fail if you plan a lesson for college students and a group of 10-year-olds shows up. In outdoor education, groups are typically part of another organization or consist of individuals who have registered independently. Before a group arrives, get as much information about the participants as possible to help you structure the content and methods for the lesson.

In some programs, an outdoor education facility allows participants to simply show up without any type of registration. In these situations it is important to gather information from the students before the lesson begins. This can be done in two ways:

1. Informally ask them about their experience and background before the lesson begins.

2. Structure an opportunity for the students to demonstrate their skills, background, and expectations.

This will allow you to gain a better understanding of the students so that you can adapt the lesson to meet their needs.

The most accurate way to determine your students' skills is to incorporate a basic assessment into the beginning of your lesson. For example, if a group wants to learn advanced canoeing skills, set up an activity that allows you to observe whether or not they have already mastered the basic skills. This could be done through travel from one place to another in a canoe or a canoe game where paddlers need to perform different skills (see chapter 8 for more on games as a teaching method). This type of assessment goes beyond having the students describe what they can do to having them show what they can do.

An understanding of age is important for effective communication as an outdoor educator. An easy trap is to communicate and use references based only in the generation you grew up in. If your participants are from a different generation, their reference points and understanding of the

Stories From Real Life: Birding Assessment

To get an idea of where the students in a birding class were at with their skills for using binoculars and their bird book, I asked them to identify the bird on the top of the tree across the field. As I watched the students I could see that more than half were struggling to find the bird with their binoculars (even closing one eye to see better), and most went through the field guide page by page to find a bird that looked similar. I saw that I would need to teach them how to adjust the eyepieces of the binoculars and have them practice finding objects quickly. Then I would go through the organization of the field guide so the students could use it as an efficient tool.

Students in a birding class learn to use binoculars.

world around them will likely be different from yours. Thus, your ability to speak to different generations and use different terminology will increase your success. Avoid the use of slang words that may be interpreted differently from what you mean. How do you learn about other generations you will be working with? Experience is the best teacher. Interact with older and younger people, and read books about what others have been through in their lives. Chapter 4 has more information on this topic.

Professional Responsibilities

Each professional educator is part of a greater community of educators. Whatever you do is a reflection upon the profession; your actions prove to the greater community the quality of all outdoor educators. Make every effort to demonstrate quality in your organization of the program, your presentation, and your commitment. There are many aspects of professional responsibility, including program organization, personal presentation, and your role in the profession.

Planning and Organizing Lessons

Plan the work and work the plan. Planning and organizing your lesson and equipment are keys to success as a professional educator. It is your responsibility to work out the logistics for a lesson, ranging from where you will meet participants and whether they will all arrive at once to what will they do after you have made camp and dinner is done. See chapter 7 for information on how to develop and write the actual lesson plan.

Table 2.1 Professional Responsibilities of an Outdoor Educator

Knows the participants	Knows the topic	Has the skills
Cares about the students' learning	Understands ecological relationships	Proficient in general camping skills and in the specific skill being taught
Enjoys teaching	Understands skills progression	Able to adjust to varying conditions of the setting
Enjoys being outdoors	Fosters student learning	Follows Leave No Trace practices (see www.lnt.org)
Prepares thoroughly	Provides for risk management and emergency response	Selects appropriate equipment and technology
Has presentable appearance	Uses varied teaching methodology	Manages group progression and dynamics
Is interested in improving the field and knows where to find organizations that guide advances	Plans the lesson and communicates effectively with the audience	
Exhibits sound judgment		

Getting organized is vital to professionalism. You should include the following considerations when planning and organizing lessons.

Communicating With the Student

Communication with the student is a whole topic in itself, but we will hit on a few important points. It is essential that students are fully informed before participation and they understand what is expected of them. All too often, students come to an activity with expectations that are different from the instructor's. They also often show up with inappropriate equipment or clothing. For example, you might be prepared to lead participants through an edible wild-plant hike, but one student expects to receive an in-depth exploration of wild edible mushrooms, which you know little about. And, despite rainy conditions, another student arrives with no rain gear. Neither one is truly prepared.

Many problems can be avoided with clear communication early on. Before students show up, determine who will communicate with the student and what information both parties need. In addition, you must respond to student questions promptly and effectively so that they feel comfortable before coming into your activity.

Equipment

Proper equipment for the activity is essential to success. Substandard equipment that fits the customer poorly will set both you and the participant up for failure. Ask yourself if the equipment you have selected or that your organization supplies is functional and is of adequate quality. There are industry standards for equipment in different types of teaching situations. Seek out experts and national organizations to find out what is appropriate. For instance, aluminum canoes should not be a part of a white-water canoeing program because they lack maneuverability and tend to stick to rocks.

Here are some equipment questions to consider:

- Is the equipment where it needs to be?
- How will it be transported?
- Is there enough for everyone?
- Does it fit participants properly?
- Is it fully functional?

When participants bring their own equipment, it is your responsibility to check it to make sure it is functional. If it is not, you need to replace it.

Materials

As mentioned in chapter 1, educators need several techniques for getting information across to students. Materials are one way to add variety to your teaching and enhance learning. Materials are items that support or enhance your instruction, such as handouts, dry-erase boards, props, audio and visual equipment, and so on. These materials can create visuals for abstract concepts. They can also reinforce what you are teaching by clearly summarizing information, as in a handout. Most good lessons include some type of supporting materials.

Here are some sample materials:

- A picture that shows the changes a piece of land has gone through over a period of time

Stories From Real Life: Failure to Check Equipment

The leaders of a college orientation backpacking trip had the route planned for a remote hiking trail. They met with the participants the evening before the trip to see if anyone had any questions and to go over the equipment and itinerary. Everything seemed in order. On the morning of departure, everyone loaded their equipment into the trailer and headed up to the trailhead, but they forgot to check the equipment of the participants. Upon unloading the equipment, one of the participants shouldered her day pack, a small backpack designed to carry just enough gear for short outings, which she considered to be appropriate for a backpacking trip. It was much too small, so the rest of the group had to carry the additional burden of extra equipment (food, camp stove, and so on) that the day pack could not hold. The leaders surely learned their lesson to check the functionality of participants' equipment before leaving!

- A model kayak and flexible kayaker to demonstrate C-to-C motion or J-lean of the paddler's upper body
- A handout that summarizes the key points of using a compass
- A drawing on a portable dry-erase board that diagrams the water cycle
- Laminated cards that show the different knots used in climbing
- Twigs that exhibit alternate, opposite, and whorled branching patterns
- Bird calls on a tape, CD, or MP3 player for participants to learn the bird calls they hear in the forest

Site Knowledge

Learn as much as you can about the location where you will be teaching. Do not teach at a site you have never been to. Visit the site beforehand to ensure that you are aware of all opportunities, distractions, and hazards at the site. Ask the following questions when you are checking out a site:

- How will you organize the students to minimize distractions?
- What may cause problems in your lesson (wind, sun, rain, and so on)? How will you minimize their effects on your lesson?
- Are there restrooms? If not, you need to train participants on what to do if they need to go to the bathroom.
- What are the hazards of teaching at that site (see the following section)?

- How can you minimize your environmental or social impact on the site?

If you cannot check out your teaching site beforehand, get as much information as possible from someone who has been there. Ask the person the questions on the previous list and get additional input on topography and layout.

Risk Management

It is your responsibility as the instructor to ensure the safety of the participants. **Risk management** is the process before, during, and after a program that strives to reduce the likelihood of accidents and health-related incidents. You must create a risk-management plan for the teaching site. Most things that could go wrong can be prevented through proper planning. Try to think of everything that could possibly go wrong and then try to determine strategies that could prevent it. For example, hypothermia is a common risk in outdoor settings. Planning for extra clothing, educating participants on warning signs, and observing participants for warning signs can usually prevent hypothermia from going beyond the first stage. Remember, most participants in outdoor education assume that they will be somewhat safe from physical injury.

Personal Presentation

First impressions make a difference in the eyes of the participant. It is your responsibility to present yourself to the participants in such a way that shows you are a professional. Your dress should be professional (leave the faded, torn clothes at home),

An overdressed instructor can intimidate students who lack advanced equipment.

but not condescending (see Stories From Real Life: Overdressed Instructor). You should present yourself so that participants look up to you and realize that your skills and abilities are achievable.

Personal presentation also includes your appearance and how you take care of your body. Look the part and play the part. Groom yourself neatly and cleanly. Another aspect is sunglasses use. Some professionals don't use sunglasses when teaching because sunglasses create a barrier between the participants and instructor—eye contact is an important part of communication. Others see the value of sunglasses for eye protection. Take off sunglasses whenever they are unnecessary so that students can see your eyes. But keep them on in the sun—eye safety is more important than eye contact with participants.

Language and communication style are also important. Use language appropriate for the group. Avoid inappropriate jokes, condescending remarks, and slang. Over time you will learn how to read a group in order to determine what is appropriate or inappropriate, though this may take hours or even days of interaction. Initially,

keep your language clean and straightforward. You will begin to establish a style of teaching, and as you do so, seek a style that focuses on the students' development.

Here are some keys to positive first impressions:

- Dress appropriately for the activity and the group.

- Arrive early, no fewer than 15 minutes before a program.

- Start on time.

- Begin to develop a rapport with students as soon as you meet them. Learn about them and interact on a personal level.

- Communicate in a way that matches the group's needs.

- Set expectations of what the group will be doing, where and how far they will be going, and so on. Clarify rules, if necessary.

- Make sure everyone has the necessary equipment.

Stories From Real Life: Overdressed Instructor

The sea kayaking instructor showed up at the small inland lake to teach a course called Introduction to Sea Kayaking. After he handed out the wetsuits and basic life jackets to the students, he donned his Gore-Tex drysuit, neoprene beanie hat, and the latest life jacket, with VHF radio in the pocket, flares, whistle, compass, and hydration system, a clear contrast to what the students were using. Later on, he climbed into his new kevlar kayak while the students climbed into their plastic boats. As the day progressed, the students were amazed at how well the instructor could do the maneuvers in his high-performance boat, while they could hardly do any in their boat. They also were intimidated by going into the cold water, even though the instructor was floating in it all the time, because of his fancy equipment.

What was wrong with this situation? There was a gap between the students and the instructor. Yes, instructors need to be comfortable in whatever the conditions throw at them, but this instructor created a barrier. He should have dressed down a bit and worked more at the students' level, using similar equipment. Think of it this way: If you want to teach high-performance driving techniques, and you are in a high-performance sports car and the participants are in pickup trucks, there's going to be a problem.

Your Role in the Profession

Where do you want to go with outdoor education? What type of audience do you want to work with? What skill or knowledge do you want to teach? Where do you want to live? As you answer these questions, you can begin to focus on how to get where you want to be in the field of outdoor education. Work with professional organizations to understand what you need to do to be the best you can be. Now is the time to begin laying out the roadmap to your professional destination.

Summary

There are many aspects to being a professional outdoor educator, including knowing what you are going to teach, having the skills to teach your topic, understanding participants, being organized, communicating with participants, understanding the use of equipment and materials, knowing your site and its potential risks, and presenting yourself properly. Almost everyone has something to work on in one or more of these categories. Your job is to understand where you are at and set goals for improving your professionalism as an outdoor educator.

Explore Your World

Once you get into a community, start networking! Get on the phone and pound the pavement to let other outdoor educators know you are there as a resource for them and to find out about their skills. They are great resources for information about the area and have a wealth of knowledge. Learn who is a natural history interpreter, who teaches canoeing, who is certified to teach rock climbing, and so on. Working with other professionals increases the potential for quality outdoor education in your area. For example, if you are an interpreter and would like to offer interpretive canoe outings but you don't have the skills to provide a safe outing, call on local canoe instructors and solicit their help. Working with other professionals also increases the visibility of outdoor education opportunities, which leads to more participants.

One helpful networking trick is to write down each person's name in your contact information file and list their skills and abilities. This will help you figure out whom to contact when you need help in a certain area.

CHAPTER 3

Theories and Foundations in Outdoor Education

CHAPTER OBJECTIVES

By the end of the chapter, you should be able to do the following:

- Explain what theory is and how it can help in teaching outdoors.
- Describe the primary theories that relate to outdoor education.

Novice outdoor educators often question why they need to bother with theories of learning, behavior, and education. One student once exclaimed, "Why do I need to learn these? All I want to do is teach!" Her teacher answered, "It is through knowing the theories that I am able to teach with purpose and meaning. The theories guide me on what and how to teach."

In this chapter, you will become familiar with learning theories that provide basic principles for teaching outdoor education. While many theories can be used to help you understand how and why outdoor education can effective, this chapter presents the theories that are germane to understanding how, why, and when you teach. The theories will help answer the following questions:

- How do you know you are teaching the correct topic?
- Why does a technique help students overcome their barrier to learning?
- Why does one person learn one way and one person learn another way?

The theories covered in this chapter include the following:

- Constructivism
- Developmental stages of environmental learning
- Personal meaning
- Experiential education
- Multiple intelligences
- Learning styles

As you read about these theories, try to imagine how they might be used in different settings or forms of outdoor education. For example, experiential education is often associated with adventure education. However, it is equally valuable in any other form of outdoor education. For that reason, none of the theories are associated with any single component of outdoor education. Further, direct experience is used as much as possible in outdoor education. You should assume that experiential education as a method for teaching about the outdoors will be used in the lessons discussed in this book regardless of the lesson setting or form.

Theories in Outdoor Education

Your teaching should be guided by an understanding of the theories behind the practice. A **theory** is an explanation of a pattern of behavior that is consistent and reliable, or mostly predictable in that it will result from deliberate effort. To be able to identify a pattern of behavior, the behavior must be systematically studied to ensure that what we think we are observing is actually occurring (Kerlinger 1986).

The more a theory is tested, the stronger it will be. Conversely, a new or emerging theory that has not yet been studied extensively is considered to be a weaker theory. A theory is not the same thing as a personal opinion. A personal opinion is a belief or value system of an individual or a group of individuals. A behavior explained by opinion will shift with a difference of opinion, whereas a theory describes a pattern of behavior regardless of one's values or beliefs.

Some theories are developmental, or explain the stages of development a person goes through, such as age or skills acquisition. Development can also be related to a stage a person goes through in learning, such as novice, intermediate, or advanced. **Developmental theories** can be related to age, such as what age is best for learning complex skills that require strength and muscle coordina-

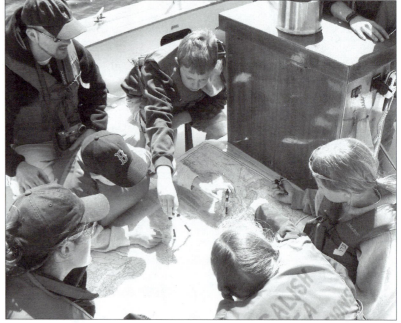

Photo courtesy of Salish Sea Expeditions.

Students at sea construct new learning through experience.

tion. They can also help explain what sequence is best for attaining complex skills. For instance, what sequence and skills in beginning rock climbing are best taught to adults versus 12-year-old children? What preexisting experience or skills are required before teaching advanced rock-climbing skills? Some developmental theories address cognitive, or knowledge, abilities, while others describe a sociopsychological influence or process. Still others refer to the relationship between physical abilities and age—for example, it is difficult to teach the use of binoculars to a child younger than 8 or 9 due to the manual dexterity required to manipulate the instrument. Finally, developmental theories usually include aspects of individual development that explain why or how a student learns or behaves.

Constructivism

The first developmental theory we will discuss, **constructivism,** is one of the most-used theories in contemporary education, including outdoor education. This theory's central theme is building on students' prior knowledge and experience to help them to construct new learning. John Dewey (1938), one of the most famous advocates of modern education theory and philosophy, was instrumental in the development of constructivism.

You have likely heard the old adage, "Is the glass half full, or is it half empty?" This is the central idea of constructivism. This approach to education assumes that students are empty vessels that the instructor needs to "fill" with knowledge, skills, and experience. Constructivism tends toward telling the student how to think or behave, and it can easily lead toward preaching.

The constructivist approach to learning claims that a student comes to a class with a wealth of knowledge, skills, and experience, all of which form the student's perceptions. Thus, this theory sees the glass as half full. The teacher's role is to determine what the student knows and then to build on the existing knowledge and experience to further the student's learning.

In constructivism, to make the lesson relevant, consider the following principles:

- Preconceptions matter.
- Make it relevant.
- Teach concepts, not facts.
- Create a challenge.
- Direct experience is important.

Preconceptions Matter

Take the time to discern student perceptions about the topic before you begin the lesson. It is best to know these preconceptions before you write your lesson plan. Don't dismiss the students' concerns because of your own familiarity with the topic. For example, a common fear for novices in a wilderness area is to think that snakes are hiding everywhere, waiting to attack. It is easy for a veteran instructor to simply pass this fear off with a laugh and a comment like, "Oh, don't worry! They won't hurt you!" Instead, stop and ask the students what they know about snakes or the area they're in. Spend some time acknowledging their concerns and explaining what they can expect to encounter and ways they can safeguard themselves.

Make It Relevant

Use examples that your students can relate to so that they can understand in their own terms what the lesson is about. An example of relevance can be seen in a lesson on body rotation in white-water kayaking. After telling students to "rotate their torso," an instructor might use the idea of twisting the lid off a peanut butter jar to illustrate the concept of twisting both the top and the bottom, but in opposite directions. Then the instructor could say, "Now apply this concept to your upper and lower torso in executing a turn." The instruction becomes relevant for the students because they can visualize twisting the lid off the jar and apply that visualization to their body.

Teach Concepts

Use facts to support concepts. Too often an instructor lists a string of facts to make a point. The students are wowed by all the knowledge the instructor has, but they have a hard time remembering the facts. Teaching facts requires learning through rote memorization. While this is legitimate for some learning, such as reading or fundamentals of math, much research has shown that students retain the lesson longer and use it more when they learn the concepts supporting the topic. For example, the concept of executing a turn in a kayak is to use the upper torso for strength and power while using the lower torso for stability, lean, and direction. Using both the upper and lower torso results in a more controlled, powerful turn. If students are simply told, "Put your paddle here and lean this way," they may be able to physically do it, but they haven't learned the turn well.

Create a Challenge

Preconceptions are symptoms of "frozen" thought, or fixed points of view. Challenging a student can help create dissonance, or discomfort, which can be a catalyst to "unfreeze" the students' preconceptions so that they can move forward in their learning. No matter what is being taught, a certain level of discomfort can lead to change. For example, it is easy for a person to see a task that is unfamiliar, such as climbing a certain cliff, and exclaim, "Oh, I could never do that!" It is a real joy in teaching to hear that same student exclaim, "I did it!" after completing the climb.

In this example, you should strive to provide a concrete set of steps to guide students in the climb, such as learning knots, then learning how to put on the safety equipment, then practicing with the equipment while on the ground. In addition, you should provide a supportive learning environment. Do not lose awareness, however, of the discomfort and anxiety that students often experience in the outdoors. Provide students with techniques and knowledge to deal with such discomfort and anxiety.

By acknowledging preconceptions and by sequentially building skills and knowledge in a physically and psychologically safe learning environment, you are providing a supportive learning environment. A supportive learning environment that includes safe procedures and discourages ridicule or peer pressure fosters learning. This approach creates a setting where students meet a challenge more easily because of the support they receive.

Use Direct Experience

Providing as much direct experience as is reasonable allows students to apply their new knowledge and skill to their previous learning. This helps create a restructuring of thought into a new frame of mind, which can be called learning. This restructuring of thought is illustrated by the five stages identified by Kolb (1984) in the figure below. By combining these steps, you are structuring a student-centered learning environment that builds on the learners' prior knowledge to create new knowledge.

Developmental Stages of Environmental Learning

The next theory builds upon constructivism. There are two parts to this theory. Part 1, developmental stages of environmental learning, is what the student experiences. Part 2, teaching stages of environmental learning, refers to the stages, or sequence, a teacher follows to foster the development of environmental literacy.

In many outdoor education programs, an important goal is **environmental literacy,** or the ability to understand the outdoors at a level where you

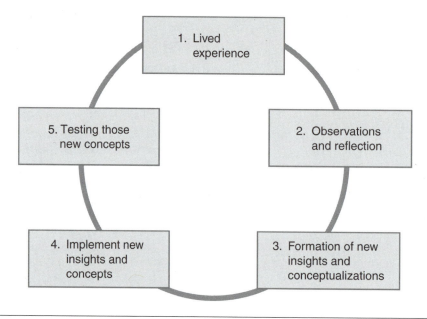

Kolb's theory of the restructuring of thought.

Adapted from D.A. Kolb, 1984, *Experiential learning,* (Englewood Cliffs, NJ: Prentice-Hall).

Explore Your World

Consider students who are learning about birds. First they learn fundamental observation skills of shape and color, and then they learn flight patterns. Next they combine shape, color, and flight patterns to notice where the bird is found (e.g., forest, meadow, water). Now they are able to identify birds in the area. Once they have learned to identify birds in the area, they are better able to identify unfamiliar birds in different regions.

are able to move comfortably in the outdoors and understand the intricacies that nature has to offer. Some of those intricacies might be related to physical skills, or they might be based in ecology, or they might be related to the ability to comfortably camp as if you were living at home. Living in, traveling through, and understanding ecological relationships demands a literacy of the natural world.

Part 1: Developmental Stages of Environmental Learning

A theory of developmental stages of environmental learning explains the stages a person goes through to become environmentally literate. These stages are less dependent on age than on experience and skill. In other words, a person can be literate in their home region but will need to become further

educated when they travel to a new area where they are unfamiliar with the environment and its flora and fauna. The speed at which individuals move through these stages depends on the extent of their skills and experience in the outdoors as well as the depth of their existing environmental knowledge.

There are four stages to environmental literacy:

- Stage 1: Survival
- Stage 2: Physical skills acquisition
- Stage 3: Relationships with the land and its inhabitants
- Stage 4: Metaphysical

When learning a subject, the goal is for the learners to attain literacy, or reach a level of understanding and skill where they can apply what they have

Stories From Real Life: From Lakes to Desert

I was asked to join a friend to spend 3 weeks backpacking through the Baja Peninsula of Mexico. I had lived my entire life in northern Minnesota, and my experience in canoeing the Boundary Waters Canoe Area Wilderness (BWCAW) extended over 30 years. I had led well over 1,000 students throughout the region, and because I knew the BWCAW as well as anybody, my comfort level was high, as was my knowledge of the area and its ecology as well as means of travel through the wilderness. However, I had never traveled in the Sonoran Desert, or any other desert for that matter. I expected to be confronted with lots of sand, rattlesnakes, and scorpions.

My first night in the desert I was apprehensive as I watched my friend lay out a tarp and place his sleeping pad and bag on it. I followed suit and then asked, "Now what?" "Let's go exploring!" was his response. As we walked through the desert under the moonlight, I soaked up the unfamiliar scents such as the fragrance of the creosote bush. My senses were keen with new sensations. I started to notice a number of holes in the ground that were about the diameter of a nickel. When I asked what caused them, my friend replied, "Oh, those are tarantula holes. Let's go find some!"

That night was mostly sleepless for me. But, as the week progressed, I became more comfortable with the desert. The tarantulas and scorpions hunted in the night but left our sleeping gear alone. By the end of the trip I noticed how I had gone from being afraid to sleep to knowing where to find the plants and animals of the desert. When we were ready to leave, I felt that the smell of the creosote bush was embedded in my mind along with the purple hue of the morning sun. I was beginning to feel like I knew the desert. I was certainly comfortable traveling in it.

Becoming familiar with a new environment will help reduce fears and misconceptions.

learned to new situations. They can gain further understanding of the subject through situations that are unrelated to or new to their experience and be able to apply their prior knowledge to their new understanding and skills.

These four developmental stages are believed to follow a consistent pattern that is not age-dependent, unlike many developmental theories. Instead, as mentioned, the stages of environmental literacy are more dependent on experience in the outdoors. To gain experience, you must improve your skills and knowledge about the area you are becoming familiar with. Thus, this theory suggests that developmental progression is more a function of time than of physical or cognitive development.

Stage 1: Survival   A person often has preconceived fears about a new place or situation. Because the situation is unfamiliar, it is natural to use what knowledge and experience you already have to make sense of the new experience. However, prior knowledge is often founded on misconceptions. For example, it is fairly common for people to think that northern Minnesota is a land of perpetual subzero temperatures with polar bears roaming about. Another misconception is that when you visit the wilderness of northern Minnesota you must beware of the lurking timber wolf waiting to make an attack.

It is not unusual for such misconceptions to be irrational fears. The important thing is to learn the truth about the fears or misconceptions. In order to do this, you must begin to become familiar with the place, which you accomplish through developing skills to take care of yourself. You also must gain an accurate awareness of your surroundings, which leads to an appreciation of those surroundings.

This phase of development is the survival stage. As people become more oriented to the setting, their appreciation of their surroundings tends to grow. This results in a certain comfort level where they are not paralyzed by fear of physical harm.

Once people realize that the creatures won't attack them or they won't wake up frozen to death, they begin to become oriented to the place, or get an overview of it. In doing this, they first fill their senses as they become aware of their surroundings, including different smells, sounds, landforms, trees, temperatures, and so on. While sensory awareness invites comfort and wonder, it also invites a motivation to work toward greater comfort. This leads to acquiring the skills required to be comfortable in the setting.

Stage 2: Physical Skills Acquisition   As awareness of the setting becomes established, people begin to improve their skills for making themselves comfortable in their surroundings. They will practice skills to establish their camp, to navigate accurately, and to refine their mode of travel. It is not unusual to spend a great deal of time, even years, in this stage of development by focusing predominantly on skills such as camp craft and canoeing. A well-practiced person can move in and through the outdoors with ease and comfort. To this person, outdoor travel in a familiar place can become as comfortable as being in their own home.

Stage 3: Relationships   Many authors have written about how time spent with a group in the outdoors usually results in a greater sense of interdependence and community among the group. This is the basis for programs ranging from Outward Bound to many wilderness therapy programs.

What also improves as people become proficient in their skills is awareness of individual species and features of the natural environment. For example, people who are familiar with a certain area may become aware of when a certain bird species arrives in the spring or where the birds can be found nesting. They may become aware of when certain flowers are in bloom. They become familiar enough with the land that they can often determine where to find a good camp, water source, or wild animal.

This is a more advanced stage than sensory awareness and skill development. Keep in mind that each stage builds on the previous one and that you should strive to maintain the achievements of the previous stages. For example, most people want to continue using their senses to appreciate their surroundings, and they are always practicing their skills.

Stage 4: Metaphysical   When a person has become familiar with their surroundings, when their skills, knowledge, and experience are integrated with the place they are in, a sense of oneness or harmony exists. Csikszentmihalyi (1975) calls this **flow.** Flow can also be considered a metaphysical state of being. It is the highest stage of development toward environmental literacy. This stage seems to be fleeting and dependent on a combined set of circumstances rather than being a static condition where you would consider yourself to have arrived. People in this stage of development often express a sense of being connected to, or a feeling of harmony with, their surroundings.

A metaphysical experience is very personal. You can teach skills and awareness to guide people toward a sense of oneness, but it is difficult to teach them to have a metaphysical experience. Consequently, you should strive to teach within the first three stages.

Part 2: Stages in Teaching Environmental Learning

The second part of the theory of developmental stages of environmental learning is the application phase. This approach to environmental learning is helpful for avoiding the trap of preaching to save the environment. Preaching tells the students how to think and feel based on the teacher's values instead of their own. This will not help the students gain their own understanding. The application phase is what you do as a teacher to foster students' learning of the environment. In this phase, you are striving to guide students toward their own understanding of the concept instead of simply having them mimic what you do or say as a teacher.

Environmental learning is a long process. You should not expect students to achieve all the stages of environmental learning in a single lesson. Literacy is a process requiring an extended period of time where skills and knowledge are reinforced through experience. Each step requires mastery of the lesson before moving on to the next level.

The stages to environmental literacy are the following:

- Sensory awareness
- Skills development and training
- Relationships (ecological)
- Environmental issues awareness and action

Sensory Awareness   To apply this theory of development, you must work with your students systematically. Start by building sensory awareness to help students feel less anxious about survival. This helps orient them to their setting. It will also help them overcome some of their preconceived fears. (Do not underestimate your students' fears. Listen when they are nervous about getting off the bus at your agency because they believe they might get lost or some creature will jump out and attack them.) Depending on your students' knowledge and experience, it may take different amounts of time to work through this stage. Finally, do not assume that adult learners don't need to learn to use their senses to become aware of and appreciate their surroundings!

Skills Development   Once your students have gained some level of awareness of their surroundings and are no longer preoccupied with survival, work on developing their skills. Skills development can be anything from practicing a specific sport such as backcountry skiing to learning general skills such as camp craft. Skills development also includes learning how to use equipment such as a pair of binoculars. For example, it is frustrating when the instructor excitedly points out a new bird only to have the bird disappear before the students can focus their binoculars on it. It is far more fruitful to teach the students how to use their binoculars and their field guide as part of the introduction to the activity.

Relationships   Following the developmental stages of learning, the students' relationship to their surroundings and awareness of relationships within nature will begin to develop when they are able to move about comfortably in the learning setting. They are now better able to look around and notice interactions in nature.

When skills and awareness are at a sufficient level to allow for a greater depth of knowledge and it is appropriate to your lesson, teach the students how the subject matter is connected to the place. Guide the students to realize connections on their own. For example, while students are gaining comfort in travel, ask them to notice where they see signs of a certain animal. Encourage them to notice that deer will bed down in the shade of certain trees, like junipers, below the southern crest of a hill. Explain how understanding the ecological relationships in their surroundings helps them better perform their activity.

Another example can be seen in white-water paddling. An understanding of geology (rock types and land forms) will help students better understand what kinds of rapids to expect. In paddling western rivers in canyon country, you can expect to find a rapid whenever a sidestream enters the river. When there are metamorphic rock types with much folding and faulting, you can expect to find pool-drop rapids.

Or, consider the case of identifying certain wildflowers. A calypso orchid is best looked for in a grove of white cedars because of the moisture, cool temperatures, and more basic pH of the soil. Understanding this ecological relationship will help students locate and identify calypso orchids.

Environmental Issues   This stage diverges from the development of environmental learning. Students may reach a point where they feel a sense of harmony with the place they are in, which can lead to a metaphysical experience. However, it is doubtful whether a feeling of harmony can actually be taught. Instead, move the students toward a greater understanding of relationships in nature. This includes teaching about threats to the value or quality of the place, if they exist. If a threat or degradation occurs, the students will become aware of an environmental problem.

Once students are familiar with the environment, they can develop their skills.

Explore Your World

1. How do you avoid getting stuck in a stage?

2. When can you move to a more advanced developmental stage?

3. Choose an area (park, nature area, wilderness) that you are familiar with. Discuss how you might guide a student from survival to understanding relationships.

4. Identify teaching behaviors that are conducive to student growth in the outdoors.

5. What are some indications that you are preaching instead of teaching to your students?

Awareness of environmental issues is an advanced form of understanding relationships. It is the development of understanding to the point where a person begins to strive toward some sort of action to protect nature. You can teach toward this commitment to protect natural spaces. The first step is awareness. While it may be tempting to immediately start teaching students how to solve environmental issues, it is essential to teach them the ability to see that the issue exists in the first place. Your job is to help your students see that improper actions can damage the outdoors.

Environmental issues include more than industrial pollution. While industrial pollution is certainly an environmental issue, so are behaviors like traveling through sensitive areas such as a wetland or deserts with fragile soil or throwing monofilament fishing line into waterways, which can entangle fish, birds, and wildlife.

Once students are able to recognize that environmental issues exist as well as understand why they exist, they are better able to take action to resolve those issues. If you have helped your students become environmentally literate, they will have gained a desire to prevent environmental issues from occurring and to help to solve existing issues.

Again, an obvious idea is to stop large corporations from polluting the atmosphere or waterways. However, if your students are able to prevent soil degradation by traveling on more hardened soil types and avoiding sensitive wetlands, you have accomplished a great deal. If your students know when and where to collect firewood, you have helped them reach the final stage of environmental literacy. It is through understanding relationships between human beings and nature that your students learn to identify environmental issues, which helps them to be better problem solvers.

Theory of Personal Meaning

It is easy to teach students according to the ways you have been taught or according to your own beliefs about the topic. However, as we have mentioned many times, understanding occurs when the learners are able to apply the subject matter to their own personal perspective.

Think back on the discussion in chapter 1 of Freeman Tilden's principles of interpretation: If it doesn't relate, it is sterile (Tilden 1957). Similarly,

Tips and Techniques

- Make prerequisite skills, knowledge, and experience clear to students so they will register for the appropriate course.

- Question your students at the beginning of the class to assess their skills and knowledge.

- Have your students demonstrate their skill level to determine their ability for your intended level of instruction.

- Start where the students are at, not where you want them to be!

constructivist theory contends that it is critical to build on what the students already know and understand. This theoretical approach to learning is called the **theory of personal meaning.** It was founded by John Dewey in 1938 and refined in 1968 by David Ausubel, an educational psychologist. Ausubel found that relying on rote memory as a measure of learning is highly limited. He wrote that learning must derive from making meaning of what is being taught. Meaning comes from symbolic representation, abstraction, categorization, and generalization. The new material is recoded into the students' personal meaning, allowing them to gain understanding and thus learn the topic.

An illustration of this can be seen in learning how to identify a tree. The learner first relates the new tree to a tree species the student already knows. The student might say, "That tree looks a lot like the cottonwoods that grow where I live." This line of thought is both symbolic representation and abstraction (How is it similar to what I am familiar with? Does it look like something I already know?). Categorization could be something like, "That tree grows in a similar setting as a cottonwood—in cool, moist soil." It is then generalized as, "It looks like a cottonwood, and it grows in similar settings, so it must be related." This recoding then progresses to the new learning that the quaking aspen is actually related to the cottonwood. The student might further turn the aspen tree into a symbol of a moment in his life that he experienced in or around the two similar trees.

This theory of personal meaning clearly builds from other theories. It can be considered developmental in that the process of building knowledge and making personal meaning of it is a function of knowledge, experience, and ability, all of which are aspects of learning development.

Learning Theories

Learning theories describe how people learn. They help you understand how to guide your students toward that moment when they say, "Now I understand!", or, "I can do it!" When that happens, it is one of the finest moments in teaching. It is especially nice when a student has learned because of the craftsmanship you have used to guide their learning.

After understanding development and when a topic or skill is best taught, the next step is understanding how people receive information and process it into their own learning. How an individual or group of people learns is called **learning theory.**

Experiential Education

Learning through direct experience has been both a method and a philosophy for centuries. It is the manner in which aboriginal people worldwide learned long before modern education came to be. As the practice of education evolved into present-day instruction where learning happens predominantly in a classroom with a lecture followed by some form of practice, a movement to recognize and use experiential learning began. The founder of contemporary theory of experiential education was John Dewey (1859-1952). He believed that learning through direct experience was the strongest form of learning, with an outcome that also builds a sense of community with the learner. Kurt Hahn advanced the application of experiential learning, applying it to adventure education when he founded the Outward Bound schools in 1941 to promote experiential education in an adventure context. Today, experiential education has gone from being a valuable philosophy and method of teaching to becoming one of the largest professional associations of outdoor education—the Association for Experiential Education (AEE).

Certain principles guide the use of experiential education as a theoretical approach:

- The experience must be authentic.
- A common activity must be used among students.
- The activity guiding the experience must be planned.
- The teacher must guide the learning.

Authentic Experience

For the activity to be experiential learning, it must be real, not contrived. If you want your students to learn about wilderness, take them to a wilderness area. If you wish to teach them about a bird, take them outdoors to observe the bird. While using audiotapes of bird songs and photos for identification is a form of education, a genuine experience is to observe the bird in its natural habitat.

Certain activities are used in outdoor education to elicit behavior or emotions that can be transferred to real life. For instance, a ropes course is a tool to encourage teamwork among group members. It uses perceived risk to challenge students' fears and self-concept. It is a common and effective tool. However, although a ropes course is a valid experience, it is not considered an authentic experience. That is, while it is a powerful tool, ropes courses are not found in everyday life. The learned behaviors of cooperation, clear communication, and teamwork are positive, but the experience on the ropes course serves as a metaphor to be transferred to applications in the students' life beyond the ropes course.

A common environmental education activity used to teach the concept of population dynamics is called Oh Deer (Western Regional Environmental Education Council 1992). In Oh Deer, students divide into groups of deer versus habitat types. It is similar to a game of tag in that deer try to tag a certain habitat. When they are unable to tag the habitat they are seeking, they shift from the group of deer to a habitat type. By keeping score of the changes in deer numbers, students learn the concept of population dynamics. This activity is an excellent game to introduce the concept of population trends. However, it is often mistaken for experiential education simply because it involves a great deal of physical action. A true experiential activity involving population dynamics would be difficult to provide in the timeframe of most learning periods. An experiential education follow-up to Oh Deer might be having students raise an aquarium of aquatic invertebrates so they can observe the shifts in population dynamics over a week or month.

Common Activity

In order to gain differing perspectives toward an experience, use an activity where the experience is similar. When students can observe similar successes and challenges, they are better able to have a discussion about what they learned. Conversely, if the activities for individuals or groups of students are dissimilar, it will be difficult for them to share their learning in a meaningful way.

Planned Experience

Do not rely only on spontaneous events that students might learn from. Instead, plan your lesson and arrange an opportunity for students to gain the relevant experience. For example, if you want to teach flower identification, scout your route before the lesson to ensure that the flowers you want to teach can be found along the trail. While you can't always predict what you will encounter during your lesson, you want to plan as much of the lesson as possible. Your students will still have a sense of discovery or feeling of wonder.

Facilitate Student Learning

Help students make sense of the experience by putting it in perspective. A student will often experience something and not realize what has just occurred or the magnitude of the event.

Take the time to discuss what the students have learned from the experience. Ask questions to increase their awareness of what they have learned:

- What skill did you learn?
- What problem did you solve to achieve success?
- How will you use what you learned today in your life beyond this activity?

© David Dahler

Exploring a cave is an authentic experience.

Stories From Real Life: Rare Bird Sighting

I was once on an ornithology field trip. We spotted and identified a Mississippi kite in northwestern Wisconsin. As novices, we did not realize that we were observing a rare event. We were told that this was only the second time ever that a Mississippi kite was spotted so far north, because their range is the southeastern United States. Knowing that information significantly enhanced the power of the experience. Through the knowledge and experience of our instructors, the event became more pronounced and memorable.

Dewey wrote that by not facilitating, or debriefing, the meaning of the experience, you run the risk of the experience being noneducative or miseducative. It is important for you to guide the meaning the student derives from the experience so its educational value is realized. Otherwise the experience may become merely an experience rather than a learning experience. Even if you put your students in a situation where the experience is intended to speak for itself, you must plan the setting, purpose, and logistics of the experience so the students can encounter it.

Multiple Intelligences

Have you ever noticed how some people are really good at physical activity? Some people can observe a skill, take a moment to think about it, and then perform it with little difficulty. Or, do you know people who can hear a song once and then be able to recite the verses and play the tune? How about people who can manipulate numbers easily and who do well memorizing scientific names and concepts? This observation that people are good at different things has led to the **theory of multiple intelligences,** which holds that there are different types of intelligence.

In 1983, psychologist Howard Gardner identified different ways that people perceive and understand the world. He labeled these different perceptions and abilities as different intelligences. In other words, modern formal education (kindergarten through 12th grade) for the most part recognizes only one style of learning, which is cognitive-oriented: The teacher presents a series of facts and concepts and the student recites them back in a written test. People who scored below average were considered to be poor learners. But Gardner recognized that this wasn't necessarily the case. For example, people who are adept at music are not less intelligent than people who are good at science; they are intelligent in a different way.

Gardner determined that intelligence can be defined as having a set of abilities. These abilities are grouped in the following ways:

- Each is mostly autonomous from the others.
- Each has a core set of ways to process information.
- Each has a distinct set of developmental stages that the learner progresses through.
- Each has valid historical roots.

While people rarely have only one type of intelligence, meaning a person can be adept in both physical abilities and cognitive intelligence, a person tends to be stronger, or more intelligent, in one or two areas rather than all of them.

Gardner identified eight types of intelligence:

1. Verbal–linguistic: The ability to use words and language, both written and spoken, as in a politician, statesman, writer, or news reporter.
2. Logical–mathematical: The ability to use inductive and deductive reasoning and the ability to use numbers and recognize abstract patterns, as in a scientist or businessperson.
3. Visual–spatial: The ability to use sight and visualization to gain understanding, as in a graphic designer, architect, or builder.
4. Body–kinesthetic: The ability to move with ease physically and have awareness of the body, as in an athlete, rock climber, or sea kayaker.
5. Musical–rhythmic: The ability to associate concepts of tonal patterns, environmental sounds, rhythms, and beats, as in a musician.

6. Interpersonal: The ability to communicate easily with others and build relationships, as in a counselor.

7. Intrapersonal: The ability to be self-reflective and aware of spiritual realities, as in a spiritual leader or consultant in team building.

8. Naturalist: The ability to observe patterns in nature, or to identify and classify objects and understand natural and human-made systems, as in a park interpreter.

So, what do you do with the concept of multiple intelligences as an outdoor educator? By being aware that different people make sense of learning in different ways, you can plan your lessons with a wider range of examples and experiences. For instance, avoid only lecturing or being overly physical without explaining how the skill works. Balance your curriculum with different approaches to teaching the topic. This is also where it is important to know your audience.

Accordingly, your lesson planning will influence your instruction. Use a variety of methods that can reach a range of intelligences to help your students gain understanding. Finally, you should plan assessment that accommodates the different ways that people learn. Avoid using only one form of evaluation. Have students describe how they understand the topic and then have them show you. For example, using art or **journaling** to indicate understanding is an excellent means for some people to show what they have learned.

Learning Styles

By understanding and appreciating different intelligences, you will notice that some students learn through different means. Sometimes this is referred to as differing **learning styles.** While similar to the theory of multiple intelligences, the idea of different learning styles is a variation of the theory.

Learning style refers to the manner in which a student learns a lesson. How a person learns is not necessarily the same as type of intelligence. Some people learn better through direct experience while others need a thorough explanation of the activity before they can begin to demonstrate it. There are two basic learning styles: kinesthetic and cognitive. While it is overly simplistic to say that a person uses only these two styles, or that a learner does not incorporate different intelligences, such as auditory or visual, into how they receive information, kinesthetic and cognitive styles of learning are the two styles you will encounter while teaching outdoors.

Kinesthetic learners want minimal explanation. They prefer a brief introduction followed by a demonstration and then practice time. These learners are typically happiest when they are doing as opposed to thinking. Cognitive learners prefer to have the topic explained to them. They strive to understand how the topic works before they begin to practice or demonstrate their learning.

These two learning styles are not the only styles that exist, but they seem to be the predominant types that are encountered in outdoor education. Notice that they are different from multiple intelligences in that two people might both be adept at body–kinesthetic intelligence, yet one is more of a kinesthetic learner while the other is more of a cognitive learner. They both will learn to perform the skill properly, but they will get there differently.

Summary

How and why you teach about the outdoors is determined by your audience. More important, knowing your audience and understanding the theories of how people learn is a tremendous tool to help you meet audience needs. The theories described in this chapter are the basic theories used in outdoor education.

Developmental theories are helpful for gaining an understanding of when a person is ready to learn a certain level of knowledge or skill, which helps you systematically guide that person toward literacy. In addition, through developmental theories like multiple intelligences, you can be better prepared to use the proper equipment, setting, and examples in teaching your students.

Similarly, through learning theories you can better understand how a person learns. They also help you understand what barriers might be inhibiting your students' progress in your lesson or course. Remember, it is sometimes about you in how you teach, but it is usually about your students in how, when, and why they learn.

Explore Your World

1. What is your predominant teaching style?

2. What theory or theories best fit how you approach your instruction?

3. How will you change your teaching now that you are more knowledgeable about educational theories?

4. Describe how your lessons are experiential.

5. What percentage of your lessons includes authentic experience? Is this percentage appropriate?

6. What is your primary style of learning?

7. How would you describe your intelligence? Where does it fit within Gardner's multiple intelligences?

8. How can you move your students to more advanced stages of development in attaining environmental literacy? How did you determine which stage to start in? How did you determine which stage to move toward?

PART II

Preparation for Teaching Outdoors

"I consider a human soul without education like a marble in the quarry, which shows none of its inherent beauties till the skill of the polisher fetches out the colours—makes the surface shine, and discovers every ornamental cloud and vein that runs through the body of it."

—Adison

CHAPTER 4

Understanding Participants

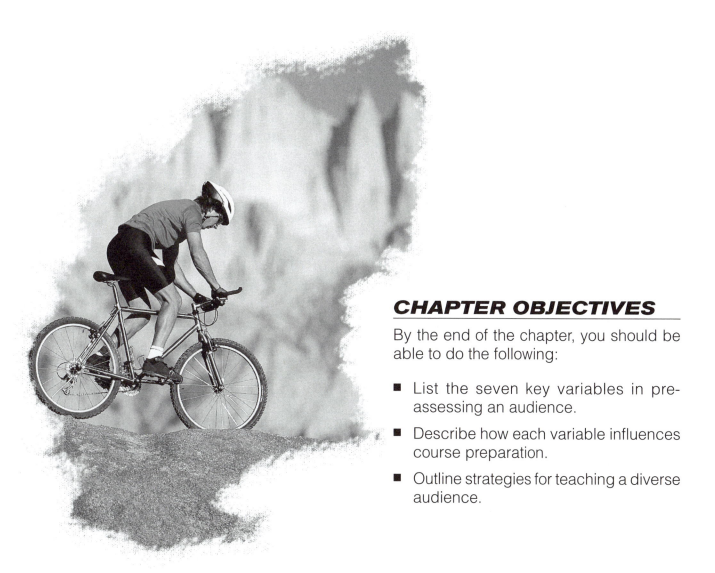

CHAPTER OBJECTIVES

By the end of the chapter, you should be able to do the following:

- List the seven key variables in pre-assessing an audience.

- Describe how each variable influences course preparation.

- Outline strategies for teaching a diverse audience.

Your understanding of participants' expectations, interests, abilities, and backgrounds will determine the success of your lesson. This chapter will help you develop the ability to understand your audience so that you can structure your lessons to meet diverse student needs.

For example, let's say the leader of a junior high chorus tries to teach his students the following song:

I drink skim milk, my toast is dry

The butter is forbidden.

My coffee's black, do you know why?

Because the cream is hidden.

The chorus leader is on a diet so the song interests him, but he has a hard time getting the students interested or excited about the song. His problem is that he doesn't understand the audience. The song has great relevance for him as a man approaching middle age and experiencing the effects of a declining metabolism. But for energetic, growing adolescents the song holds no relevance at all.

In this chapter, you will learn **GAME FACe**, the seven key variables to consider when assessing your audience: **G**ender, **A**ge, **M**edical conditions, **E**xperience, **F**amiliarity of group members, **A**bilities, and **C**ulture and **e**thnicity. Consider these variables when planning your courses so that you can avoid the chorus leader's mistake and construct meaningful lessons that will engage a variety of learners. Through thoughtful preparation and planning, the success of your lessons will skyrocket.

Audience Assessment

GAME FACe is an acronym that will help you remember the key variables of audience assessment. Initial audience assessment uses indicators based on scientific evidence to predict audience developmental levels and behavior, which will help you plan an appropriate, meaningful learning experience for your students. Before beginning any lesson development, collect as much information about your audience as you can. Once the audience arrives, you will be able to more accurately assess their characteristics and adjust content and activities accordingly. Your lessons should reflect audience needs and interests. Regardless of student age or experience, ask yourself what is relevant to them. What major life questions are they facing? How does the experience you are about to share with them relate to their past experiences and inform their future choices?

Effective audience assessment begins before the audience's arrival. Have audience members complete a questionnaire concerning their related experience, personal habits that reinforce or interfere with learning, physical needs or limitations, and what they expect from the course. A sample audience assessment questionnaire can be found in appendix B ("Pretrip Questionnaire," p. 190). If the students are registering directly with your organization, you can collect this information with their registration. If you are teaching schoolchildren, the classroom teachers can collect this information from their students. Use this information to craft a course

---

Stories From Real Life:
Building on Student Knowledge

My friend and I were teaching a weeklong summer science camp for 4th and 5th graders. We had planned an active curriculum based on field science experiences. However, as we started to receive the pretrip forms from our future students, we noticed that many students expected to build forts as part of the week's activities. This was not at all what we had planned!

We sat down and looked at our curriculum for the week and found a place where we could include fort building. Neither of us liked the term *fort* or its violent and military implications, so we changed the focus to animal adaptations. By using fairy dust we transformed the students into make-believe animals. Then groups of animals made a "nest" for themselves in the woods. We integrated the nest-building activity into the animal adaptations part of the field research. The students were so excited that they saved their nests to show to their parents on family night. The families helped the students deconstruct the nest and restore the area to its natural state.

that is challenging and pushes students' limits but is based on the constructivist idea of building on what the student already knows and understands. This strategy works for students regardless of age and experience. Collect preplanning sheets from all of your students, whether they are senior citizens, adults, schoolchildren, families, or clubs. Through this information you can inform yourself of essential medical information, student expectations about the course, and student experience with the skills involved in the course. Start with what the students already know and use their knowledge and natural interest to guide their exploration and learning.

Variables in Audience Assessment: GAME FACe

- Gender
- Age
- Medical conditions
- Experience
- Familiarity of group members
- Abilities (cognitive and physical)
- Culture and ethnicity

Stereotyping

GAME FACe consists of the major factors in audience assessment. Stereotyping is different from assessing your audience. Stereotyping is projecting your personal expectations onto your audience. Stereotypes are usually narrow, inaccurate expectations of people based on limited direct experience.

The human mind has the capacity to find what it seeks. For example, if you expect a female audience to be passive or less physically able than a male audience, you will notice those behaviors and your stereotype will be reinforced. If you expect those same females to be strong and capable, you will notice and reinforce those behaviors.

Stereotyping doesn't stop with sexism. It includes racism, ageism, and homophobia. It can even extend to personal appearance, socioeconomic status, and physical ability.

As an outdoor educator you are responsible for creating safe opportunities for all your students to push themselves and grow. If you approach your audience with internalized stereotypes, you will not create equal opportunities for your students. In addition, an outdoor educator must be able to affirm a student's ethnicity, gender, or sexual orientation, not ignore it. This requires awareness

Educators must assess their students' abilities.

of your own attitudes and assumptions as well as knowledge about different ethnicities and cultures and age and gender issues. Outdoor educators must also be prepared to combat racism, whether personal or institutionalized, and help students do the same.

It is beyond the scope of this book to help outdoor educators uncover their own biases. But it is your ethical responsibility as an outdoor educator to begin this exploration and to continue it throughout your career. Racist, sexist, and ageist assumptions are dangerous tools in the uninformed educator's hands. Many excellent resources exist to facilitate exploration of your assumptions. Please refer to Cultural Literacy for Outdoor Educators in the bibliography (p. 204) for useful references.

Gender

Current research shows that males and females are "hardwired" differently—male and female brains are structurally different and the different genders use parts of their brains differently (Jensen 2000; Sousa 2000). In addition, cultural expectations from family and community members are more likely to influence girls' performance than their genetic ability (Jensen 2000; Women's College Coalition 2003). However, boys and girls share an overwhelming number of similar characteristics.

In addition to their social expectations of performance, outdoor educators often relate to girls and boys differently. For example, many outdoor educators tend to "rescue" girls from difficult problems or situations. As an outdoor educator, create your lesson plan to provide appropriate challenges to students regardless of gender.

Tips for Gender Equity

- If you had a male trail leader yesterday, choose a female today.
- Keep track of student participation and create opportunities for less vocal students to speak up or participate.
- Females are often stereotyped into the role of secretary when performing scientific research. Set up research projects using cooperative learning techniques and expect every student's handwriting to appear on the worksheets.
- Allow females to struggle with problems the same way you allow males to struggle with problems.

In addition to performance expectations, consider the dynamics between males and females in class. When preparing for your course, note the number of males and females registered. If the genders are unevenly represented, divide the class into smaller groups for activities. For example, if your field group has 12 students (10 female, 2 male), divide them into three working groups. Two groups of 4 students will be all female. One group of 4 students will be half male and half female. This allows the underrepresented gender to work in a gender-balanced atmosphere.

Age and Cognitive Development

The human brain and body develop in generally predictable ways. The first step in designing effective lessons in the outdoors is to understand your audiences' predicted cognitive development based on age.

Human Development

Human development describes how children and adolescents change socially, cognitively, physically, and emotionally as they grow. Jean Piaget, a founding researcher in the field of human cognitive development, began his work in the early 1920s, exploring how children learn about their world. Piaget's **cognitive development theory** (2001) describes four developmental stages children progress through:

1. Sensorimotor stage (birth to 2 years old). Understands the world through own behavior and perception, but only thinks about objects seen (object permanence).

Stories From Real Life: Assessing Developmental Levels

Day 2 during a weeklong outdoor education experience for a group of 10th graders was designated as a leadership hike day. Our goal was a challenging hike with several thousand feet of elevation gain and loss. Each group member rotated through the lead position throughout the hike. Each one received a leadership saying such as, "The river would be silent if you removed the rocks," to share with the group. The goal was to have the students reflect on these sayings and apply the metaphors to the hike and then to their lives. In this example, the river was a metaphor for life and the rocks were a metaphor for the challenges we face each day. If we removed the rocks from the river, the river would lose its melodious song, much as life would lose its interest if the challenges were removed. Each leader was to read, think about, and then relate the quote to the leadership role and the hike. The hike was permeated with wonderful moments of insight and sharing about the qualities of an effective leader and the role of challenge in our daily lives.

The next week the students were 7th graders and we did a similar activity. However, this time the students were unable to interpret the sayings. We got no deeper than, "Well, if you took all the rocks out of a river, it wouldn't make noise anymore." Reflecting on the day, I realized the leadership challenge was appropriate for the developmental level of the older students, but the younger students were still developing their abstract thought processes so the activity didn't work for them.

2. Preoperational stage (3 to 7 years old). Begins to think about objects out of direct view, but reasoning is illogical and egocentric.

3. Concrete operational stage (8 to 11 years old). Reasons logically, but limited to concrete thinking.

4. Formal operational stage (12 to 15 years old). Reasons logically and abstractly as well as concretely.

In the early 20th century, while Piaget was doing groundbreaking work in human development, Lev Vygotsky was conducting similar research in Russia, though unfortunately his research wasn't influential on Western thought until his work was translated decades later. Vygotsky's theory, the **social development theory,** considers how the social system in which a child learns influences the child's development (1962). Vygotsky's theory describes how a child's elementary mental functions, such as senses and hunger, transform into higher mental functions, such as language, memory, perception, and problem solving, through the influence of culture. These higher mental functions are culturally patterned activities (1980). Another key component of Vytgotsky's theory is the **zone of proximal development (ZPD)**. The ZPD is the difference between what a child can accomplish independently and what a child can accomplish when guided in a social situation (1980). An effective educator can assess what a child can do independently and assist the child to a higher level of function, helping the child learn.

Today, researchers continue to explore patterns of human development. The discussion of what influences human development, whether external factors such as social system and culture or internal factors such as genetics and neurological development, rages on. The most important point to remember is to view human development as moving though a pattern (see table 4.1).

The process is malleable, not rigid. Think of cognitive development as a hike up a mountainside. As you gain elevation, you gradually move from one life zone to another. Changes occur and you move through various definable zones. However, while the pattern of change is predictable, the life zones are not bounded by rigid lines. Transitions are gradual.

Table 4.1 Age Characteristics

3-4 years old (early childhood)	5-11 years old (elementary school)	12-17 years old (adolescence)	18 years and older (adult)
• Egocentric • Need attention and supervision (1:5 teacher–student ratio) • Developing physically, lack fine muscle coordination • Developing language skills (speak in short sentences, encourage students to speak) • Concrete, literal thinkers • Have short attention spans (limit activities to <30 minutes) • Need regular snacks, drinks, and bathroom breaks • Express selves through drawing or dictating stories	• Gathering information about who they are and what they can do • Developing better understanding of how to get along with others • Improving physical abilities • Learning to use language to express themselves more completely • Interpret language literally • Change multiple variables at once while solving a problem • Lack understanding of fractions and proportions	• Undergo dramatic physical changes (both genders experience puberty and growth spurts) • Develop higher-level thinking skills, abstract thought, operational reasoning • Attention span grows • Develop independence from parents and other authority • Feel uncertain about themselves due to physical changes • Need to feel competent, accepted, and affirmed • Developing attitudes and values about life and work	• "Vote with their feet," and usually have the freedom to leave • Bring knowledge and experience to the learning situation • Want to be involved in decision making about their learning • Want life- or problem-centered learning rather than subject-centered learning • Are motivated by intrinsic factors

Familiarize yourself with developmental theory to help you plan your courses, but be prepared to constantly assess student development throughout the course and adjust the curriculum as needed. This is a constructivist concept called **scaffolding.** Audience age can help you form general expectations, but don't make decisions about audience development based on age alone.

Adult Learners Versus Child Learners

The human brain is born knowing how to think. However, you can teach the brain strategies for more efficient learning. Some differences between child and adult learners arise because the brain and nervous system are still growing in children. Other differences are a result of knowledge, experience, and learning strategies.

Learning occurs when new information is linked to old knowledge. Since adults have acquired more knowledge and had more experiences, they have more potential connections for new learning. They also have more practice making some of those connections. However, growing brains are quicker at making connections.

People spend their lives learning how to learn. Some master the skills better than others, but adult learners are more efficient at learning than children because of the strategies they have learned. For example, adults may know how to "chunk" learning (or divide into understandable parts) to maximize their short-term memory, they may know how to rehearse more effectively, and they have practiced these strategies until they are proficient at them.

When you are teaching children, in addition to covering the content you should also teach learning strategies to help them become effective learners. When teaching adult students, pay attention to signals they give you about how they learn. For example, some adult students will consistently take notes or ask you to write things on the board, while others will need to talk to peers to extract meaning from the information. As you pick up these signals from students, begin to include similar strategies into your teaching plan.

Generational Differences

Cultures change over time, and technology has greatly influenced the speed of cultural change. Even within your own culture, each generation has different points of reference. Subtle things such as the language you choose, the clothes you wear, or references you make in class will make your course relevant or irrelevant to your students. For example, when teaching schoolchildren, you might refer to current children's movies and pop culture. If you were teaching the same content to a group of retirees, you might change your references to adult movies, especially those with actors whose ages are similar to your students', and refer to music from a time period when your students were adolescents.

Medical Conditions

To prepare a safe and challenging experience for your audience, before they arrive you should familiarize yourself with any medical conditions they may have. Following is information about the most common medical conditions you will need to understand. This information is not a complete list,

---

Stories From Real Life: Talking About My Generation

When leading a workshop with teachers, my coinstructor, a teacher in his late 20s, made a reference to the children's television show, *Sesame Street.* He asked the teachers to raise their hand if they remembered a particular song Bert and Ernie sang. He may as well have asked everyone under 40 to raise their hand, because only the younger teachers raised their hands. *Sesame Street* had cultural relevance to the younger students, but not to the older students. The instructor used Bert and Ernie's song to build a metaphor to a key concept in the class, and half of the teachers, those who were over 40, were mystified. My coinstructor needed to work harder to move beyond what was meaningful to him and to educate himself about the culture of all the students.

---

nor is it a substitute for first aid training. You will need to meet the medical training requirements of your organization, which will work with a medical doctor who will help create a protocol for your work situation. For example, the protocol will dictate whether you can administer over-the-counter medications, such as acetaminophen or ibuprofen, to your students. It will identify who will hold prescription medications for your students, how they will be held, and who will dispense those medications. The protocol will also cover a variety of situations specific to your work situation. You are legally bound to respond according to the protocol, so be thoroughly familiar with it. In addition, collect your students' medical histories before their arrival so you can anticipate problems and prepare a safe yet challenging experience.

Asthma

Asthma is a temporary medical condition where the airway swells and spasms, resulting in impaired breathing. Asthma can be triggered by many things including cold weather, exposure to allergens such as pollen and dust, and exercise. Students with asthma usually carry inhalers, either over-the-counter or prescription. Students with severe asthma may also take medication. The key to asthma is prevention of a major attack. Know if any of your students have asthma, check to see that they always have their inhaler and other prescription medication, and watch them carefully during physical exertion. Stop and rest to avoid triggering an asthma attack. It is better to stop than to create a medical emergency because your student is having difficulty breathing.

Allergies

An allergy is hypersensitivity to a specific substance. Almost any substance can be an allergen. The most common allergens are foods (nuts, seafood), pollen, and insect bites. After exposure to an allergen, the body releases excessive amounts of histamine. The reaction can range from mild and local (rash or swelling) to life threatening (anaphylaxis). Typically your students will know if they have allergies and will carry appropriate treatment. In addition, your organization may choose to provide you with an allergy response kit, including injectable epinephrine and an antihistamine. Follow your organization's protocol for carrying the kit and responding to allergic reactions.

Cardiac Emergencies

Ventricular septal defects (VSD), heart murmurs, heart attacks, angina, and congestive heart failure are potential cardiac concerns. While the chance of these diseases occurring increases with age, don't expect only older patients to manifest heart conditions. VSD and heart murmurs are congenital conditions present in children. For a heart patient of any age, the increased exercise and stress in an active outdoor program may exacerbate an existing heart condition. Collect medical histories from your students to learn about specific cardiac conditions that may influence their participation in your program.

Seizures and Epilepsy

Seizures are sudden, uncontrolled electrical activity in the brain. Students who regularly experience seizures have epilepsy. Diagnosed epileptics may take prescriptions to control their seizures. However, other medical situations may also cause a person to have a seizure. Be aware of students who have epilepsy. You need to consider their disease when putting them in physically risky situations such as standing at the edge of a cliff or belaying a partner while rock climbing. If a student is not diagnosed with epilepsy and has a seizure, treat the situation as a medical emergency.

Diabetes

Diabetes is a disease where the body cannot moderate the amount of sugar in the blood. Too much or too little blood sugar can create a serious medical situation. If you have students with diabetes, help them manage the disease. Their input (food and rest) needs to equal their output (exercise and stress) in order for their bodies to remain in balance. Make sure diabetic students test their blood sugar regularly. Let them know the physical rigors of the course, and plan stops, snacks, water, and rest.

Brittle Bone Disease

Brittle bone disease, or osteogenesis imperfecta, results from abnormalities in the protein structure, or collagen, of the bones. The disease causes bones to break more easily than normal. Brittle bone disease is a congenital condition present in children.

Experience

Understanding your audiences' interests or previous experience in similar skills or settings will help you adjust the content of your lesson to meet your audiences' needs. Be clear about the level of skill you are teaching—you would approach an introductory backpacking trip very differently from an advanced backpacking trip.

Assess the range of experience in your audience. If students have similar previous experience, assess that experience and begin instruction and practice. If students have widely different experiences and abilities, group students according to ability. Have more advanced students mentor beginning students.

If a known skill is too similar to the skill being learned, the student may experience a negative transfer of knowledge. What students know about one skill may actually inhibit their learning of the new skill. Address this problem directly with your students and help them prepare to learn something different. Often this requires more concentration, effort, and methodical practice than learning an entirely new skill for the first time.

Group Familiarity

When assessing your audience, reflect on how well the group members know each other. Are they strangers who enrolled independently in an organic gardening course? Are they a school class that has been together since they were young? The group dynamics will be strongly influenced by the familiarity of the participants with eachother.

It's important to set a tone of welcome and inclusion right from the start. You are striving to create a psychologically safe environment where people can take risks in order to learn and grow, and students should feel free to be who they are and to test new boundaries without fear of teasing, ridicule, or exclusion from the group.

If group members are well acquainted, plan experiences to challenge and extend that acquaintance. Help them see each other with new eyes. Often during field courses you hear comments such as, "I never knew Wajida could do that!" and, "I didn't know Steve was such a strong leader!" For such growth to occur, individuals have to be able to push their own limits and the group needs to accept a broader view of its members.

If your audience is a group of strangers, plan some time for them to become acquainted before beginning core activities. This is particularly important if physical or psychological risk is involved. Depending on the course students will be outside their comfort zone and will need to trust the other group members. Part of the art of teaching is knowing when to encourage students to push their limits and when to offer support. A good rule of thumb

A blindfolded walk can help build group familiarity.

© David Dahler

is to start out safe and set a fun, accepting tone. Then provide challenges in a deliberate process, first increasing the social risk, then increasing the physical risk. As the group succeeds with each level of risk, allow individuals to reflect on their learning and growth and generalize their learning to other situations. Then provide them with the next, greater challenge. Changing one variable at a time allows the group to meet the challenges in a series of steps.

Abilities

Audience members will vary in their physical and cognitive abilities. While you can make some assumptions based on age, often other factors influence how well students can participate and learn.

Physical Abilities

Encourage participation from all students, including those with some type of physical impairment. Be careful not to make a student's physical condition the "challenge" for the group. Check in regularly with students to make sure they feel included in respectful ways. When you know you have students with physical disabilities, plan activities the entire group can do. Include any necessary adaptive equipment, such as larger handles for students with gross motor skill impairment or large-print handouts for students with vision impairment.

Remember that physical condition does not imply cognitive or developmental delays. Students with cerebral palsy, for example, may appear to have developmental delays because of a damaged language center, yet their cognitive function is completely unimpaired. Get the facts about your students before the start of the program so you can be prepared and professional.

Mobility

Assess your audience for mobility differences. If mobility differences are caused by disease, such as cerebral palsy, stroke, arthritis, or muscular dystrophy, familiarize yourself with other ramifications of the disease that may come up during the course. Check in with your student at the beginning and throughout the course to assess comfort and participation level.

Adjust the distances you plan to cover, the surfaces and gathering areas you'll use, and the activities for the group so that every student can participate. Locate adaptive equipment such as all-terrain wheelchairs or pulks (sleds) to increase participant comfort and mobility.

When hiking, the rule of thumb is that the group goes as fast as its slowest member. The goal isn't to get to a certain destination, it's to travel as a group. Engage all students by planning activities at various points throughout the hike.

If students are in a wheelchair, avoid touching the wheelchair without permission. Ask if they would like assistance before giving it. Get down to their eye level when you are speaking to them. If they have a personal aide, speak directly with them, not through their aide.

Deaf and Hard of Hearing

Many students will have some measurable hearing loss. This includes permanent loss as well as temporary loss due to ear infections (Alexander Graham Bell Association 2003). Since any hearing loss may interfere with a student's ability to learn, awareness of deaf and hard-of-hearing techniques will increase your effectiveness as an outdoor educator.

Deaf and hard-of-hearing students may speak American Sign Language through an interpreter, use sound-enhancement devices, have cochlear implants, read lips, or use a combination of these techniques and aids.

Working With Students and Their Interpreters

- Speak to the student, not the interpreter.
- Keep the interpreter in visual contact with the student at all times.
- During night hikes, slide shows, or other dark settings, make sure the student can see the interpreter.

Some deaf or hard-of-hearing students may ask you to wear a personal FM system that magnifies your voice for the student. Switch this device on when you are speaking to the entire group or the deaf student, and switch it off when engaging in casual conversation with other students, as your conversation becomes a distraction for the deaf student.

Teaching Deaf or Hard-of-Hearing Students

- Use a normal tone of voice.
- Provide a clear view of your mouth and face.

- Ask students to repeat themselves if you don't understand them.
- Avoid being backlit.
- Enforce a rule of having one person speak at a time.
- Use visual aids frequently.
- Choose quiet areas for conversation and study.

Visual Impairment

People who are visually impaired can and should have wonderful experiences in the outdoors. Speak with these students before the course begins about how to safely include them in the activities. Include aides or helpers in the conversation and learn how they will participate as well.

If a student who is visually impaired uses a service animal, remember that the animal is working, not a pet. It is allowed in places where pets are not allowed, and you should not touch it or otherwise distract it from its job. Discuss the situation with the whole group so people feel comfortable asking questions and everyone feels welcomed as a member of the group.

Teaching Students With Visual Impairment

- Introduce yourself immediately to students who are blind.
- Give clear, specific directions.
- Use a normal tone of voice.
- Ensure your route is clear of unnecessary obstacles.
- Speak instructions as well as write them.
- Orient blind students to the learning space.
- Enforce a rule of having one person speak at a time.

Developmental Delays

Several medical conditions can create developmental delays in students. These delays may range from being barely detectable by untrained personnel to severely influencing learning and participation. You should find out about the conditions your students have and their level of function.

Three of the more common conditions that may affect your students' learning are autism disorder, Asperger's disorder, and fetal alcohol syndrome. Autism disorder and Asperger's disorder are spectrum disorders, meaning they have a broad spectrum

Plan to include students of different abilities.

of symptoms and characteristics. Two people with the same diagnosis may have completely different symptoms. Autism and Asperger's disorder are the two most common subgroups of a larger diagnostic category called pervasive developmental disorders (PDD). The causes of autism and Asperger's have not been clearly identified, but the disorders are more common in boys than girls. Other than this gender preference, autism and Asperger's are not limited to specific ethnic, socioeconomic, or geographical groups. Autism, Asperger's, and fetal alcohol syndrome are lifetime conditions. The symptoms may diminish with education and treatment, but the disorder persists throughout a person's lifetime.

If you have students with any of these or similar disorders, collect as much information about the students' specific symptoms as you can. Since these disorders exhibit a huge range of symptoms and severity, the more information you can gather before beginning your course, the more you can adapt the course to your students' needs.

Autism Disorder

Autism is a developmental disability resulting from a neurological disorder that affects communication and social interaction. Symptoms include highly patterned behavior, resistance to change, repetition, difficulty mixing with other people, little or no eye contact, attachment to specific objects, and unresponsiveness to social cues.

Asperger's Disorder

Asperger's is sometimes referred to as verbal autism, although the relationship between Asperger's and autism is not clear. Asperger's disorder tends to appear later (after 4 years old) than autism. People with Asperger's disorder express symptoms like social isolation, clumsiness, repetitive patterns in speech, repetitive motor mannerisms, lack of social reciprocity, and a restricted pattern of interest.

When you teach students with autism or Asperger's disorder, choose a quiet environment, minimize potential distractions, and keep the atmosphere as calm as possible. Set clear behavior guidelines to minimize inappropriate behavior. Use props and pictures to reinforce the spoken word.

Fetal Alcohol Syndrome (FAS)

FAS consists of a wide range of effects from alcohol use during pregnancy. This disease is not limited to heavy drinkers or routine alcohol use but can come from a single alcohol binge during pregnancy. Symptoms include heart, liver, and kidney problems; vision and hearing problems; slow growth; poor coordination; difficulties with math and reading; and physical deformities such as a small head or abnormalities of arms, legs, feet, and hands.

Students with FAS may manifest a spectrum of abilities and behaviors, so make sure to assess each student individually. Typically, students with FAS have poor concentration skills and can be easily distracted. Their fine motor and large muscle skills may be poorly developed. Some students with FAS may experience social awkwardness or emotional difficulties. They may lack the skills to manage impulse control.

When teaching students with FAS, create as quiet, nondistracting, and calm an environment as possible. Keep the student near you to help her or him focus and manage their behavior. Teach in short sessions and allow all students frequent breaks.

Speak slowly, give adequate time after questions, and use visual reinforcement as much as possible. As always, remember to encourage effort, growth, and success.

Learning and Attention Differences

Students of all ages represent many different learning styles and abilities. If students have predictable learning difficulties over an extended period of time that significantly affect their ability to learn, they may be evaluated and diagnosed with a learning disability or attention disorder. Learning disabilities are not the same as attention disorders, although both may occur in the same person.

- **Attention deficit/hyperactivity disorder (ADHD)** is a condition affecting children and adults that is characterized by problems with attention, impulsiveness, and overactivity.
- **Learning disorder (LD)** is an umbrella term covering a vast range of conditions. One student may have language processing difficulties, another student may have difficulties in social interactions, and another student may lack physical coordination. All of these conditions may be considered learning disorders.

Learning disabilities and attention disorders can cause repeated failure in school. Consequently, a student's self-image can be severely damaged by their learning or attention disorder, as Dr. Mel Levine notes in *Educational Care* (2002, 1):

Children who experience too much failure too early in life are exquisitely vulnerable to a wide range of complications. When these students are poorly understood, when their specific problems go unrecognized and untreated, they are especially prone to behavioral and emotional difficulties that frequently are more severe than the learning problems that generated them. It is not unusual for such students to lose motivation, to become painfully (and often secretly) anxious about themselves, to display noncompliance, to commit antisocial acts (including substance abuse and delinquent activity), and to lose ambition.

The number of children diagnosed with learning or attention disorders continues to increase

(U.S. Department of Education 2000). Collect as much information as you can about your students' learning and attention disorders before meeting the students. If you are working with a school group, converse with the classroom teacher and ask about the strategies the student uses in the classroom to achieve success. All students with special needs have an **individualized education plan (IEP)** that guides their strategies, treatment, and progress in the classroom. Teachers will not disclose the contents of the IEP, but they can discuss strategies the students are familiar with and help solve specific situations.

Fortunately, outdoor education provides an active approach to learning that reaches both the mind and body of the student. Many students who are unsuccessful in the classroom experience success in an outdoor learning situation. However, you still need to be knowledgeable about learning and attention disorders and develop deliberate strategies to help your students succeed.

Teaching Students With Attention Disorders

- Keep the student near you during focused activities.
- Develop a secret signal such as a wink and smile or gentle touch on the shoulder to help the student focus.
- Quickly establish a daily routine.
- Begin each day with a review.
- Establish clear rules, limits, and expectations for all students.
- Anticipate problems and make a proactive plan.
- Gain the student's attention before beginning.
- Give brief instructions.
- Use concrete, relevant, interesting examples.
- Celebrate the student's strengths and contributions.
- Allow the student to move frequently.
- Choose quiet, nondistracting study sites.
- Write as well as speak, and use props.
- Encourage taking notes in journals.
- Encourage good eating and sleeping habits.
- Become more knowledgeable about learning and attention differences.

© Mandy Vance

Outdoor educators must understand cultural and ethnic differences.

Stories From Real Life: Social Conventions of Speech

Our environmental education graduate program attracted students from all around the world. Students were required to be proficient in English before they were admitted to the program. However, social conventions of speech are usually not taught during English courses in other countries because the conventions vary from English-speaking culture to English-speaking culture.

An example of the role of social conventions is the phrase, "Hello, how are you doing?" As dominant-culture Americans we might use this greeting whenever we met someone. However, we wouldn't pause to allow the other person to respond to the question; it is merely a routine greeting. Foreign students in the program were usually aghast at the rudeness of Americans asking such a question and then walking away. It typically took a foreign student several months to realize this was simply a form of greeting, not an authentic question requiring a response.

Culture and Ethnicity

Teaching is a social endeavor. Our cultural values are deeply embedded in what we teach, how we choose to teach it, and how students are expected to engage with the material. Our culture and ethnicity frame our past experiences and help create our worldview, or the lens through which we see the world. Each of us is constantly interpreting what we see. The meaning we extract from an experience is influenced by our previous experience, which is guided by the culture we live in.

Not all Americans share the same culture and ethnicity. Dominant American culture is generally defined as white, male, Christian, young, thin, affluent, able-bodied, and heterosexual (Rothenberg, Schafehausen, and Schneider 2001). If you fit the cultural norm, role models for your identity infuse your daily life. If you differ from the cultural norm, you will develop your cultural identity without the benefit of role models and against the backdrop of the dominant culture (Tatum 1997). Finding positive role models with whom you can identify is more difficult for people of nondominant cultures than for people of the dominant culture.

In addition to your culture, how long you have lived in a culture influences your worldview. With immigration on the rise, many of your students may be recent immigrants or first-generation Americans. They may or may not be fluent in English and they may or may not understand American cultural currencies and social conventions. An understanding of the cultures from which your students come as well as the challenges of coming from a nondominant culture is essential as you strive to build connections with your students and provide them with meaningful experiences.

As an outdoor educator it is important that you understand the cultural and ethnic perspectives of your students. Not only do you need to understand and accept individual and cultural differences, you must create a learning environment where everyone feels valued and accepted. In addition, you must be able to reflect a positive self-image toward students of different cultural backgrounds. This means affirming when students engage in positive behavior valued by their culture. To know how to do this, you must understand your students' background and culture.

Building Your Cultural Awareness

- Read books and watch movies that depict different cultures.
- When you watch dominant culture movies or read books, inventory how often people from nondominant cultures are portrayed in a negative or stereotypical manner.
- Subscribe to publications that represent a variety of cultures.
- Learn about leaders from a culture other than your own and articulate their achievements. Use these examples in your teaching.
- Make friends across cultural boundaries.
- Attend local cultural events.
- Make sure your props fairly, accurately, and positively represent a variety of cultures.

- Choose stories and illustrations that reflect a culturally diverse audience (see page 204 in the bibliography for ideas).

Language

If you and all your audience members share the same primary language, you only need to appropriately reflect the developmental level of the audience in your vocabulary choice. Challenge your students to learn new terms and stretch their vocabulary, and avoid speaking over their heads. If they can't understand what you say, they won't learn from you.

English language learners (ELL) are people whose primary language is not English and who are learning English. In the United States it is estimated that 1 in 5 students speak a language other than English at home (U.S. Census Bureau 2003), and numbers are increasing every year.

ELL students will challenge you to use varied teaching methods. Depending on your students' English proficiency, you will need to slow down verbal instruction, provide strong visual support, review frequently, and assess student learning carefully before progressing. Keep in mind that ELL does not mean cognitively slow. ELL students will show the same range of cognitive ability, from gifted to challenging, as students who speak English as their primary language.

In addition to learning vocabulary and grammar, ELL students are learning the social conventions of speech. Socially accepted ways of arguing, interrupting, changing the subject, and so on vary with culture. Provide guided practice for vocabulary, grammar, and social conventions of speech as part of your course instruction for ELL students. Speak with ELL students early on to set appropriate goals and objectives for them throughout the course. They may be more interested in improving their language proficiency than learning natural history content or mastering a new skill. One strategy for the outdoor educator is to use student interest in language proficiency to teach vocabulary and content related to your topic.

Techniques to Use With ELL Students

- Use simple language and keep jargon and new vocabulary to a minimum.
- Create appropriate props to support the spoken word.
- Make sure props and vocabulary are developmentally appropriate for your audience.
- Create learning situations where students speak to each other.
- Assess learning to assure ELL students grasp main concepts.
- Review regularly.
- Encourage drawing as well as writing.
- Show interest in students' cultures by learning a few words of their native language.

Stories From Real Life: Body Language Barrier

I invited an environmental education professional from Guatemala to join our staff at an environmental learning center in the United States as an instructor. As a staff, we frequently talked about acceptance, tolerance, and diversity issues, yet it soon became apparent that the Guatemalan instructor was not being accepted by the other instructors. When I talked to the other instructors, the only thing I could learn was that the Guatemalan instructor talked too much and was "pushy." When I spent some time with the Guatemalan instructor I realized what the problem was. The instructor stood close to people when she spoke and she spoke in a loud voice, gesturing energetically with her hands as she spoke. At a staff meeting I told the instructors what I had noticed, and they learned to accept the close physical proximity, which had felt invasive to them. The instructor from Guatemala learned that Americans prefer a larger personal space and a quieter speaking volume than she was used to at home. With a few subtle changes in behavior, this cultural miscommunication was corrected and the year progressed successfully.

- Choose examples and role models from students' native cultures.
- Encourage students to be proud of their cultural heritage by honoring and respecting it.

Outdoor education programs are working to expand their appeal to underrepresented audiences. The North American Association for Environmental Education (NAAEE) dedicated its 2003 annual conference to the topic of diversity issues, and many state organizations are making similar efforts. Individual organizations are creating diversity initiatives or incentives to provide scholarships to socioeconomically challenged students. Your organization may make a commitment to recruit staff and develop programs to reach more diverse audiences. Second language proficiency is becoming an asset for outdoor educators.

Body Language

In addition to the words we speak, the language of our bodies communicates much about us. Body language, like verbal language, can vary from culture to culture. Because we are often habituated to our cultural norms and perceive body language unconsciously, it can be an unperceived barrier to intercultural communication.

One familiar example of body language as communication is personal space. Personal space is the envelope of empty space we keep around us, allowing only intimate acquaintances inside. When someone invades our personal space without our permission we feel uncomfortable or downright panicky.

Cultures require a varying amount of personal space. Some require more, some less. You've probably had the experience of listening to someone who has a smaller personal space than you have. The speaker gets closer and closer to you, feeling you are too distant. Meanwhile you keep backing away as your personal space is invaded. You find the speaker pushy or aggressive, while the speaker perceives you as aloof or distant.

The volume at which we speak, our facial expressions, the amount and length of eye contact, the ways we position our bodies, what we do with our arms, and the clothes we choose to wear all contribute to nonverbal communication between people. Realizing that cultures have different nonverbal norms will help you enter situations with more acceptance and understanding of these differences.

Strategies for Teaching Diverse Audiences

Use the audience assessment sheets from appendix B or a similar tool to collect information about your audience. Then start to create a big picture of your audience by copying and completing the assessment worksheet in table 4.2.

Once you have an overall picture of your audience, begin writing lesson plans, including content, route, and teaching methods specifically designed to meet the needs of your audience. You won't teach everyone perfectly all the time, but make sure you're providing a meaningful experience for everyone.

When you're done, scrutinize your overall strategy. Your teaching methodologies should be active (e.g., measure the circumference of a giant Sequoia rather than just talk about it), varied (write, speak, draw, act out) and appropriate (for the age and developmental level) for the audience.

Summary

What you teach, how you plan to teach, and even where you teach are determined by your audience. One of the first steps of preparation is assessing your audience before their arrival. You can put on your GAME FACe by considering your audience's gender, age, medical conditions, experience, familiarity with each other, abilities, and culture and ethnicity before writing your lesson plans. Based on these variables, you can begin to craft a curriculum to meet your students' expectations and needs.

This is not an exhaustive list, but it is a solid beginning in planning an experience that is appropriate, safe, and challenging. Once a course begins, keep an open mind and stay alert to signals you receive from the audience. Always expect the unexpected, and respond to the audience once you meet them face to face and can assess how the experience is going.

Table 4.2 Audience Assessment: Putting on Your GAME FACe

1. Gender	a. What is the gender makeup of your group? b. How will that influence their experience? c. How will you divide tasks among group members?
2. Age	a. How old are your students? b. Are they similar (school groups) or different (family camps) in age? c. What can you anticipate about their developmental level based on age? d. What other factors have influenced their developmental level? e. Describe generational differences your students may manifest.
3. Medical conditions	a. List the medical conditions group members have. b. Describe actions you need to take to respond to those conditions.
4. Experience	a. Describe the previous experience audience members have relating to your coursework. b. Does the audience have similar or different experience levels? c. What similar knowledge does your audience hold that may interfere with their learning?
5. Familiarity of audience members	a. How well do group members know each other? b. How will that influence your teaching? c. Outline a plan to introduce members to each other.
6. Abilities	a. What do you know about the physical abilities of your audience (mobility, hearing, vision)? b. How will you adapt to your audience's physical abilities? c. List any adaptive equipment you may need. d. What do you know about the cognitive abilities of your audience? e. What considerations will you need to make in your lesson planning to accommodate the cognitive abilities of your audience?
7. Culture and ethnicity	a. What is the ethnic and cultural makeup of your audience? b. Describe what you know about these cultures. c. Describe how your verbal examples and teaching props will positively and accurately reflect these cultures. d. List body-language considerations you will make. e. How many audience members speak English as their primary language? f. How many English language learners (ELL) are in your group? g. List the languages you and your audience members share. h. Are students first-generation Americans, recent immigrants, multigeneration Americans, or foreign visitors?

From Ken Gilbertson, Timothy Bates, Terry McLaughlin, and Alan Ewert, 2006, *Outdoor Education: Methods and Strategies,* Champaign, IL: Human Kinetics.

Explore Your World

1. Discuss seven ways to preassess an audience.

2. Describe how each of these influences your lesson preparation.

3. Explain how you can adapt your lesson to meet special needs of your audience (mobility, sight, hearing, language).

CHAPTER 5

Creating the Learning Environment

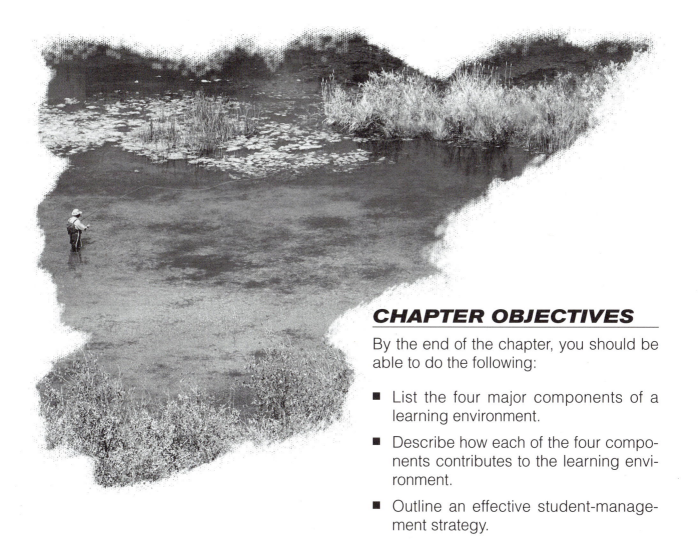

CHAPTER OBJECTIVES

By the end of the chapter, you should be able to do the following:

- List the four major components of a learning environment.

- Describe how each of the four components contributes to the learning environment.

- Outline an effective student-management strategy.

The learning environment is created through the outdoor educator's interpersonal skills, which encourage the students to interact and participate so that everyone in the group succeeds. This is a challenging part of teaching but also can be very rewarding. This chapter will explore the elements of a good learning environment, including managing students and the places where teaching occurs.

A successful learning environment is one that fosters learning in appropriate ways. One approach is to ensure that each learning opportunity is safe (physically and psychologically), challenging, and relevant. To do this, you must attend to four elements: the presenter, the pupil, the interpersonal process, and the place.

Foundations of the Learning Environment

Specific factors that contribute to a successful learning environment vary from learner to learner. However, as an outdoor educator there are some basic factors you can manage when creating the learning environment. These factors include making the learning environment physically safe, psychologically safe, challenging, and relevant to the student's life.

Physical Safety

When creating the learning environment, begin with physical safety. Nobody should get hurt and everyone's physical needs should be attended to. There should be snack and drink breaks, and students should know where and how to go to the bathroom. Students should understand the physical risks of the environment and be comfortable enough to engage in learning.

Psychological Safety

Once you've addressed physical safety, consider psychological safety. To learn and engage, people need to feel supported to take risks and be who they are. Participants should feel cared for and encouraged. They should feel they are a valued part of the group and have something to contribute and to gain from the group and the experience.

Challenge

Challenge must be present for learning to occur. Challenge can be intellectual, such as learning new information; it can be social, such as meeting new people or functioning in a new situation; or it can be physical, such as learning a new skill or building on existing skills. Challenge can also be a combination of any these forms.

Relevance

Learning must connect to students' lives and be relevant to their previous experience. Consider the daily lives of your students when crafting the learning environment and make deliberate links between the students' daily lives and their new experience. For example, imagine you are taking a group of inner-city students on a caving trip. To prepare them for the experience, you might address fear, trust, and working as a team. Following the experience, you would debrief the group, helping them link how they addressed their fears, how they were willing to trust others and act in a trustworthy manner, and how they worked together as a team. You would generate concrete examples from their daily lives in which they need and use these characteristics, and then have them set a specific goal for a behavior change at home. How will their caving experience continue to help them at home? What barriers might they run into when implementing this new learning? How will they deal with these barriers? In this manner, the caving experience informs their daily lives.

When designing an outdoor experience, clearly identify your outcomes and goals. Outcomes and goals will reflect the relevance the experience has for the students. You have to figure out how you will know if you've created a successful learning environ-

Explore Your World

Think of a learning experience that you found particularly fulfilling. Describe it in detail. Were you alone or in a group? Did the group have a leader? What elements contributed to your feeling of fulfillment? What parts of the experience blocked or inhibited your learning?

ment. Is your goal for participants to have fun? Pass time safely, such as in an after-school program? Learn a skill? Learn about themselves? The first step in creating a successful learning environment is identifying how you will measure success.

Components of Successful Learning Environments

Now that you have identified how you will measure success, build your learning environment by attending to the four main components: presenter, pupil, interpersonal process, and place.

Presenter

Your personality, management strategy, and team-building strategy all set the stage for the learning environment. Use your passion, knowledge, skills, and humor as tools to create the environment. There is an old saying in teaching, "You teach who you are." Your personality, enthusiasm, and passion for the topic will teach more than your words possibly can.

You bear a large responsibility as the course leader. You are responsible for the safety of the course, even if you choose to delegate some safety responsibility to your students. Your energy and enthusiasm for the material provide a role model for your students. You may choose not to be on center stage throughout the entire course, and you probably shouldn't be if you want to practice student-directed learning and constructivism. However, it remains your responsibility to facilitate a safe, involving experience for all students.

Take care of yourself, getting enough rest, healthy food, and exercise before beginning a course. Prepare the course content and teaching materials well in advance so you can respond to last-minute changes and emergencies. Spend some time reflecting on your own strengths and weaknesses so you are familiar with what you bring to the process and where you may need support.

Pupil

Each student brings a unique combination of interests, motivations, course expectations, willingness to engage, physical condition and limitations, and needs to the course. Once the students arrive, begin immediately to build **rapport** by making a connection with your students. Learn each student's name immediately and use it frequently. Begin having conversations with your students to get to know them. Notice who is quiet and who is boisterous. Notice what diversity is in your group (males and females, ethnicity, physical ability, age, and so on). These are all factors that will influence the dynamic among group members.

Immediately begin to build student **motivation** to learn. Motivation is a student's intent to learn (Hunter 1982). Outdoor educators frequently use the student's interest in the topic and their own energy and enthusiasm to build motivation. Interest and enthusiasm can be effective motivators, but using a variety of motivation strategies will make you a more powerful and flexible educator. When student interest starts to flag and your enthusiasm isn't enough to carry the course, it's nice to have alternative plans.

One way to motivate students is to give a course overview, letting them know what will happen in the course. Often this gets students excited about the activity and content, and it reassures students who may have unrealistic concerns about the course. Keep in mind that your students are probably much less familiar with the outdoors than you are. Simple things like where they'll go to the bathroom or whether they'll have to sit on the ground and get dirty may distract students. Keep them focused on the content of the course.

Stories From Real Life: A Motivating Overview

A group of graduate students showed up bright and early for a full day of birding. As soon as they were settled, I gave them a quick overview of the class. We were going to use binoculars to identify common species, band birds with a local bander, monitor behavior of a local species, and do a habitat reconstruction project. One student's hand went up as soon as the overview was complete. "We get to do all that today?" she wondered, clearly excited. I had no question that the overview had its intended effect on her motivation.

Other motivational strategies include helping students understand the immediate relevance of the information. You can use verbal cues to help students discern the most important information. For example, you might say, "Pay attention to this next part because in 30 minutes you'll be on the orienteering course by yourself and you'll need to know how to use the compass correctly." Or you might say, "Listen carefully to what we cover next. We're going over what to bring on the trip and how to pack your backpack."

Empowering students is an effective motivator. By giving students choices, making them leaders, or allowing them to determine the content of class, they will engage more readily. They will learn to be responsible for their own education. This is especially true of adult students. Adults like to exert control over their own experience. Guide them by giving them choices and clarifying the risks and benefits involved with each choice.

Photo courtesy of Salish Sea Expeditions.

Motivation through engagement.

Early in the course assess each student's expectations of the course. You also may have collected some written information from the students before the course. Check in with the students to discuss their expectations. This provides an opportunity for you to influence unrealistic or inappropriate expectations as well as hone in on what the students would like to learn in the course. For example, a student expecting to execute a roll in an introductory

kayaking class needs to understand the complexities of kayaking. Learning how to roll a kayak is a great long-term goal, but it is not an appropriate goal for a weekend introductory course. During longer courses, check in with students throughout the course to assure that they feel it is meeting their expectations. Encourage students to be open to readjusting their expectations once the course is underway. Often new goals open up as the student gains knowledge about a subject.

Student expectations also provide excellent closure to courses. Revisit the expectations at the end of a course. In what ways were the expectations met and not met? What surprised the student about the course? What new goals does the student leave the course with?

Interpersonal Process

The dynamic among group personalities, skill and knowledge levels, maturity, and leadership skills affects how smoothly course goals are accomplished and contributes to the success of each student. In addition to who you are as the educator and who the individual students are, the interaction among group members is a vital component of the learning environment. Each student brings strengths and weaknesses, interests and dislikes, and unique personality traits to the group. How those different characteristics blend and how the outdoor educator sets the tone and manages the group will influence the success of the learning environment.

Begin each course on a strong, positive note. Take charge of the group energy immediately and focus it on a fun, meaningful activity right away. Be prepared with props and tools. Start on time and with high energy.

The beginning of the course or lesson is when your students are most interested in what it will be like. You set the tone with everything you do, so it's best to attend to administrative details before the course begins. Some details must be attended to after the start of a course, but don't do them right away. Engage the group immediately in an activity and come back to paperwork or other details after a couple of hours.

Some courses, such as corporate retreats, family trips, and personal growth experiences, focus on interpersonal and intrapersonal growth and challenge. Even in courses that do not focus on group process, spend some time developing the teamwork and engagement of the group. In a short course this may mean playing a fun game to introduce group members to each other and then moving on to content. During longer courses you may choose to provide a team-building experience every day.

Managing Students

An important component of the interpersonal process is managing student behavior. This applies to school-aged children as well as adults. The outcome is the same regardless of age: a safe learning environment where all students can engage, learn, and grow. Even the process is similar regardless of age. The biggest difference is the method you employ to accomplish the process.

Effective management is a symphony of student engagement, motivation to learn, and ability to participate. The outdoor educator is the conductor, establishing clear limits, expectations, and guidelines for the experience. Because of its multifaceted structure, effective management can be subtle and difficult to master. In addition, beginning outdoor educators are often uncomfortable with their position of authority. It is possible to use a respectful, compassionate approach while still providing appropriate structure, but it takes time and practice.

In an outdoor experience, there is the added challenge of the novel outdoor setting. Students may perceive you as a substitute teacher. To minimize misbehavior, address these concerns privately, directly, proactively, and consistently. If course content and activities encourage intrinsic interest from students, it is easier to minimize misbehavior. Your goal is to set a positive, safe tone for class, so keep your demeanor positive, smile frequently, and expect your students to behave, not misbehave.

Another challenge for beginning outdoor educators is managing an audience of students who are older than themselves. Whether this involves managing the participation of teachers and chaperones who accompany school-aged children or leading a workshop for teachers, beginning outdoor educators may feel awkward and uncomfortable in their role. Keep in mind that you are the expert and you understand the consequences of students' behavior choices in the outdoors better than anyone else. Treat people of all ages with respect, have reasons for your decisions and rules you enforce, and you can effectively manage every audience.

An outdoor instructor encourages team building during lunch.

Management Strategy

There are many schools of thought on effective student management. Behavior management, which is described in the following section, is one strategy. As you build your skills and gain experience, explore other options. You likely won't find a single strategy that fits all situations. Your management strategy will continue to refine and develop throughout the course of your career.

Behavior management involves setting guidelines for safe student participation. Effective management skills are essential for creating a physically and psychologically safe learning environment. The more involved the students are in the establishment of these guidelines, the more motivated they will be to participate. Promoting student involvement in the management process also promotes their growth and development. Do not compromise student safety while attempting to create an inclusive environment. Even in adult courses, you are responsible for judgments involving the safety of the group. Tailor the degree of control to the students' developmental level.

Establishing Expectations

Expectations are rules for behavior. These can range from requiring everyone to participate to requiring written assignments to be typewritten. One of the first things you should do after meeting your students is set course expectations. By clearly defining expectations from the beginning you are being proactive, and students understand how to behave. It is essential to involve the students in the process of establishing expectations. You are not listing the dos and don'ts of the course. You are establishing a process for communication among all participants. You are responsible for setting the tone of the course and establishing the process for communication, but the expectations ideally come from your students. Younger students need more guidance in this process, while older students can have more autonomy. Assess the developmental level of your students and adapt your approach accordingly. It's better to be conservative, so if you aren't sure of students' developmental level, take more of the lead.

Some outdoor educators choose to begin by playing games or doing a mixer to set a fun tone. For example, you might learn students' names by tossing a small object around the group. Each student says the name of the person they are tossing the object to. As you and the students master the names, add one or two more objects to the toss.

This will speed up response time and help group members hone in on names. Then follow up the game with a discussion on behavioral expectations. If you choose to start with a game, keep an eye out for unsafe situations and intervene immediately.

How to Set Expectations

Have students sit in a circle in a comfortable setting where they won't be distracted for about 15 minutes. Depending on the age of the students and the tone you want to set, you can use a talking stick that, when held, gives the holder the right to speak. A stuffed animal, a ball, or a natural object like a feather or rock will also suffice.

Everything you do during these first few minutes sets a tone. In addition to listening to your words, students are watching your every move. Be deliberate in the choices you make. For example, ask a question, give adequate time for students to think, and then ask who would like to answer first. For certain questions you will want a response from every student. For other questions you can collect a sampling of responses. Students can pass the talking stick around the circle or gently toss it to the next speaker. Use a chalkboard or paper and marker to summarize student comments. Be sure to reward good listening behavior and prevent interruptions or disruptions.

Begin with a warm-up question such as, "Give one word that describes how you are feeling about the upcoming (day, week, trip, or whatever applies)." This gets students talking and familiarizes them with your methods. Another strategy is to have students discuss the question in pairs before discussing it as a group.

Follow up with a question about what each student expects from the experience. It's important that each student respond. First, explain that as a class they have a lot of exciting activities to do and places to visit. You and they need to make sure that everyone is safe and that everyone can participate. What rules or expectations should the group have? List the suggested expectations on the board, categorizing similar suggestions under one heading. Suggest ideas to fill in any omissions once the students complete their suggestions.

After looking at the list of expectations, ask if anyone has questions about why some of these are necessary. Allow discussion and make changes to the list as appropriate. Edit the list and group the expectations so you have two or three main expectations. For example, a lot of behaviors can be condensed under a single expectation for respect.

Once the list is complete and students understand the necessity of each expectation, get all students to agree to the list. Use a signaled response, such as nodding or a thumbs-up. Their agreement is essential because they are setting up guidelines for their experience.

The group expectations will depend on the age of the students and their reasons for attending the course. When leading adults, go around the group and have individuals share what they expect from the course. Follow with your expectations or framework. For example, when leading teacher workshops you might share two things immediately. First, write the word *educere* on the board, explaining that it is the Latin root of *education*, which means "to draw forth." Tell them they can expect that from you as a teacher. You view them not as empty glasses to fill with information but as knowledgeable professionals who have a lot to share with the group.

Second, write, "The person doing the talking is the person doing the learning." Explain that the students are expected to talk because it's through talking and teaching that one truly explores and masters new information. With these two expectations on the board, frame your expectations of the students: They should share what they know and expect to participate in the course, or they should be active learners.

Expectations for a class are based on the expected developmental level of your students.

- Preschool students get very clear but playful expectations such as, "There is glue on your seats. You will stay put until I come and touch you on the head. Then your glue will release and you can stand up."

- Elementary school students get concrete expectations such as, "Show respect for yourself, others, and the environment." Then explore what respectful behavior looks like.

- High school students get more abstract expectations such as, "Act appropriately. Sometimes that means running around and laughing, sometimes that means listening quietly. You need to decide what appropriate behavior is at every point in class."

- Adults get clear expectations with reasons such as, "I will start class promptly on time

every session. This is how I show respect for all class participants. I also expect you to show up prepared and on time."

Adapting expectations by age level is a bit of an art form, but much can be anticipated before the class by thoughtful planning.

Rewarding and Acknowledging Behavior Rewarding behavior means noticing and responding when students adhere to the expectations. Acknowledging behavior means providing gentle reminders to students who forget or ignore the expectations. In class, especially early on, be sure to enthusiastically reward appropriate behavior and correct inappropriate behavior.

Examples of Rewarding Appropriate Behavior

- "Thanks for waiting your turn, Juana."

- "You showed good active listening behaviors during that discussion, Steve."

- "Nice job as trail leader, Yo. You kept the group together and set a reasonable pace for everyone."

These comments are directed toward individuals and give feedback for specific behavior. Broad generalizations such as "Nice work!" are less effective than statements about specific behavior such as "Thanks for picking up after lunch."

To keep a positive tone and to help students understand what you expect from them, pay attention to appropriate behavior choices. Appropriate behavior is easy to overlook, while misbehavior gets attention by being disruptive or distracting. Train yourself to notice appropriate choices, both quietly to yourself and aloud to your students.

Acknowledging inappropriate choices must be done as quickly and as personally as possible, such as in a quiet conversation with the individual. Avoid discussing inappropriate behavior in front of the entire class unless the entire class is involved. One of your goals is to preserve and enhance the self-esteem of your students, so address inappropriate choices as quickly and privately as the setting allows.

Examples of Acknowledging Inappropriate Choices

- "Jose, the rule is no throwing snow. The next time you throw snow you will sit out of the rest of the activity."

Stories From Real Life:
Two Minutes to Positive Leadership

Lao was a remarkable 10th grader but in an awkward phase. He was physically uncomfortable with his recent growth and he was socially awkward. His behavior would swing from kind and insightful to disruptive. Lao wasn't the most challenging student in class but he certainly made his presence felt.

About 3 days into the program we were traveling across campus to our challenge course. We hopped on a shuttle bus for a 10-minute ride to the course. The shuttle was empty, and Lao sat near the front. I sat down next to Lao and took advantage of the situation to start a quick dialogue.

"Lao, how's this week been going for you?"

"Great, I'm having a lot of fun."

"How are you feeling about our group?"

"I think they're really fun. We're having a good time."

"How do you feel about your role in our group?"

"I dunno."

"Can I share something I noticed? You are a strong leader. People in this group listen to what you say and watch what you do. Sometimes you use your role to help people in the group, and sometimes you use your role to interrupt what's going on. Use your superpowers for good, Lao, not evil."

Lao nodded, and he stayed in the role of strong, positive leader for the rest of the week.

This is a good example of a teacher-led discussion. It would have benefited Lao's development if we had a longer discussion during which he elucidated the role he saw himself in and his strengths and weaknesses in that role. However, I was looking for an early opportunity for a discussion with Lao and when the short bus ride presented itself, I took advantage of it.

- "Marin, you pushed in line in front of Jane. Go to the back of the line."

- "That behavior is disrespectful, Sarah. What would be a more respectful choice?"

- "Quinn, alcohol is not allowed on backcountry trips."

The first sentence in each interaction is a brief observation of student behavior. Throwing snow and pushing in line are observations. Disrespectful behavior is a judgment on the behavior observed. Jose received a warning about the consequences of his behavior, Marin received a consequence for her behavior, and Sarah is about to take part in a discussion about behavior choices. Quinn is an adult who is about to hear your organization's alcohol rule. Once he understands the policy and has a chance to respond, the two of you will pour out the alcohol together.

When Talking Isn't Enough You've involved the students in setting clear expectations. You have verbally rewarded appropriate choices and acknowledged inappropriate choices, but behavior doesn't improve. What do you do? It's time for consequences.

If a student disregards an expectation more than twice, consequences are necessary. The best consequences are those that relate directly to the misbehavior. For example, if students go outside in the rain without rain gear, they'll get wet. If student behavior is disrespectful, a simple consequence related to the behavior should immediately follow.

In an outdoor setting, sometimes it can be difficult to identify an appropriate consequence. The goal is not to punish the students. The goal is to let them experience the consequences of their choices. Use natural consequences whenever you can. For example, 8th graders who insist on

Tips and Techniques

- Be consistent.
- Keep consequences short, simple, and related to the behavior.
- Stand close to the student for privacy.
- Use direct eye contact, but don't be intimidating.
- Remain calm and use a soft voice.
- Affirm what's appropriate.
- Be firm and free of anger.
- Listen to the student's side of the story and show understanding.
- Don't allow excuses or bargaining.

wearing tennis shoes in the snow can be allowed to do so. Make sure they understand that the snow will be slippery and their feet will get wet and cold. As long as the students experience discomfort and not real physical pain or frostbite and they understand the consequences when making the decision, let the students make the choice. However, if safety is at stake, overrule their decision.

Sometimes natural consequences are difficult to identify. In these situations, try to relate the consequence to the behavior. For example, if the expectation is no running on the trail, an appropriate consequence for running would be for that student to walk at the back of the group. If the expectation is respectful listening and the student chats with a neighbor instead of listening, an appropriate consequence would be to separate the two students. Follow up both of these consequences with a quiet, private conversation with the student as soon as the opportunity arises.

Some outdoor educators have a difficult time allowing students to experience the consequences

of their choices. Keep the attitude that consequences such as these are no big deal. We all experience consequences in our daily lives.

Managing Troublemakers

"To see [our students] clearly and see them whole, and respond to them wisely in the moment, requires a fusion of Freud and Solomon that few of us achieve."

Parker Palmer, *The Courage to Teach* (1998)

Sometimes an individual student consistently challenges limits and expectations. An outdoor educator can quickly come to expect certain students to misbehave. This expectation will influence the student's self-perception and the student will quickly fill the role of troublemaker.

When the same students challenge expectations again and again, it can be hard to break the cycle. Begin by understanding that the behavior stems from the students' frustration in trying to get their needs met. Find ways to build a positive relationship with these students and look for their strengths

Stories From Real Life: Consequences for Adult Behavior

A friend of mine had just entered law school. He knew he would be penalized for turning work in late. He was upset when he was docked 10 points for turning in a paper 2 minutes late. He asked me my opinion as a teacher. My response was, "Well, your professor is setting clear limits. You know exactly where you stand with her. And chances are, you won't turn in a paper late again, so her strategy worked."

and contributions, not just their misbehavior. Make a point of spending extra time hiking on the trail or just chatting with the students. Make a connection with them as a person and try to meet their needs in a more positive, direct manner.

Strategies for Managing Misbehavior

- Separate the action from the student.
  - "I like you, not your behavior choice."
  - "I want you to stay in this class, but your behavior has to change."
  - "I appreciate the leadership you've shown; you've contributed a lot to the success of this class. But your behavior choices are affecting others."
- After implementing a consequence, forgive the student and allow the student to rejoin the group with a clean slate. Don't hold a grudge.
- Visit with the student on the trail and build rapport. Send the student the message that you enjoy her company; she is not a bad person.
- Encourage appropriate behavior choices. Create opportunities for the student to succeed.

- Notice improvements and discuss those with the student.
  - "The tone of voice you used just now was much more appropriate than the one you used earlier."
  - "I saw you put a lot of effort into waiting for others during the last activity. Keep up the good work!"
  - "I noticed you checking in with Sally to see how she was doing on the hike. That shows you are concerned about others."

Anger Management Outdoor educators are human and experience a wide range of emotions when teaching. It's the feeling of making a human connection that drives most of us to teach. But what happens when those emotions turn negative? Especially in situations involving behavior management, outdoor educators can feel angry, manipulated, and ineffective.

Your emotions reflect what's happening between you and the student. If you're angry, that's important information. Because anger is a masking emotion, meaning that other emotions are behind the anger, warning signs can vary. People get angry when they feel hurt, scared, or threatened, and warning signs may include difficulty breathing,

---

Stories From Real Life: Managing a Troublemaker

Ryan, a 10th-grade student, had been a handful all week. He routinely showed up for class late and unprepared. While other students volunteered to help carry gear, Ryan never stepped forward. The group constantly waited for him as he fumbled with his gear and backpack. Even his physical appearance was untidy, with long hair hanging in his face, a sullen expression, and baggy, ragged clothes.

The second day of the course Ryan's classroom teacher accompanied us on the trail. I noticed her rapport with Ryan. He stuck to her side like glue and seemed to light up when talking to her.

While students were engaged in an activity, I chatted with the teacher. "Tell me about Ryan," I said. She smiled. "He's a handful, isn't he? His parents are divorced and he lives with his mother. She's working two jobs trying to support her three kids. She's never at home."

With this new understanding I went back to class. I sought Ryan out for conversations on the trail. I asked him to help out with tasks like setting up lunch. When he contributed to discussions I affirmed his effort. I made sure the activities were challenging but things he could succeed at. I kept high expectations for the behavior and involvement of all the students in the class, including Ryan. When Ryan made poor choices, I still enforced appropriate consequences for him. By the end of the week Ryan was participating in class and opening up to sharing thoughts, knowledge, and insights.

Yelling at students is ineffective management.

Because you are the responsible adult as well as a role model, you cannot lose control and behave angrily with a student. Force yourself to appear calm. Calmly revealing your anger is appropriate and can be very effective. Acting angry and expressing anger are two different things. You can calmly say, "I'm feeling angry and hurt right now," without yelling or losing control.

Guiding Your Growth

Learning how to effectively manage students is an imperfect science. No outdoor educator does it perfectly. Keep your sense of humor and be patient with yourself as you develop your own style of effective management. Conversations with your peers can help you through challenging situations. Strive to set a positive tone by noticing appropriate behavior in students. Spend time reflecting after a class and notice what you did well and what you want to improve. An effectively managed group will learn more and be more enjoyable for you to teach.

Managing Adult Audiences

Many of the principles discussed thus far work for adults as well as children. You want to set clear guidelines immediately. Work hard to be proactive, preventing misbehavior whenever possible. When adults make poor choices, connect with them immediately to let them know. When necessary, implement consequences. The same process works for all audiences regardless of age. However, managing adults involves more diplomacy, more explanation

increased heart rate, dilated pupils, coughing or choking, and feeling flushed. Act before you get angry. Notice your warning signs and know your triggers.

© Ira Estin

Explore Your World

The following is a true story. At each "What do you do?" stop and write down how you would respond in that situation before continuing.

It's Monday morning and your 5th-grade students are about to arrive for their 3-day field trip to your residential environmental education school. Since the students live so close to your campus, they arrive around 10 a.m. and bring their own lunches for the first day of program.

Your group arrives and drops off their sleeping bags. They gather at the designated spot, arriving one at a time. You greet and chat with students as they arrive. Two male parent chaperones are quietly watching the students arrive. The students arrive with appropriate clothing, backpacks, journals, lunch, and water bottles—everyone except Tammy, that is. Tammy arrives without a backpack. She is pacing around and can't seem to stand still when she is talking to you. She says she has everything she needs in her pockets. She doesn't have lunch, but she says she never eats lunch. She claims to have left her lunch at home on purpose.

(continued)

(continued)

What do you do?

Tammy is clearly sending signals that she needs help. She is unprepared and appears agitated. Fifth-grade children shouldn't skip meals because their body and brain are still growing and need energy to learn. Tammy will also need water frequently. If possible, check in with Tammy's teacher to get his insight into how Tammy behaves in the classroom and if there are techniques he employs to include and manage Tammy. Before you leave the campus, short day or not, you need to get Tammy a backpack, water, lunch, journal, and anything else you expect her to have to successfully participate. Pair one of the adult chaperones with Tammy to encourage her, give her attention, and keep her on task.

****

Because the day is so short, you skip your rule-setting session during which you normally have students come up with rules and expectations that they agree to abide by. You jump into activities, planning to set the tone and grab the students' attention through the activities. You have planned a team challenge, a journaling activity in the touch-and-see room filled with plant specimens and stuffed animals representative of the area, and then a 1-mile hike to an aesthetic point.

You play the group game to assess where the students are as a group. They accomplish the task, but they communicate poorly and don't seem to trust each other. Tammy participates, but she stays at the back of the line, taking part only minimally, and asks you to repeat instructions as soon as you finish giving them.

What do you do?

Tammy needs clear behavior guidelines. Even though you feel rushed for time, in the end skipping over the rules doesn't save time and may put students at risk. Take the time to develop rules with the students and get their agreement to abide by the rules. Be sure the rules are concrete and clear, because these students are 5th graders (see chapter 4). Try giving Tammy a little extra attention and developing a good rapport with her. Set her up for success by establishing clear guidelines and boundaries, encouraging her appropriate behavior choices, and giving her challenges she can accomplish.

****

You only have time for one activity, the group challenge, before lunch. Since the morning was so rushed, you decide to debrief the group game during lunch. Tammy doesn't have lunch, so she has lots of time to talk during the debriefing. Tammy dominates the discussion, but the other students don't seem interested in participating and chat quietly among themselves. Tammy frequently stands and mills around the lunch circle. She isn't eating and she doesn't show any interest in eating.

As you prompt students in debriefing the group activity, Tammy gives ridiculous answers to your questions. For example, when you try to make an analogy between the team game and basketball, Tammy insists that basketball isn't a team sport and one person can have the ball all the time. Whenever you ask a yes-or-no question, Tammy gives the opposite answer of what you are looking for. You keep trying to get Tammy to admit that basketball is a team game, but she won't budge. You end up arguing with her to no avail.

What do you do?

A power struggle between you and Tammy is developing. Avoid the power struggle. Begin by finding some common ground with Tammy. For example, when she mentions sport teams, find out if she likes a certain sport or team and ask her to tell you more about that team. If you are looking for a specific answer to a question, rephrase the question to allow students to use critical thinking rather than just repeat a response. Use a hand-raising rule to manage Tammy's

(continued)

shouted or inappropriate answers as well as to allow other students a chance to respond. Tammy is not your only concern at this point. The other students aren't engaging in the discussion. Lunch may not be the best time for such a structured discussion. Regroup after lunch when everyone can focus on the task at hand, and conduct a structured discussion where everyone can contribute.

****

After lunch you choose to do a quiet drawing activity in the touch-and-see room. When you ask students to get their journals you notice for the first time that Tammy doesn't have a journal. You are busy getting other students on task so you quickly direct Tammy to borrow a blank page from someone else and get to work.

You work intensely with the other students during the drawing activity, so it takes you awhile to notice that Tammy hasn't gotten paper or a pencil or started work on the assignment. You ask another student for a piece of paper and a pencil and instruct Tammy to begin the assignment. Tammy takes a long time looking around the room, choosing something to draw. Finally she settles on a small bat.

Tammy asks you if a bat is a mammal and you tell her it is. She challenges you that all mammals have hair, but this bat doesn't have hair. You try to get her to admit that the bat she is looking at has hair, but she won't admit it. You are so exasperated with her argumentative behavior, you exclaim, "How simple do I have to make this for you?"

Tammy finally settles into drawing and finishes a rough sketch in about 2 minutes. She spends the rest of the time wandering around the room.

What do you do?

By this time, you should be aware that Tammy will need attention in order to succeed at the activity. Watch Tammy immediately after you give the group the assignment. If she isn't engaging with the activity, give her clear guidelines, such as "Tammy, I expect you to draw this bat. Include the outline as well as five other details you see. This should take you at least 10 minutes. If you get done sooner than that, look over your work carefully to make sure you've followed directions." Ask one of the chaperones to sit near Tammy and keep her on task. Give Tammy lots of encouragement for her effort and continue to build rapport with her. And don't forget that Tammy is only one of your students. What do your other students need right now to be successful?

****

This story illustrates how effective management has ripple effects all through a class. As outdoor educators we may never know the labels the students bring with them. Tammy may or may not have been diagnosed with attention deficit/hyperactivity disorder (ADHD). Is it important for you to know Tammy's diagnosis relative to hyperactivity? Why or why not? Can you effectively manage her behavior without this knowledge?

---

of reasons, more discussion, and more choice on the part of the student. The following examples will help you understand the range of situations you may have to respond to:

- A teacher uses profanity with her school-aged children.

- Some college students bring drugs along on a backpacking trip.

- Several teachers enrolled in a workshop for college credit were out late partying last night and didn't show up for class today.

- A small family leaves your family weekend program to spend time exploring on their own.

- A group of adults goes sledding on an off-limits hill during free time.

This is not an inclusive list, nor are these situations common in outdoor education. Most participants, whether child or adult, take part in your course because they want to be there and are interested in and excited about their experience. However, be prepared to respond to whatever a situation brings. Following any kind of management situation, reflect on what you learned and how you might avoid a similar experience in the future.

Place

The first three components of the learning environment involve people. The presenter, the pupils, and the interactions among group members all influence the learning environment. The final component of the learning environment is the physical environment itself: the place. The weather, remoteness, popularity, and physical structure of the site shape the success of the learning environment. Environmental hazards are the objective parts of a learning environment. These cannot be controlled. The subjective parts of a learning environment are leader and student behavior, gear, and training, all of which can be controlled. A successful outdoor educator understands and evaluates the **objective hazards** and plans and controls the **subjective hazards.**

Leave No Trace Ethics

Leave No Trace ethics consist of seven principles of behavior to minimize human effects on wild areas. These principles include the following: plan ahead and prepare, travel and camp on durable surfaces, dispose of waste properly, leave what you find, minimize campfire impacts, respect wildlife, and be considerate of other visitors (Leave No Trace 2004). The Leave No Trace Center for Outdoor Ethics is a national nonprofit organization dedicated to promoting responsible outdoor recreation through education, research, and partnerships. Leave No Trace education builds awareness, appreciation, and respect for nature. When teaching in outdoor settings, practice Leave No Trace ethics and teach them to your students. Your efforts will help preserve wild and natural areas for the future.

Logistics

Logistics consist of getting, maintaining, and distributing personnel and materials to a study site.

Logistics range from arranging food and transportation for your students to setting up an evacuation plan in case of an emergency. The more routine and systematic your programs are, the simpler the logistical arrangements. Create a template of your program and use that template whenever possible to make logistical arrangements easier. Customized programs usually involve more logistics than standardized programs.

Logistics demand organizational skills. Make checklists and timelines and keep accurate records to minimize mistakes and avoid overlooking details. If others are helping organize logistics, create clear communication plans so tasks are clearly defined and responsible leaders are identified. Check and double-check the key logistical points to make sure everything goes smoothly when the program begins. The more organized your logistics are when your program begins, the more you can concentrate on your students and provide a meaningful program.

When planning a course, keep these key points in mind:

- Know who owns and manages the property where you'll hold your course.
- Arrange for permits or permission to use the site as necessary.
- Begin with a site reconnaissance so you have direct experience with the site before the program begins.
- Familiarize yourself with any special logistical or safety concerns of the site.
- Locate bathrooms for student use or be prepared to teach students appropriate methods and ethics for going to the bathroom outdoors.
- Arrange for food, snacks, and water as necessary.
- Practice Leave No Trace ethics.
- Before leaving an area, do a small cleanup project to remove traces of your use and leave the area better than when you arrived.
- Understand that you are a representative of your organization and your profession. Make sure your behavior is exemplary. Be a role model for others to follow.

Transportation is a major part of logistics, and getting students to and from your study site is an important part of course planning. If students are meeting you at the site, make sure they have maps or are familiar enough with the area that they will arrive on time. If you are taking a bus or van, arrange for parking or for another driver to shuttle your vehicle to a suitable parking area. Consider the length of the drive when planning your courses. Be prepared for bathroom breaks en route to the study site. Be aware of motion sickness. Let students prone to motion sickness sit in the front of the vehicle. Open a window for fresh air for the student if necessary.

Safety

Safety is becoming more and more of a concern when planning outdoor education experiences. Every ethical outdoor educator works to keep students safe from harm. Some risk is inherent in an outdoor setting, and often participants choose the experience specifically because of the risks involved.

Students may feel at risk while rock climbing.

© University of Minnesota Duluth Outdoor Program

Perceived risk is the danger or harm the participants believe is present. **Actual risk** is the real risk that is present. If perceived risk and actual risk of an experience are similar, the participant has an accurate assessment of inherent risk. However, perceived risk and actual risk can be different. For example, students may feel greatly at risk while taking part in a rock-climbing experience. Their perceived risk is high, but their actual risk is quite low due to the safety measures in place. In the car on the drive home, the students' perceived risk may be quite low. They are probably used to riding in cars and are quite tolerant of the risk involved. In reality, actual risk for the trip is at its highest point during the drive due to the frequency of car accidents.

If perceived risk is too high, it will interfere with a student's ability to learn and participate in your course. Manage perceived risk to keep it at a reasonable level, and make sure you understand and can manage the actual risk your students are taking.

It is incumbent on outdoor educators and their parent organization to manage risk. Carefully consider the risks you are exposing your students to. Every organization should have an explicit safety policy and every employee is responsible for reading, understanding, and implementing the policy regarding risk management. There are two elements to risk management: incident prevention and incident response.

Incident Prevention Your first goal is to prevent harm to your students. Become aware of the apparent and hidden risks of your study sites. Make sure you understand the medical history and conditions of your students. Manage your students and their experience to minimize exposure to unnecessary risk. If you don't feel you have sufficient control of your students or if your students are not developmentally ready for an experience, don't engage in the experience, regardless of the students' expectations. Be aware that students' intellectual, physical, emotional, and psychological developmental levels can vary. You may have a group that is intellectually well developed for their age, but their emotional development lags behind the norms. If you assess a group's development in one area, don't assume similar development in another area. Assess each area independently, and assess each student individually and the group as a whole. Your goal is to provide a safe yet meaningful experience for every group member.

The organization you work for will have first aid training requirements. Make sure your training is current and you can respond effectively to incidents. Carry the first aid equipment issued and required by your organization and become familiar with it before the course begins. Bring communication equipment such as cell phones, radios, or two-way radios that your organization provides and requires. Double-check batteries and cell phone coverage so that your communication tools will help you in the event of an incident. Work with your organization to develop evacuation plans. Know those plans and protocols and carry written copies of them with you in the field.

Incident Response The second aspect of risk management is incident response. You have thoroughly explored an area and are familiar with inherent risks. You have set group limits to keep students safe. Yet someone gets hurt, sick, or lost. Your response to the incident is defined in your organization's risk-management protocol. Familiarize yourself with the protocol so you can respond efficiently to any incident. Now is the time that your equipment, first aid training, and communication network are essential. Respond to incidents calmly and professionally. Keep accurate records of the incident as it occurs and involve other rescue personnel as the situation warrants.

Following an incident, complete all documentation required by your agency. Reflect on why the incident occurred so you can learn from the experience. Did it occur due to failure by the outdoor educator to not notice a risk or to communicate rules clearly and early? Was it a failure by the student to follow the rules? Many accidents are preventable. A tree falling unexpectedly or a rock falling from a cliff may constitute a true accident, but even then location of the group in a high-risk zone, such as a rock-fall zone, calls into question the nature of the accident. Prepare for your courses by scrutinizing the study area for safety concerns. When incidents do happen, know how to respond. Turn hindsight into foresight by reflecting on the incident to learn from the experience and translate that learning into future prevention practices.

Summary

An effective outdoor educator understands the subtleties and complexities of creating a learning environment that is safe and engaging for all students. When planning a course begin by considering yourself, the presenter. What are your strengths and weaknesses? How will you take care of yourself so you are healthy when the course begins? Remember to plan well in advance to allow flexibility for last-minute changes.

Next consider the pupils. What are your pupils' needs? How will you meet them? What are realistic goals for this course? What is your plan to build rapport between yourself and your pupils and among the pupils? How will you motivate your students to learn?

The third consideration is the process. How will you greet students, set the tone, and manage their behavior effectively?

Finally, consider the site where the course will take place. The location will influence your course. How remote is it? How will you achieve access to it? How popular is it? Arrange logistics, such as transportation, permits, food, water, and bathrooms, well in advance. Keep good records and develop systems or templates whenever possible to minimize future planning. Have a solid risk-management policy so you can anticipate and prevent incidents. If incidents do occur, have a response and evacuation plan in place.

Consideration of these four variables will allow you to design an experience that is compelling, interesting, and appropriate for your audience.

Explore Your World

1. Describe ways to build rapport with your students.

2. List four techniques to motivate your students.

3. Identify three effective management strategies.

4. Describe safety management for your teaching site.

CHAPTER 6

Outdoor Education Settings

CHAPTER OBJECTIVES

By the end of the chapter, you should be able to do the following:

- Describe the characteristics of an instructional setting that meets student needs.

- Explain the strengths and limitations of an indoor setting versus an outdoor setting.

- Explain how to manage transitions and logistics between settings within a lesson or course.

- Describe unique features of the night as a learning setting.

- Discuss how to build your own resource file to complement instructional settings for your outdoor education courses.

In chapter 1, we discussed the definitions of formal, nonformal, and informal educational settings. The type of setting is determined by the students' learning expectations, the length of the education experience (hours, days, weeks), and the type of evaluation and its implications (whether one advances to the next level versus confirming how much learning has occurred for that lesson).

This chapter will discuss how to prepare the learning site, or setting. Now that you are actually at the site, what preparations will help your class run smoothly? The outdoor educational setting is different from the traditional classroom setting because you can't control for weather, distractions, or unforeseen occurrences such as a tree falling down at the site where you had planned to teach. Given these circumstances, you want to select the best site possible, know the features that will enhance and limit your lesson, and be prepared for possible unforeseen situations that can help or hinder your lesson.

Site Selection

Your site is the place or places where your lesson takes place. It is the physical location that provides optimal learning for your students. The well-chosen site allows you to use different teaching methods, has outdoor features that foster experiential learning, and allows for minimal logistics for transitions within your lesson. Further, it is a place with minimal distractions and potential dangers. For example, teaching sea kayaking at a popular beach for swimming in midsummer results in unwanted onlookers during your dry-land instruction and the need to dodge swimmers while trying to practice on-water skills. On the other hand, choosing a beach that is secluded, has a gentle slope of access, and is sheltered from the wind or competing noise such as a roadway is much preferred.

As a rule, try to begin and end your lesson in a controlled location such as an indoor classroom or a pavilion. It is best if the control, or base, location is close to the area of experiential activity to minimize time spent moving between locations. Close proximity of the activity area and the base location also allows equipment to be laid out and ready for use because it can be supervised while you give your introduction or conclusion.

Ideally, the base site should have amenities such as bathrooms, electricity, shelter from weather (sun, cold, rain, wind, noise), and visual aids such as a blackboard or dry-erase board. It should also allow your students to be comfortable while learning (such as having chairs to sit on and a table for course materials such as notebooks, handouts, books, and drawing supplies). It is common to begin or end a lesson with a video or some sort of visual aids such as maps, books, or tools. However, sometimes simply setting up a tarp to protect students from wind, rain, or sun will be the best option for a base. The key is to set up a comfortable starting point that minimizes distractions and keeps the group together.

The activity site needs to serve the abilities and development of your audience. Be sure you know your audience before selecting the site. Ensure that the site will accommodate your students' level of experience and skills. For example, does the activity site match your students' abilities? Having them use a ski slope or a climbing route that is below or above their skills will interfere with skill development.

Stories From Real Life: Classroom Rapids

While teaching white-water kayaking to a class of beginners, my coinstructor and I liked to bring the class to a rapid that we thought was easy (class II) and an ideal introduction to white water. The rapids were immediately downstream and within view of the parking lot. For the most part, the rapids were ideal for the sequence and level of the class. Because of these qualities, the rapids were called classroom rapids. However, the day we brought our class to the rapids, the river was in a spring-runoff state of high volume and very cold water.

When our class went on the river, most students were intimidated by the size and volume of the river, even though they were not near any rapids. When we floated down to the classroom rapids, we floated through them and stopped in a large eddy to begin our lesson of boat handling in moving water. One student was so intimidated by the river that he was unable to perform any of his kayak skills. The student needed to be escorted off the river to wait out the class by the van. This situation might have been avoided had we simply selected a similar rapid in a river with much less size and volume.

Learning Barriers

In addition to selecting and preparing your teaching site, you need to be aware of potential barriers to learning. Barriers to learning are circumstances or situations that are distracting or inhibit students' learning. Sometimes these are social, such as being overly concerned with what others might think of them if they fail (Ewert 1989). Barriers can also be physical, such as in the story from real life about classroom rapids. Physical learning barriers are distractions caused by aspects of the natural environment such as temperature extremes, wind, or insects. This section will describe barriers to your students' learning and explain what steps you can take to minimize or prevent the barriers.

Physical Barriers

Physical barriers to student learning are aspects or occurrences in the natural environment that cause a distraction, which hinders learning. Examples of these barriers include the following:

- Distracting sounds (e.g., airport, roadway)
- Bright sunlight
- Wind
- Temperature extremes
- Being wet
- Physiological needs

The physical site must lend itself to ease of learning. The most common barrier to learning is noise. Proximity to roadways, people who are not part of the group, or natural features such as high winds or rapids can be distracting. The distraction can be as basic as a student's inability to hear what you are saying. Outside noise can increase your students' anxiety by inhibiting them from focusing on essential aspects of the lesson such as a specific maneuver or technique.

Weather can also be a barrier to learning. Extreme temperatures, wind, rain, or snow necessitate proper clothing and make learning in a systematic manner difficult. While learning in the outdoors is a desired part of outdoor education, extreme weather can be distracting to students' learning, especially when the students are novices. As suggested in the discussion on environmental learning stages in chapter 3, ensure that your students are protected from extremes. If it's windy, do your lesson in a sheltered area. Set up a tarp or teach in a pavilion. Ensure that everyone is properly dressed.

A fundamental rule in teaching outdoors is to place your students with their back to the sun to keep sunlight out of their eyes. The inability to clearly see is as much a barrier to learning as the inability to hear.

Protecting your students from physical distractions will greatly enhance the quality of your lesson, but students' physical needs must also be

An instructor must keep the group together while traveling to the learning site.

© Ira Estin

acknowledged. When basic physiological needs are not met, the capacity to think or act is reduced. Although this may appear obvious, it is easily overlooked if you are gauging the class based on your own needs. Take the time to ensure hydration and energy needs are met. If students are dehydrated or their energy levels are low because they have not eaten for several hours, they will struggle to pay attention because they are more focused on their hunger or thirst, not to mention their energy is diminished. Similarly, provide adequate bathroom breaks. An hourly bathroom break is helpful and also allows time for individual questions.

Finally, be sensitive to students' fitness levels. Variances in fitness will affect the pace of the class as well as personal performance. This often occurs in a setting with mixed ages and with beginning and intermediate skill levels. All too often young, fit, enthusiastic instructors are intent on sharing their knowledge and skills while being oblivious to their students' fatigue. While you cannot control for uniform fitness, insensitivity to people with lower fitness levels will discourage those students, resulting in a significant barrier to their learning.

Social Barriers

Social barriers to learning are distractions that are caused by other students in the class, by the individuals' self-confidence, or by people not involved in the class, such as bystanders. The instructor can also inadvertently become a barrier to student learning. Common social barriers to learning include the following:

- Fear of failure
- Humiliation
- Unfamiliar clothing or equipment
- Distracting sights (other people not in class, pets, other group members)
- Instructor influences
  - Sunglasses
  - Face obscured by hat or clothing
  - Clothing or grooming that is inappropriate for the setting
  - Voice volume that is too low

When students are in a new learning situation, particularly when outdoors, anxiety seems to influence their self-confidence. Of course, there is also excitement about the setting and the lesson. Yet the combined influences of a new setting, a new

skill, and unfamiliar classmates can be stressful. Fear of being unable to perform well in front of other people is perhaps the greatest social learning barrier. Ewert (1989) found that fear of failure and the accompanying humiliation ranked as a higher concern than risk of injury. In addition, students often feel silly or awkward when first wearing protective equipment. For example, body image is often a concern when standing around in a wet suit, and some people are concerned about their hair when first putting on a helmet. Having to wear a large floppy hat to protect against sun or rain or wearing an unflattering rain suit can also embarrass some people.

Students thus may be concerned about their ability to perform the skill or activity well and also feel uncomfortable in their equipment and protective clothing. Add bystanders watching, and you have a big distraction from the task at hand.

Instructor Behavior

Another social learning barrier, though typically unintended, is inappropriate actions of the instructor. Students have entrusted you to guide them in their acquisition of skills, knowledge, and experience. Accordingly, they expect you to behave professionally and appropriately for their level of ability. The manner in which you present yourself not only represents the agency you work for, but also influences the behavior of your students, or determines the norms of your class. The learning culture you develop will greatly influence the setting.

For example, sunglasses that prevent eye contact and clothing that obscures your ability to communicate can distract from learning and sends the message, "This class is casual and not very important to me." This image can become a barrier for those who are expecting more from their instructor. You are expected to use fundamental teaching techniques such as a loud, clear voice. Wearing clothes that are professional and appropriate to the skill level are also basic means of inviting your students to learn.

Showing up to class with equipment that is considerably higher performance than your students creates a barrier by making you unbelievable as an instructor. For example, when an instructor shows up to a skiing class dressed in racing clothing and equipment while the students are using touring skis and wearing blue jeans, some students will dismiss the instructor as too far beyond them. Others will mistakenly believe that to be good, you have to be a racer. Conversely, an instructor who wears a hat that hides the face or eyes, is poorly groomed, and is dressed haphazardly will project an uncaring attitude.

Ultimately, your goal is to create a safe and inviting learning environment, which means fostering a comfortable atmosphere. Thus, never comment to a struggling student, "It's easy! Just do it like me." Instead, acknowledge the newness of the situation and respect your students' concerns by deliberately addressing them. For instance, "This equipment may feel awkward to you at first. It is intended to protect you this way. . . ," or, "We all might look a bit silly in this gear, but this is how it will help you be more comfortable in these conditions. . . ." Provide a comfortable place to change into or out of clothing. Locate your class in a quiet space away from bystanders or environmental distractions. In short, always be sensitive to these types of barriers to learning.

Removing Barriers

You must strive to remove barriers to student learning so you can intentionally foster an optimal learning setting. Removing barriers to promote learning is commonly used in association with Maslow's hierarchy of needs (1986). Maslow stated that before people can feel complete or self-actualized, they must first go through a series of stages. First, their personal physical needs must be met. They must not be hungry, thirsty, cold, or uncomfortable. Second, they must feel safe, both socially and physically. Third, they must feel as if they belong. Their social group must be inviting and accepting. Fourth, they must feel as if they are able; that is, their self-esteem must be high. These stages lead to a sense of "I can," or self-actualization. This chapter's discussion refers to those stages, yet another reason why it is important for you to understand your students is so you can teach where they are at, not where you want them to be.

While you can't know every aspect of a person or situation that might get in the way of course delivery, it is helpful to select and then know your setting well enough to avoid creating a barrier to learning. Finally, your choice of setting along with your behavior within that setting will greatly influence your students' learning.

Equipment

Whether the setting is indoors or outdoors, it must allow for the use of necessary equipment and materials. If you are teaching canoeing, it is necessary to have a setting that allows easy access to canoes. Thus, a typical school classroom is not an ideal setting for teaching canoeing. Likewise, if you need to use a dissecting microscope to identify flower parts, you will need a setting that protects sensitive equipment from the weather.

Accessory equipment, such as paddles and life jackets for sea kayaking, must also be accessible. This means you must be near storage and checkout so students can access the equipment in an orderly fashion that maintains the flow of the class and allows for inventory of gear. Often, it is the small items that disrupt the flow class because accessories are overlooked, inaccessible, or cannot be properly protected from weather. When teaching inside a classroom it is difficult to manage large or bulky equipment, and when teaching outside it is difficult to manage small, sensitive, or lightweight equipment.

A setting must allow for access to and protection of equipment to keep it safe from weather or inappropriate use. Use the equipment and materials within the setting to foster the flow and sequence of instruction. It is also helpful when a setting allows you to set up a table that is sturdy enough to prevent movement. Something to sit on helps, too. You must be able to haul the gear to the site in an efficient manner.

Another method for investigating the outdoors is collecting samples and then bringing them to a laboratory where the samples can be observed and studied. This requires a setting where the samples are relatively close to the laboratory and a laboratory setting is available with the necessary equipment and materials to meet your learning objectives.

Logistics

It is best to start and conclude your lessons from a site that is protected from weather and distractions, or a **control site.** This means you usually need at least two different settings for your lesson. When moving students, equipment, or materials from one setting to another, a certain level of logistics is required to accomplish the transition seamlessly. Well-planned logistics can enhance a lesson, while poorly planned logistics can ruin a lesson. Logistics are the way you move materials and equipment, as well as students, from one setting to another.

Because of time limits, smooth logistics are essential to your class. The setting determines the extent of necessary logistics. For example, for canoe instruction, if an aquatic center is located on a beach

Collecting specimens in the field can involve complex logistics.

Photo courtesy of Wolf Ridge ELC, 6282 Cranberry Road, Finland, MN. www.wolf-ridge.org.

you have your equipment and materials storage on-site. You also have a control point to start and conclude each lesson. The transition from indoors to outdoors is minimal.

On the other hand, if you are teaching bog ecology and you are beginning your lesson indoors using posters, terrariums, and a drawing board to introduce bogs and their ecology, then moving your students outdoors to examine an actual bog will involve more complex logistics. You will also need to move your students back to the indoor classroom so they can closely examine the specimens that they have collected. You will need to prepare materials to facilitate equipment use and the introduction and conclusion of the lesson. You will also need know exactly how you are going to move your class to the bog.

Record Keeping

Record keeping is recording what occurs in each lesson and course. It includes keeping track of attendance and monitoring student progress step by step. It also records what course is taught by whom and to how many students, which is necessary to receive certification for activities such as first aid, lifeguarding, and coastal kayaking instruction.

Maintaining up-to-date, accurate records of your lessons will aid in your evaluation of your students. It lets them see in writing what they have accomplished in their course. In addition, you will have a concrete means of reporting your classes for certification and supervisory evaluation.

Record keeping can be done with paper and pencil, a specific form, or electronically such as on a computer. Whatever means of record keeping you use, it should be consistent with record keeping by the rest of the agency so that other instructors use similar procedures. Refer to appendix B for sample forms.

Special Settings: Lessons in the Night

One unique aspect of outdoor education is teaching during the night. It is actually quite rare in a formal learning setting (classroom) to experience an educational lesson in the dark. Because of the likelihood that you will be conducting some type of outdoor education at night, this section covers methods and strategies that are unique to low-light settings.

A lesson at night can be an exciting and stimulating learning experience. Listening to nocturnal creatures such as deer and owls is often a new experience. Learning how our eyesight adapts to low light can open up a whole new world to explore. Taking the time to examine the night sky or learn new smells of the night can be enlightening. Using sight and motion to hide in the dark is a great tool for understanding how animals survive at night, which is difficult to teach during the day.

Humans are largely diurnal, meaning we are accustomed to adapting daytime elements to be comfortable in the dark. In many ways, we are unfamiliar with the night because we are rarely in it thanks to artificial lights, staying indoors, and traveling in vehicles. The sounds, sights, smells, and feel of the night have become foreign experiences to most people. Because of this unfamiliarity, teaching a lesson in the night can be exciting for students. However, this unique setting also presents some potential barriers to learning. Following are special guidelines for teaching in the night. Also see the example Night Hike lesson in chapter 11.

Tips and Techniques

Know Your Site

While it's still daylight, walk the route or area that you will be using with your class. Note where there are places that can confuse students, such as areas that become an apparent dead end. Also note where students might become confused about which route to take while traveling. It's best to know your setting well in daylight and then revisit the area in the dark to ensure that you are also familiar with it in low light. Because of the degree that we rely on eyesight over our other senses, it is easy to overlook a hazard such as a small dip in the trail or even a tree root. Try to identify any potential hazards and be able to locate them in the dark.

Start With What Students Know

Before you venture out into the dark, acclimate your students. Acclimatizing is both a physical and psychological endeavor. Have your students sit quietly in a spot with no light nearby. Give them a few moments to allow their other senses to adjust to the dark. They will find that their senses of smell and hearing are heightened. This activity will also allow the students to calm down about being in an unfamiliar setting. Darkness is typically avoided because it represents the unknown and therefore is something to be feared, and in general people are taught to fear the night in urban settings.

Prepare in a Controlled Setting

Ensure that all students have warm clothes, sturdy shoes or boots, and a hat and gloves. Explain to them the general plan—how long they will be out, how far they will go, and expected behavior (discourage behavior that scares others, like grabbing someone from behind; encourage silence).

Get Used to the Dark

Go to an easily accessible location away from light and human sounds. An open field is a good place to go. Sit in a circle and ask your students what things they are afraid of in the dark. While you maintain a supportive environment by respecting students' fears and concerns (whether you think they are rational or not), you will learn what psychological barriers may be blocking their learning. Ask them what they need to do to avoid that fear. Explain to them what you will do to address their fear or concern, such as traveling slowly with frequent stops.

Sensitize Students to Night Activity

Take the time to sensitize the students to physiological aspects of night activity. For instance, point out how their eyes adjust to the dark. Direct their senses of hearing and smell to the noises and smells of the night. Spend 15 to 20 minutes at the site getting used to the dark. Establish student comfort such as warmth and dryness before you proceed.

(continued)

(continued)

Educators should take steps to prepare their groups for night lessons.

Doing Activities

Travel slowly and within visual or voice contact (unless it is a cloudy, moonless night, there is typically adequate light to see shapes in the dark). Have students place one hand on the shoulder of the person in front of them, or hang onto a rope, or walk closely enough that they can see the person in front of them. Pause often (every 50 to 100 feet or 15 to 30 meters if walking) to allow people to catch up, listen to the night, and maintain comfort levels. Set explicit physical boundaries in which you want your students to stay, and do not allow students to stray outside those boundaries.

When hiking, use trails that are wide and flat such as abandoned roads or ski trails. When traveling by water, use a route that is easy to navigate and end at a landing that is easy to find and disembark at.

Conclusion

Before entering your control site—typically a building—conclude your lesson by emphasizing what experiences the students gained, what skills they acquired, and what new awareness they found. Warn students that lights will appear very bright because their eyes are adapting to rely on rods more than cones.

Here are some tips for preparing for a lesson in the night:

- Address psychological fears and concerns before you begin.
- Know your setting both in daylight and in the dark.
- Travel slowly with frequent stops.
- Show students how to stay warm and dry.
- Bring a first aid kit, a flashlight, and spare batteries.
- Discourage inappropriate behaviors such as scaring other people, making excessive noise, and moving outside established physical boundaries.

Summary

Teaching a successful lesson in the outdoors involves the proper selection of one or more settings. Each setting should have physical characteristics that reduce distractions and foster optimal learning. The setting should allow for storage, presentation (layout), and efficient use of equipment and supporting materials. It also should require minimal logistics for transitioning between settings or topic changes. Finally, an ideal setting for outdoor education has minimal barriers to student learning, whether those barriers are social, physical, or emotional. A special setting—the night—can be an especially effective setting for fostering outdoor learning.

Explore Your World

1. Choose an outdoor education topic and write down what settings best meet the education goals of that topic. What are the pros and cons of the settings?

2. Identify the barriers that you should be aware of in the settings you just identified.

3. Discuss what subjects and skills are good topics to teach in a night setting.

4. Make a list of materials that support a lesson in a night setting and identify where to find them.

5. What safety considerations should you make when choosing an outdoor setting to teach in?

CHAPTER 7

Designing Lessons

CHAPTER OBJECTIVES

By the end of the chapter, you should be able to do the following:

- Describe the value of a lesson plan.

- Write a lesson plan with the necessary components.

- Explain the components of effective introductions and conclusions.

- Describe the role of reflection in the lesson and ways to incorporate reflection.

- Define assessment and give three examples of assessment techniques.

Lesson quality begins with planning, and at the heart of planning lies the lesson plan. All outdoor educators need the skills to lay out an organized plan that meets the needs of their particular audience at a particular teaching site. This is not to say that you need to start from scratch every time you teach a different group or at a different site. Often you can modify one of the thousands of outdoor education plans that are already in existence. The lesson plan has key elements that help you succeed in delivering your message or skill. Leave out pieces of the plan and you will reduce your likelihood of success.

Advantages of Lesson Plans

Now that you have spent considerable time learning how to teach a topic, it is time to create the actual lesson. Many people shy away from writing a lesson plan because they think it is busy work, yet a lesson plan is a useful tool that accomplishes many things:

- It helps you organize your thoughts.
- It focuses your teaching toward appropriate goals and objectives.
- It helps you stay on schedule.
- It helps you remember items that you plan to teach.
- It serves as a record of your teaching.
- It allows you to see weaknesses and oversights in your lesson before you are in front of students.
- It contributes to a professional demeanor.

- It helps you make informed adjustments as conditions merit.
- It provides a tool for follow-up and evaluation.

A lesson plan becomes the roadmap for your lesson. For the same reason we need good maps for navigation, we need good lesson plans for teaching. Both provide an understanding of where you are and where you are going. They even help provide flexibility in getting to your destination. When navigating long distances, we often need multiple maps, particularly when we want detail of the area traveled. Like maps, we need multiple lesson plans when the educational experience addresses multiple topics or lasts a long time. This chapter will help you discover the components of good lessons in outdoor education. Concepts apply to short lessons as well as multiday experiences.

Format

You should write a lesson plan whenever you teach. When you are first learning the terrain of an area (lesson topic), you need to use a map (lesson plan) to find your way. Once you have visited the area (taught numerous times) your reliance on the map decreases. When you first start, use lesson plans regularly, and as you develop, rely on lesson plans to enhance content and flow. Good lesson plans have a number of essential components (see pages 88-89). Keep in mind that first and foremost, the lesson plan is written for you. Since you likely are working for a larger organization, your notes should also be complete enough that others can pick up the lesson plan and use it.

The starting point in writing a lesson plan is to determine goals. These are your destinations, or

Stories From Real Life: Planning Saves the Lesson

The two students in our outdoor education methods class thought they had the world by the tail and they definitely knew the topic they were going to team-teach to a group of 4th-grade Cub Scouts. What they didn't do was spend time working together to develop a lesson plan. Sure, they had a sketchy outline of what they would cover, but it had little detail and no objectives. Much to their surprise, the lesson went poorly. They were not able to clearly describe to the participants what they would be doing, transitions were disjointed, they reacted to discipline problems rather than prevented them, and the students learned little. The two instructors quickly regrouped after the lesson and created clear objectives, organized a plan of activities and transitions, and clarified how they would introduce the lesson as well as wrap it up. Needless to say, the lesson went much better the second time around with a different group.

Discover Outdoor Education

Consider your favorite outdoor activity and your favorite group to work with. Come up with one goal and three objectives for the group to learn about that activity (see pages 88-89). Make sure you are able to observe or measure whether students achieve that objective. For example, if your audience consists of 16-year-olds and your goal is to teach them how to put up a tarp, one objective might be, "Students will be able to tie a taut-line hitch."

where you want to go and what you want to accomplish with this lesson. In other words, your goals are the big picture of what you want your students to do (for example, a goal for a backpack trip may be to learn the ecology of an area). Next, and one of the most difficult tasks in writing a lesson, is developing the objectives. These are the observable or measurable outcomes of your lesson (for example, related to the goal of ecology, an objective might be to identify five bird species and describe the habitat they would be found in). Over time writing lesson plans becomes easier and easier and it eventually becomes second nature.

Structure

The organization of the lesson content and methods is critical to the success of the lesson. Certain components need to be included in each lesson, such as an introduction and conclusion. The lesson flow should follow a certain pattern. This pattern and all content and methods used in the lesson should be well planned before you meet with your group.

Introduction

Your introduction is the initial attention-grabber for your students. Get your students' attention early, and you'll have it for the rest of class. Enthusiastic, energetic, well-planned introductions are vital!

An introduction should be like watching a commercial for an ice-cold glass of lemonade on a hot summer day. The commercial will make you thirstier than you were before. It will entice you to get excited and act on your excitement by buying some of the lemonade. That's exactly what an introduction should do: It should entice the students to be enthusiastic about the topic and anticipate the next experience you are about to share.

Components of a Good Introduction

1. Be positive! Have a "This class is going to be fantastic!" attitude.

2. Have high energy. If you expect the students to have a lot of energy and enthusiasm, you should set an example.

3. Manage students. Make sure everyone knows what is expected from them. Be clear and positive.

4. Be organized. A well-prepared introduction should flow smoothly from one point to the next.

5. Develop rapport with the students. Learning names and using them is one way to accomplish this.

6. Have a sense of humor and have fun.

7. Include an overview of activities the class will include.

8. Motivate your students to be involved in class. Your students will walk in to class curious. Capitalize on that initial interest and make the class relevant to them.

9. Cover your main ideas right away. What is the purpose of the class?

10. Connect the class to students' daily lives. Help them immediately see the relevancy of what you are teaching.

11. Assess students' initial knowledge. To begin where the student is, deliberately assess knowledge, skill, experience, and interest in the topic.

You can use several techniques to grab the attention of the students, including role-playing and storytelling. For role-playing, you could become a lost hunter for orienteering class, a drill instructor for the ropes course, or a tree for trees identification. Role-play catches attention and educates at the same time. For details on using role-playing, see chapter 8. For storytelling, sit on the floor in a circle, on sleeping pads, around a campfire ring, and so on. Get the students thinking right away by challenging them with a problem. Storytelling is a great way to pull people into an activity. People love stories, and stories teach at

The following is an outline designed to guide you in developing lesson plans. The lesson plan is an effective tool used to enhance your instruction. Please approach it as a tool rather than a burden. Think of it as a road map to guide the journey!

I. *Title—Name it!*

Be creative, draw the reader in!

II. *Goals—The big why!*

Goals are the general rationale or purpose of what you want to teach. Goals speak to the broad outcome of a lesson.

Example: "This lesson will encourage sensory awareness toward natural objects."

III. *Objectives—The specific why!*

Objectives are the measurable and observable outcomes of your lesson. They are the specific reasons the lesson is created or used.

Example: "From this lesson, students will learn to

a. describe five different natural objects,
b. write their awareness clearly in a brief essay,
c. describe a different object using each of the human senses, and
d. perform a diagonal stride using full arm and leg extension with correct body lean."

IV. *Audience identified—Your students.*

Identify your audience in terms of

a. age group,
b. affiliation (e.g., Boy Scout troop, recreation undergrads, grade 5 class, etc.),
c. number, and
d. learning expectations (level, scope, or sequence of material to be taught).

V. *Duration—Time involved.*

a. How long is the lesson? (preparation included)
b. How long will it take to get to the site? (travel time)
c. How long will it take to follow up the field experience or lab experience?

VI. *Location—Where?*

a. Where will the lesson be taught?
b. How will you get there?
c. Any specific safety concerns?

VII. *Content and methods—The substance of your presentation and how you will teach it.*

This is the major portion of your lesson plan. Typically, a lesson has three key elements: an introduction, a body (including opportunities for reflection), and a conclusion.

A peer educator should be able to pick up your lesson plan, understand your content, and be able to follow your procedural steps to successfully present the lesson.

Take time here to lay out your lesson properly and it will pay off during your lesson.

a. Include the information that is readily usable for your presentation (background), the information you want to impart to the students. Content is finding the factual knowledge and blending it into a conceptual plan so that the receiver can make sense of it—that is, learning through personal meaning and building on past experiences. This information must be organized into a usable form for you, the presenter. Further, include additional background information designed to support other educators preparing to use this lesson.

b. Describe, within the content, the methods that will be used to present that information and work toward achievement of the objectives. For example, if you are teaching tree identification, explain how you will teach tree identification and describe the specific activities that might be

Lesson-plan format.

(continued)

a part of this (games, role-play, experimentation, demonstration, observation, etc.). Provide specific directions of procedure to accomplish the planned lesson (e.g., step 1, step 2 . . . part a, part b . . . etc.).

VIII. *Management and safety.*

Depending on your audience, you will need to consider different things for management of the group and prevention of injuries.

    a. How will you manage the group (keeping the group together, rules, discipline, supervision, etc.)?

    b. What are potential risks at the site you are using with the activities you are conducting? How will you minimize the students' exposure to the risks?

IX. *Equipment—What you need!*

    a. What equipment or materials will be needed?

    b. List each specific item and quantity.

X. *What is a foul weather alternative?*

Strive to avoid simply going indoors in inclement weather. Rather, be prepared to accommodate student comfort and your lesson delivery by protecting your class from weather distractions. For example, you could provide a clothing list, set up a tarp, bring lanterns, provide extra clothing, or move your learning site to a more sheltered location outside.

XI. *Evaluation—Assessing learning.*

Provide a specific plan for assessing learning. The plan may be a test, a group discussion, a rubric, a product completed for the student portfolio, demonstration of ability, etc. Be deliberate about how the learning will be assessed; your tool should help you address the following questions:

    a. How do you know that the lesson was successful?

    b. Were your objectives met?

    c. How were you successful as an instructor?

XII. *Follow up—What's next?*

Each lesson should link to the next lesson of a deliberate sequence (scope and sequence) within a broader context. This is especially important for all formal and nonformal educators—lessons are rarely stand-alone without a connection to other learning.

    a. What is the next lesson?

    b. How will you prepare your students for the next lesson?

XIII. *Reference materials to support your lesson.*

Lesson plans must have some reference source that supports your content. The reference must be valid (books, journals). Unless a person is recognized in their field as a leading expert, people are not necessarily valid resources (e.g., the camp director at Camp Kookamunga may not really teach proper canoe stroke technique, even though he is the main instructor at the camp). Be wary of Web resources.

    a. Provide any source information, and cite it properly!

    b. List at least three references for additional information.

XIV. *Connections to established standards.*

Often, outdoor educators work with groups from formal education. When this occurs, it should be clear how the lesson connects to the standards established by the appropriate school district or state education agencies. Standards vary widely from district to district and state to state. Work with the classroom teacher(s) to determine how your lesson will support their efforts to meet standards. Ultimately, it is the responsibility of the classroom teacher to determine how student learning connects to the standards they are required to follow.

Lesson-plan format. *(continued)*

many different levels. See chapter 10 for ways to do storytelling.

The first 10 to 15 minutes of a class are crucial. Now more than any other time during class you set the mood for the entire class. Student responses during the conclusion begin right here. Following a well-planned introduction, your students should be "thirsting" for more!

Balancing Cognitive, Kinesthetic, and Affective Methods

As discussed in chapter 3, it is important for teaching to combine mental activities, physical activities, and emotional activities. Since different people have different learning styles, you should present opportunities for mental, physical, and emotional activities. Often you won't know which learning style each student prefers, so it is your responsibility to try to reach all learning styles by using a variety of teaching methods.

Let's look at an activity for teaching how to build a campfire. This activity should incorporate a component on understanding the mechanics of fire and

safety (cognitive) as well as the actual building of a fire (kinesthetic and affective). All too often, outdoor educators spend too much time lecturing or explaining how to do something and leave little time for actually doing something (although occasionally they go the other way and explain too little). Different topics and different learners demand a different balance of cognitive, kinesthetic, and affective components. Experience will teach you how to balance these effectively.

But how do you flow from one component to another? Which comes first? There are two common ways to create a sequence that balances cognitive, kinesthetic, and affective learning. The first is describe, demonstrate, do, and the second is whole–part–whole.

Describe, Demonstrate, Do

The first sequence of development is widely known as **describe, demonstrate, do,** or the 3-Ds. In this strategy, instructors first describe the skill or topic to be learned. They then demonstrate how to do the skill. Finally, the students have the opportunity to do the skill. Savvy outdoor educators can mix up the order to better meet the needs of the students and provide outstanding opportunities for learning.

© Ira Estin

The second step of describe, demonstrate, do involves showing students how to do the skill.

Stories From Real Life: Signals of Effective Teaching

Each candidate for coastal kayaking instructor was assigned a topic to teach to their peers in the certification course. It just so happened that two of the candidates got the same topic: the use of signaling and safety devices. The first person put together a detailed lesson plan that included all of the necessary content. In following this lesson plan, the instructor spent the entire time describing how and when to use various flares and signaling devices—she even included a handout.

The next instructor also had a well-planned lesson, but his was a bit different. After a short discussion on when to use signaling and safety devices, he proceeded to demonstrate the actual use of such devices on the beach (since some devices are pyrotechnics, he checked with the coast guard for approval). Then each participant had the opportunity to use each of the devices.

Needless to say, the second lesson had each component of describe, demonstrate, do and thus was very effective. The first lesson, on the other hand, only included description and the participants learned little of the actual skill.

Whole–Part–Whole

The second way to establish a lesson sequence is the **whole–part–whole** method. This sequence can be blended with the 3-Ds for an effective lesson. In this progression, typically used when teaching complex skills or tasks, instructors demonstrate the entire skill. Then they use the 3-Ds to teach each of the pieces of the skill. For example, in teaching a kayak roll, the instructor first demonstrates the complete roll. Then the instructor works with students on the various parts of the roll (setup, sweep, hip-snap, recovery), one part at a time. Finally, the students bring all the pieces together in a complete roll. The advantage of starting with the whole is that students can see the objective of learning each piece. Essentially, this method is a visual demonstration of the lesson objectives.

Coaching

Coaching contributes to the skill development of participants. Look beyond the typical perspective of a coach as someone who helps the team succeed. In outdoor education, coaching helps everyone succeed. It is not a tool for subjecting a person to criticism or comparing them to a standard. It is a technique for developing cognitive and kinesthetic skills. Coaching thus becomes synonymous with feedback. Coaching feedback does the following:

- Provides positive reinforcement of what students are doing successfully

- Informs students of what they need to improve
- Motivates students toward success

It is important for the coach to have the ability to see what students are doing right and what they need to improve and to be able to communicate that information to the students. Coaching goes hand in hand with both describe, demonstrate, do and whole–part–whole since the success of the skill development often depends on coaching by the instructor.

Guidelines for Effective Coaching

- Know the difference between evaluating (giving feedback, coaching) versus judging. You must be nonjudgmental—you are not judging abilities, but trying to help someone learn.

- Strive for positive comments that are genuine. It is appropriate to show students what they are doing correctly or incorrectly and explain how they can improve.

- Be supportive—the goal is learning.

- When giving feedback, you must be realistic, accurate, and concrete. You may have to take notes—if you are inaccurate or vague in your feedback, it will be ineffective.

- Make direct statements rather than beat around the bush. This does not mean that tact gets thrown out the window, but do not tiptoe around an issue.

- Do not apologize for your views. (For example, "Maybe it's just me, but I thought. . .")
- Set a positive tone for giving and receiving feedback.
- Be positive. Acknowledge what people are doing right.
- Immediacy is important. Coach and give feedback as soon as possible.
- Correct errors one at a time.
- Avoid making an example of a student's inabilities.
- Try group feedback—discuss common errors in the group.
- Be specific and make your comments understandable.
- Use peer coaching, making sure peers know how to do the skill properly.
- Provide time for practice and reflection.
- Use the sandwich-cookie method—give two examples of what the person did well (cookie) and one thing to work on (filling).
- Be able to demonstrate both incorrect and correct skills.

Good coaching skills come from experience, practice, and patience. Your ability to help students gain cognitive or kinesthetic skills comes from you knowing the skills inside and out. Success is also a result of your ability to structure the skill development into a proper progression and coach students along the way.

Wrapping Up the Lesson

Effective lessons do not just end. Numerous factors can help complete a lesson and increase the success of learning. An effective wrap-up includes looking back at the experience, extracting key lessons, generalizing those lessons, and applying the lessons to real life. Wrapping up is often omitted from outdoor education due to timing and a desire to prolong the experience. However, the conclusion can be one of the most important factors if your goal is to provide a transformative experience for your students.

Imagine the following scenario: You did a great audience preassessment, so you were prepared when the group arrived. Your curriculum planning was without a fault, clear and meaningful and carefully building key concepts through direct experience. You chose varied methods depending on the conditions and audience needs. Tomorrow the group goes home. Now what?

The end is often the most difficult part of a course for outdoor educators. Too many times, outdoor educators do nothing because they don't know what to do. Or they fill up every available minute with activities and experiences, because that's what the audience came for, isn't it? Not necessarily.

Extracting meaning and extending the learning from an experience requires some time and expertise on the part of the outdoor educator, but the audience leaves with a deeper understanding of themselves and how the experience informs their daily lives. It's through reflecting about themselves and their experience and then transferring their learning to their daily life that your students become transformed. Without effective **reflection** and conclusion, much of the potential meaning and transformative powers of the outdoor experience can be lost.

Reflection

Reflection requires quiet time to think back on the experience. Reflection can be as open-ended as simply providing the students time and a reflective atmosphere. Reflection can also be a guided process with the outdoor educator providing prompts to stimulate and direct the student's thoughts. Your decision on structure should be based on student development and needs. As a general rule of thumb, the younger the student the more structure is needed. However, this is not always the case. Eighth-grade students who are accustomed to a lot of structure will need as much as 5th-grade students who are used to independent direction. Adults who are unfamiliar with reflection benefit from a structured reflection assignment.

For some outdoor educators reflection is always done last: last thing during class, last thing before dinner, last thing in a trip. But reflection has the greatest effect when it occurs close to the experience. When laying out your curriculum, identify key experiences and schedule time for reflection shortly following those experiences. If you habitually leave reflection for last, you may lose opportunities for learning while the experience is still fresh in the student's mind. And too often, when reflection is the last thing on the schedule, it gets dropped because you run out of time.

The word *reflection* conjures images of sitting silently by oneself, deep in thought. However, discussion and conversation are an important part of reflection as well. As people struggle to make meaning from new information or experiences, verbalizing their thoughts can help them clarify questions

Reflecting on an experience is essential.

and create links between what they know and what they are learning.

Timing   Timing is one of the hardest parts of effective reflection. There is so much to do—can you really carve out time to think and talk about what you did and what you learned? If you want your students to gain insight from their experience and apply it in new settings, then the answer is yes.

Set aside reflection time based on the length of the program as well as the richness of the experience. A rule of thumb is to spend 30 minutes reflecting for every 6 hours of instruction. So, at the end of a teaching day, spend 30 minutes reflecting and making meaning. At the end of a teaching week, spend 90 minutes reflecting on and extending the experience. It's more effective to have continuous reflection time rather than 5-minute chunks here and there. If you've done a good job reflecting and making meaning throughout the experience, you can hook into that for your final reflection.

Setting   Choose an aesthetic setting where students won't be distracted. The setting helps create the tone for closure. During inclement weather find a sheltered site so students will be comfortable and can concentrate.

The setting can be a metaphor for reflection and closure. A high point can symbolize the peak the students have just reached. A lake symbolizes stilling the waters so you can see into the depths. The setting should also allow students to disperse safely, have private places to sit by themselves, and converse without distracting others.

Trust and Self-Disclosure   Reflection is by nature very personal. Make sure you've created a safe learning environment so students can take risks and feel accepted. When it's time to share, give students the option of sharing only part of their work if they choose. Students must feel empowered to say no. If the same students choose not to share time after time, consider having a conversation with them. What part of their thoughts are they comfortable sharing? Do they feel as if they are pushing their limits and working outside their comfort zone? Doing so is important because that's when growth occurs.

Approaches to Reflection

Following is a list of four approaches that can be used to reflect on experiences. They are included here to show the range of learning opportunities you can create during reflection.

Hooking Into Past and Future Learning

Have students write responses to the following questions in their journals or on a blank piece of paper:

- What did you learn about?
- How does this relate to what you already know about the topic?
- How can this help you in the future?
- What new questions do you now have about the topic?

Give students 15 minutes to write about what they learned and how it may apply to their life, then gather the group and share highlights of their reflection.

Dyad Discussion   Pair students and give pairs a list of questions to discuss. Regroup and discuss insights with the full group. Here are some sample questions:

- What surprised you about yourself today?
- Describe how you can continue to face challenges at home.
- List the obstacles that may get in your way.
- Make a quick plan to overcome these obstacles.
- How will you continue to learn about yourself?

Concept Map   In making a **concept map,** students extract key ideas and terms from class and plot them visually to show relationships among them. The students establish a visual representation of relationships between concepts that may have only been presented verbally.

To make a concept map (see p. 95) have students write the key concept in the middle of a blank sheet of paper. For example, the main concept may be "water cycle" or "challenges." Students then write

down all facts and subconcepts they can think of that are related to the main concept. Encourage students to think freely. If it pops into their head, they should write it down. As the students are writing down related facts and subconcepts, have them relate the subconcepts to each other and to the key concept. Have students draw lines between related facts and subconcepts and the key concept. The final result is a web of related ideas and information.

If students are unfamiliar with concept maps, give them an example. Choose a different topic for the example than the one you will give to students to allow them opportunity for creativity and fresh thinking.

When students are done drawing, gather and share maps.

Self-Portrait   Hand out a blank sheet of paper. Instruct students to draw a picture of themselves. Have students label parts that have grown and changed during the experience. For example, their legs have gotten stronger from hiking, or their heart has gotten kinder from sharing with others. Share portraits as a group.

This activity is a nice **framing** activity. Framing means using an identical activity at the beginning and at the end of a course. Since the activity is identical, any changes reflect student learning during the course. Have students draw a self-portrait the first day of the course and then another one the last day. How have they changed? What did they expect? What caught them by surprise?

Lesson Conclusion

Following an effective reflection session where students connect their new learning with previous knowledge and transfer their learning to their home life, take a few moments to conclude the experience. The conclusion is just as important as

Explore Your World

Picture a group of students and the experience they've just shared. Perhaps you're completing a 10-day backpacking trip focusing on leadership skills. Maybe today is the last day of a 3-day school experience at a residential environmental education center. Or perhaps you're wrapping up 5 days with classroom teachers who have come to learn about environmental education and how it links to their classroom.

Which technique would you choose for wrapping up with your group? Describe why you would choose that approach. What other approaches would you consider? Describe the effects of your choice.

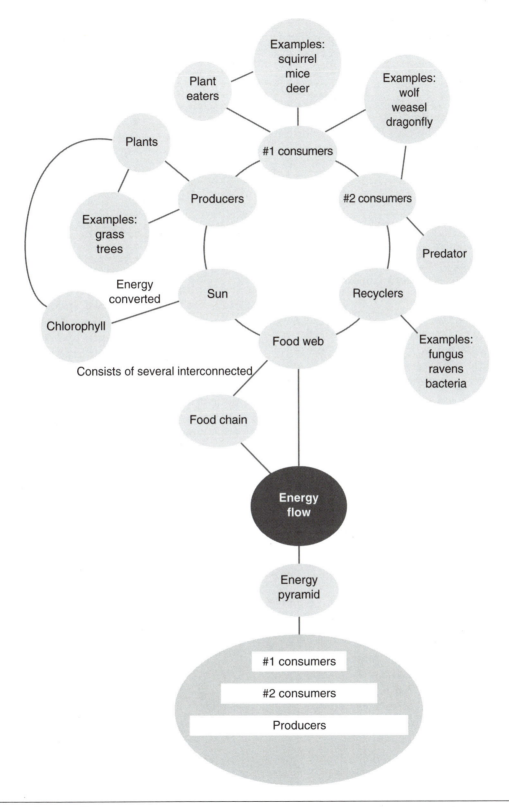

Concept map of energy flow.

the introduction. It should be dramatic and an attention-grabber. You should never skip or slight a conclusion. After spending time in your class, you and your students deserve a grand ending.

Conclusions, just like introductions, should be well planned and organized. Be prepared and professional. While the introduction entices students into enthusiasm for the class, the conclusion ties the class together. It's the students' final impression of class, the last thing they hear and the beginning of what they will be thinking about when they leave.

Elements of a Good Conclusion

1. Plan time for a conclusion. Great conclusions don't just happen, they're planned, starting with leaving sufficient time at the end of class.

2. Review the entire class. The students have probably just completed a great activity, and that's what is foremost in everyone's mind. But what has happened throughout the entire class? Stir up memories to set the stage for a conclusion. For example, have students get into a comfortable position and lead them through a guided imagery of the experience. Include key activities in the review and touch on main concepts.

3. Tie in the concepts. Everything you did in class had a purpose, and you should show that purpose in the conclusion. Process information rather than having students regurgitate it. For example, spread out a poster-sized sheet of blank paper and scatter several colored markers around the edge. In the center write, "What we did today." Have students fill the sheet with words that describe what they did during the shared experience. This effectively reviews the experience. To process the information, turn the sheet over and write, "What did we learn today?" in the middle of the sheet. Have students fill this side of the paper with the learning behind the activities.

4. Make it personal to the students. Help them figure out how the class affects their daily life. Explore pertinence at home and around the world. For example, after stream-study class how can they conserve water at home?

5. Involve the students. As a teacher, you need students' input to evaluate their understanding and progress. Let the students do some of the talking, sharing insights, stories, hopes, and dreams.

6. Get feedback. You need to know how you did as an instructor. Ask the students what they felt was effective and what could be improved (now they are coaching you!). You can hand out a short evaluation form (see the example in appendix B) or have a sharing circle that focuses on the topic, the presentational methods, and you as an instructor.

Assessment

There is a difference between teaching and learning. Learning is an action that only the students can accomplish. Even the best lesson in the world cannot teach. It can only be learned. In order for learning to take place, the students must be willing to learn.

Learning is influenced by what the students already know. Just as outdoor educators have a certain perception of the world created by their past knowledge and experiences, so do your students. While you may intend a student to learn one thing, they may very well be learning another. To know what your students learned, you assess their learning.

Too often outdoor educators treat education as an action that the teacher, not the student, engages in. Many educators may not think of assessment

Feedback is an important assessment tool.

as part of outdoor education. Assessment was not expected in nonformal settings and not done in informal settings in the original definition of formal, nonformal, and informal education (Tamir 1990).

The field of outdoor education is forming stronger and stronger links with formal, or classroom, education. As such, the pressures for assessing student learning will increase. Outdoor education is becoming recognized for its influence on learning by providing students with a meaningful context for their learning. In every setting a responsible educator will assess student mastery of basic concepts before building on that knowledge base with more complex concepts. For example, if a student doesn't understand the definition of an herbivore, carnivore, omnivore, producer, or consumer, you won't be able to teach the concept of energy flow and food webs. To build on what the student already knows and understands, you must first assess what the student knows and understands.

Develop an assessment strategy as you develop your objectives and activities in a lesson plan. Assessment can take several forms and is most effectively conducted all throughout a lesson (formative), not at the end of a lesson only (summative).

Formative assessment is conducted during a lesson while ideas are still forming. Formative assessment helps the students measure their own progress and helps the outdoor educator adjust the content and flow of the course based on student needs.

Receiving feedback on how their learning is progressing can motivate students to continue to learn. By seeing their growth and learning, students are rewarded for their effort. Formative assessment also helps students identify specific areas where they need additional growth, which helps them direct their energy and attention to those areas.

Formative assessment can be simple or complex. It may be as simple as noticing how a student is using a compass: "You're doing a good job working with the map to figure out your next bearing. You're lining up your bearing on your compass with great accuracy. Now pay some attention to shooting a bearing, or looking ahead directly along your bearing, to choose a path to walk." More complex skills require formative assessment that is more complex. Using the whole–part–whole technique, break the complex skill up into components. Then assess student mastery of each part before moving on to the next step.

Summative assessment is conducted at the end of a lesson. Summative assessment tallies learning that has taken place throughout a lesson. Skill-based courses such as first aid or kayaking, which offer certificates of mastery, usually have a required summative assessment at the end of the course. The summative assessment often takes the form of a written test and a practical skills exam, which must be passed before the students receive the certificate authorizing their skill level.

Effective assessment is useful both for the student and the outdoor educator. It offers the students useful feedback on their learning, and seeing their growth and learning can motivate them to continue the effort to engage and learn. Effective formative assessment can help the students focus energy and attention on areas of weakness. For outdoor educators, assessment helps track the effectiveness of their teaching. Are students progressing as anticipated? Based on assessment outcomes, the outdoor educator can alter teaching strategies to better meet the

Tips and Techniques for Assessment

"Teachers engage in the act of observing students while students engage in the act of observing phenomena."

—Madeline Hunter, *Mastery Teaching* (1982)

Everyone is familiar with written tests, quizzes, and other pen-and-paper forms of assessment. They can be effective tools, but don't limit your assessment plan to them. Often these are awkward in an outdoor setting. Instead, engage students in conversations with each other and with yourself and assess the outcomes of those conversations. Give students projects to complete and presentations to do. Have students develop projects to add to a portfolio that represents their best work. Read student journals to gain insight into their learning.

needs of the students. Every student is unique, and while you try to anticipate your audience in as many ways as possible, there is no way to plan a perfect lesson until you have met and interacted with your students.

Rubrics

A **rubric** is a grid of essential behaviors, knowledge, and skills necessary for mastery of a topic or skill. Rubrics also weight the importance of each component. Rubrics are one method teachers use to help students understand how they will be assessed, what behaviors and knowledge will be assessed, and the weight attached to each characteristic.

You can develop your own rubric and share it with your students. (See example below.) Begin by identifying key concepts and skills in the activity. Be clear about what parts of the process and the product you will evaluate. For example, if students are giving a group presentation on the pioneer history of their hometown, key concepts may include time of settlement, lifestyle, industry, farming, and recreation. These are all products of their learning. In addition, since students are working in groups, you may choose to assess how well the students work together, use their time, and share responsibility. These skills and the skills of effective presentation are the process part of the rubric. Once you've identified key concepts and skills, create a scale to evaluate how well the students

Sample Rubric for Cross-Country Skiing Diagonal Stride

Key parts	Outstanding 4 points	Competent 3 points	Developing 2 points	Nonmastery 1 point
Body position	Forward, athletic, ready position: eyes forward, knees/hips/ankles flexed, forward lean (hips over the feet).	Forward, athletic, ready position with two out of three components: eyes forward, knees/hips/ankles flexed, forward lean.	Upright position with knees flexed.	Upright position with little or no flex in legs; weight often back (leans or falls back).
Arm–pole movement	Forward angle at pole plant; arm comfortably flexed at elbow and wrist when planting; arm fully extends behind skier; arm recovery is a straight relaxed arm swing; arm motion remains at skiers side throughout—does not cross in front of body in plant motion.	Forward angle at pole plant; partial arm extension; arm motion remains at skier's side throughout—does not cross in front of body in plant motion.	Vertical pole plant; arm extends only to hip; arms may cross over in front of body in plant motion.	Backward angle at pole plant; little or no arm extension; arms cross in front of body in plant motion.
Leg and body movement	Alternating push-off from one ski onto gliding ski; forward body position; flex in hips, knees, and ankles; strong push from the whole foot is down and back; leg is fully extended back (knee and ankle straighten) while forward leg remains flexed for balance and next push.	Movement as described in "Outstanding" but without a strong push or full confidence in balance on glide.	Skier exhibits push mechanics or glide position yet is unable to sequence both motions in succession.	Skier shuffles skis in tracks without a recognizable push and glide.
Timing	Opposite arm and leg movement in diagonally opposite directions; push occurs when feet come together; opposite pole is swung forward and planted.	Opposite arm and leg movement in diagonally opposite directions; push occurs early or late of feet coming together.	Opposite arm and leg movement in diagonally opposite directions without push or glide—essentially a diagonal walk motion.	Same-side arm and leg movement; arms in same-side synch with leg shuffle.

Reprinted with permission by Tom Beery, 2005.

expressed that concept or showed that skill. The scale can run from 1 (not shown or covered) to 5 (exceeded expectations). Now you have a rubric for assessment. Students can see the rubric before completing the task so they understand how they will be evaluated.

Another strategy is to have students develop their own rubric. Student-directed learning takes time but engages the students more deeply in the learning process. This teaches metacognition, or "thinking about thinking" skills. Imagine a student reflecting on what knowledge and skills are necessary to successfully master a topic. Student-created rubrics answer the question, "How will you show yourself and me that you've succeeded in learning?"

Journals

Journals play many roles in outdoor education. They can provide insight into student learning and an alternative mode of communication between the outdoor educator and the student. Journals can be a means for personal reflection as well. A useful trick that allows one journal to serve both as an assessment tool and a reflection tool is to hand out paper clips to your students. The students can clip together any pages that are off limits for the outdoor educator. In this manner you can respect student privacy and still have access to the assignments in the journal that are less personal.

Asking Questions

Simply asking students questions is another assessment tool. Questions engage students in learning by having them actively think and solve problems. Questions also give you feedback on what your students are learning and how well they are mastering it.

One challenge in asking questions is assuring that all students have the opportunity to respond. Following a question allow adequate time, 3 to 5 seconds, for students to formulate an answer. As soon as you call on a student to respond, you are signaling the other students to stop thinking about the question. Deliberately call on different students during the discussion so you get a broader view of student understanding. Don't put students on the spot, however, by calling on people who are unprepared to answer. Vary your techniques so everyone can have a chance to think about the question and respond. For example, you might pair students up and give the group a question. Allow partners to discuss the question and then share the results of their discussion with the group. With this technique every student has a chance to think about the question and to respond.

Good questions ask students to demonstrate their knowledge. For example, asking students to touch a sugar maple shows you how many students can correctly identify the tree. Once students have mastered knowledge, move to more complex questions that require students to manipulate the knowledge. For example, "Does this forest exhibit biodiversity? Be prepared to explain your answer," requires students to correctly identify the trees, estimate how many different kinds of trees there are in the forest, and evaluate the health of the forest based on those parameters.

Don't look for one correct answer from your students. You are teaching them how to think, not how to guess what's on your mind. "Has the Ojibwe culture changed significantly over time?" is a question loaded with judgment and value. If you use it to open a discussion of how the culture has changed and what the effects of those changes are, you are encouraging students to think. If, however, you are trying to get students to say yes or no in agreement with the answer you have in your mind, you are teaching students to guess what you think rather than think for themselves.

Questions are powerful tools. Plan questions as you lay out your curriculum and list the questions in your lesson plan. Begin with knowledge questions to introduce students to new material. Then progress to more complex questions that analyze, synthesize, or evaluate the material as class progresses. These questions will help you keep in touch with the content your students are learning and how well they are processing that information.

Authentic Assessment

In the context of outdoor education, authentic means real-to-life. Authentic assessment has students demonstrating what they have learned. For example, if the goal of your lesson is to teach the skills to build a Leave No Trace campfire in a hardwood forest, have the students build a Leave No Trace campfire. By observing the actions of the students you quickly will be able to determine if your goal was met.

Following are examples of objectives and the techniques to assess them. Read through them and then answer the question at the end.

1. List four essential components of habitat. Assessment: Following the habitat game, students will draw a picture of a habitat of their

choosing. The drawing must include the four components of a habitat and describe or show the links between the habitat components.

2. Demonstrate how to correctly hold a canoe paddle and execute the J-stroke, draw stroke, and forward stroke. Assessment: Each pair of students in a canoe will demonstrate all four skills before paddling freely on the lake.

3. Outline a group management plan for Leave No Trace travel in a designated wilderness area. Assessment: Teams of four will present their plan to the whole class. Each plan must include at least three components of Leave No Trace practices.

Question: What are two ways you can assess objectives from your favorite lesson? Write down your answer.

Assessment is quickly becoming an essential part of outdoor education. Assessment can be a useful tool for the student as well as the outdoor educator. An effective assessment plan incorporates a variety of methods throughout the entire course.

Professional Reflection

Just like participants, instructors should reflect on their experiences. We all have areas we can improve. Use the available opportunities to become a better outdoor educator. Take the time to reflect on the lesson you have given and jot your thoughts on what worked and what didn't. You can use these thoughts later to improve the lesson.

When it comes to evaluation, keep an open mind. Seek out a means for getting evaluation from participants, peers, and supervisors. This could be written or verbal feedback (see example on p. 101).

If your organization does not require evaluation, it is up to you to make it happen. Seek input from others on your teaching performance, your organization, your contribution to the field of outdoor education, and your overall effectiveness as an outdoor educator.

Once you have received feedback, take the time to reflect on specific strategies for improving your teaching. Begin working on easier items, but quickly prioritize the items that will have the biggest influence on your teaching.

An example of a teaching flaw that is easy to improve is repetitive phrases. Many beginning outdoor educators use repetitive phrases such as "Um" or "OK" or "You guys" when referring to a mixed-gender group. Have an observer follow you in the field and tally any words you use inap-

propriately or repeatedly. Some outdoor educators use the same expression six times in a minute! If no observer is available, self-evaluate by taping yourself. If neither option is available, listen to yourself while you teach.

Once you have identified which phrases you use, categorize how you use the phrase. Do you say "OK" to close a topic and make a transition? Do you ask "OK?" to check your students' understanding? Once you know what phrases you use and how you use them, develop alternative language to replace your repetitive phrases.

A more difficult item to work on is inclusion of all students. While this is more difficult because it requires a variety of methodologies, it will also have a much bigger impact on your effectiveness as an outdoor educator. For example, it's common to respond to more assertive or vocal students. However, every student deserves an opportunity to participate. In addition, unequal student participation may have gender, ethnic, or learning-disability overtones. Do boys dominate your class? If you have only two Hispanic students, are they given equal opportunity to participate? Do you allow students to shout out answers rather than having students raise their hands? If so, you are encouraging fast-thinking students to respond and closing out many other students in your class.

Begin by having an observer tally how many times each student in your class responds, noting whether the students volunteered the response or if they were called on. Have your observer draw sketches of the physical arrangement of your students. Was everyone included in the group or were some students closer to you, the props, and so on? Is it always the same students who are close and who are far away?

With this self-awareness, develop a strategy to correct any noted inequities. For example, routinely alternate between female and male volunteers. If students are quiet, be careful not to put them on the spot. Quietly spend time with them, building rapport. Connect with the quiet students and learn about them. Then gradually invite their participation in the class. Begin by having them share easy responses, slowly working into more difficult answers or a deeper level of self-disclosure. Smile and affirm students whenever they participate in class. As you can see, correcting this inequity is more difficult than simply breaking the habit of a repetitive phrase. But the outcome for your students is much richer. The end result of working on your skills is personal growth and awareness and more effective teaching.

Sample Teaching Evaluation

Presenter _____ Evaluator _____

Date _____ Presentation topic _____

Audience: K-3   4-6   7-12   college   adult   family

1. **Prelesson**

   Lesson plan organization: none   poor   fair   good   excellent
   Comments:

2. **Presentation**

   Comment on each of the following areas.

   Delivery (voice, repetitive expressions such as "uh," body language, confidence)

   Awareness of students (understanding their level, handling discipline, answering questions, reading the audience, using teachable moments)

   Message (clarity, organization, pace, impact)

   Techniques used and their effectiveness (imaging, games, role playing, and so on)

   Content (quantity of information, use of ethics and values, and so on)

   Summary (conclusion)

3. **Improvements**

   Provide a concise list of areas in which the presenter could improve.

From Ken Gilbertson, Timothy Bates, Terry McLaughlin, and Alan Ewert, 2006, *Outdoor Education: Methods and Strategies,* Champaign, IL: Human Kinetics.

Stories From the Real World: Trying Something New

My coinstructor and I had taught a lesson on the logging history of the area many times using discussion, lecture, games, and guided discovery. We knew the content thoroughly and could work with the participants to improve their understanding of the role of logging and its relationship to the ecosystem. Our objectives were clearly met in these lessons. But, after teaching this same lesson plan many times, our enthusiasm was waning. It was time to try something new. We chose to try characterization as the teaching method. One of us portrayed a logger from the early 1900s and the other portrayed a logger from the 1970s, and we used the setting of an active sawmill. The first time through was a little rough since the dialogue was new. But it was fun for us and the participants had a great time being involved in a discussion between two loggers and actually using some of the tools of the trade. With time the lesson improved and has become a hit with participants. This lesson has been much more successful because we tried something new and we were enthusiastic.

It is difficult to improve your teaching without trying new things. Once you are comfortable with certain methods and strategies, try variations on those methods or try new strategies. This will invigorate you and it may be a more successful way for you to teach. It is OK to fail occasionally with a method as long as the failure does not compromise safety. Gain new ideas by observing others teach, reading books and current research, and attending professional conferences.

© University of Minnesota Duluth Outdoor Program

New methods enhance learning.

Summary

With a well-written lesson plan and proper planning, you are more likely to deliver an outstanding lesson. From that base you can be more creative and flexible with your lesson. All good lessons have an introduction, body, reflection, and conclusion. The outdoor educator should have a clear understanding of how these will be conducted through methods that balance cognitive, kinesthetic, and affective learning.

When planning lessons, particularly skill-based lessons, incorporate the 3-Ds: describe, demonstrate, and do. If the skill is complex, use the whole–part–whole technique to break the skill into manageable parts. Recognize your role as a coach for the entire group. You are there to tell your students what they are doing well and to suggest areas they can work on. Plan assessment strategies into your lesson so you can give meaningful feedback to your students during the course (formative assessment) and at the end of the course (summative assessment).

When you first begin to write lesson plans you will probably find they take a lot of work and time. It's tempting to fly by the seat of your pants and begin instruction without a lesson plan. However, a well-written lesson plan will greatly improve your teaching and make you more conscious of the choices you are making. And don't forget, writing lesson plans becomes easier with practice.

Explore Your World

1. Describe how a well-written lesson plan influences the quality of the lesson.

2. Explain the basic components of a lesson.

3. Provide two examples of objectives.

4. Discuss how you would use reflection within a lesson.

5. Write four ways to assess a given topic.

PART III

Methods and Delivery of Outdoor Education

"The thing that is so important at this moment is an awareness of the totality of the person. One of the greatest stumbling blocks that people have today is understanding that one cannot experience life from the neck up. . . . If I could I would wave a magic wand and have them be automatically convinced that brain existence is only a small part of their lives. They are missing out on a whole fantastic world."

—Jean Berry

CHAPTER 8

Physical Methods

CHAPTER OBJECTIVES

By the end of the chapter, you should be able to do the following:

- Describe what physical methods are and how they pertain to outdoor education.

- Explain how to apply the development of physical skills to a topic.

- Demonstrate physical manipulation to teach a specific outdoor skill.

- Describe when and where to use games, activities, and competitions in a lesson.

- Present a lesson using theatrics or characterization to learn about the outdoors.

- Explain how initiatives are used in outdoor education.

Physical methods are methods that have a hands-on, kinesthetic element. Not only can these methods be used to teach skills, but they also can be used to teach concepts. Often viewed as the most effective method for teaching, these techniques enable students to get involved with their body as well as their mind. Lessons involving ropes courses, skill instruction, trips, and therapeutic settings regularly use physical methods to help people develop physically, mentally, and emotionally.

Physical Skills Development

It is difficult to imagine education in an outdoor environment without some kind of physical activity. The learning of physical skills is often the purpose of the course or activity. In physical skills development, one of the initial considerations is the needs of the individual. Much has been written about the needs of both individuals and groups in an outdoor environment, including acceptable energy levels, body temperature, shelter, food and water, personal security, self-actualization, and fear reduction (Ford and Blanchard 1993). More recently, some have advocated the **performance triad** of hydration, nutrition, and pacing as a model for helping students perform and learn. That is, outdoor educators need to ensure that their students are properly hydrated and have eaten sufficient calories to be successful in the tasks demanded of them, which should not be too fast paced. In addition, students need to understand the importance of monitoring their health and energy levels during an activity to ensure sufficient energy reserves in case of an emergency or other contingency.

After dealing with the psychological and physiological needs of the learner, effective teaching of physical skills involves the following principles:

- Skill instruction should be timely and relevant. Schedule your instruction for a time when the learner is ready and needs to learn the skill. Teaching a skill that will not be used for several days requires you to reteach the lesson later.

- Use multidimensional teaching techniques. Use a variety of senses, experiences, and examples in your lesson plans. For example, in teaching a concept such as the water cycle, you can expose the students to the different components of the cycle through techniques such as direct experience (e.g., rafting down a river), observation and introspection (e.g., using a journal to record thoughts and observations regarding cloud formation, rain, and thunderstorms), and analysis of watershed through the use of maps and aerial photographs.

- Use the power of association by drawing on the learners' past experience and background to help make connections with the material being taught (theories of personal meaning and constructivism).

- Use repetition and practice in direct proportion to the importance of the material. For example, if the activity involves elements of risk, integrate numerous opportunities for practice and assessment before trying out the real thing.

- Instill confidence and trust in your students by giving them appropriate levels of responsibility and offering timely feedback on their performance and your expectations. Anticipate the 80% rule—students will watch you do an activity and emulate 80% of what you do. Beware of the assumption trap, or assuming that students can perform a physical activity because it's easy or the students have done the activity before.

- Whenever possible and appropriate, use **sequencing** and **progression.** Sequencing an activity involves teaching a foundation of skills and knowledge and then engaging the learner in activities that require the use of these foundational skills for more complex tasks. Similarly, progression involves moving from simplistic and relatively low-risk tasks to more complex and risky activities. Using a ropes-course scenario, the students would start with initiative activities (see page 113), move to a low ropes-course setting (i.e., a ropes course relatively low to the ground), and then move to a higher ropes-course environment.

Introduction

In the introduction, the instructor sets the stage for the learning experience by getting the attention of the students and helping them understand why it is important to learn certain physical skills. For example, having students look at sections of the river they will be canoeing is often an excellent prelude to teaching specific canoe strokes and skills. Students' observations of the moving

INTRODUCTION

Understand students' needs.

Plan teaching/learning opportunity.

Select appropriate time and setting.

Get students' attention.

Establish need to learn from student perspective.

PRESENTATION

Unfold the learning opportunity.

Utilize past experiences and background of students.

Develop foundational learning, then more specific learning.

Use effective questioning and visual or physical aids.

Check for understanding.

Develop and demonstrate interest in the subject.

PERFORMANCE

Demonstrate ➡ Practice ➡ Evaluate ➡ Correct ➡ Practice

Provide immediate feedback.

Encourage self-assessment and self-correction.

Explicitly state standards or criteria for success.

Sequence of effective instruction.

water will motivate them to learn the proper procedures and techniques because they will be using those skills shortly, thus creating an immediacy of need.

Presentation

During the presentation phase, the instructor unfolds a logical and well-planned learning sequence that incorporates the past experience and background of the learners. For this phase you should do the following:

- Select an appropriate place and time to teach the lesson. Pay attention to the physical and psychological needs of the learners. Are they hungry or cold? Is the sun in their eyes? Are they focusing on the fire, river, or other components of the outdoors rather than the lesson?

- Be organized and use notes. Even if you have a great deal of experience with the subject, using notes and a lesson plan helps ensure that important information is not left out.

- Speak clearly and with inflection while maintaining eye contact with the audience.

- Use visual aids, real-life examples, and props to help illustrate important points of the lesson.

- Periodically check for understanding. One way to accomplish this is to break up the lesson with actual practice.

- Be enthusiastic about your teaching and the subject. Good instructors use theatrics, humor, storytelling, and other techniques to make even boring topics interesting, positive learning experiences.

Practice

In the practice phase, provide opportunities for the students to learn by doing; that is, provide direct experience. This is also the phase where skill assessment is critical. Providing timely, accurate, and helpful evaluations of the student's performance of a particular skill or activity can help preclude the learning of incorrect procedures and help the student successfully learn the skill required for the activity.

Application

Finally, in the application phase the students have to perform the skill in a real-life context. Similar to the practice phase, the instructor is present to provide immediate advice. Upon completion of the activity, providing a summative set of observations for both the individual and group often allows the learners to put it all together and use past experience and reflection to complete the learning of the physical skills or activity.

Physical Manipulation

Often in outdoor education, it is necessary to complete a skill in a precise manner for effective technique and efficiency. But how do we get to that point of skill mastery? One tool for helping people understand how to move their body to accomplish a skill is called **physical manipulation.** This technique involves simply moving the student's body into the proper position so that the muscles can begin to memorize the unfamiliar motion. Imagine yourself as the artist and the person as the clay—you need to adjust the body to get it into the proper position.

A simple example of physical manipulation is teaching a Duffek stroke to a person paddling in the bow of a canoe. Beginning paddlers often do not understand the arm, torso, and paddle placement for this stationary stroke. You could ask participants for permission to move their body into position, and then gently turn their torso and place their arms into position for the stroke. You are physically guiding the students through the proper motion so they can feel the correct technique.

Physical manipulation can be used in many settings and with many different skills. A word of caution, however—not all participants like to be touched. Ask permission before you use this method.

Activities, Games, and Competitions

Activities, games, and competitions add an element of fun to the lesson and enhance motivation to learn. They are also effective tools for evaluation. This sec-

An educator uses physical manipulation to teach correct paddle position.

tion describes how to use the methods of activities, games, and competitions in your lessons.

Activities

An activity involves action rather than sitting and listening. Activities are the basis for all hands-on education, and experiential learning requires activity in the learning exercise. Being active engages your students' minds and bodies. Activity can also be useful to change the pace of a lesson and promote interaction among your students. The key to this method (as well as games and competition) is to use it to deliberately foster learning about the subject matter.

Games and Competitions

Games and competitions are activities that are sometimes interchangeable but not always. Games focus the students' attention on a specific activity that has rules and that may or may not result in a winner. Competitions, on the other hand, almost always result in a winner of some sort.

One common type of game is the **initiative,** where participants work together to accomplish an assigned task that requires problem solving and teamwork (more about initiatives later in this chapter). Games can range from board games to running games. What you incorporate into your game is determined by what you want to accomplish with the game, or your objective. If your objective is to burn off steam with a group of 5th graders, then a running game may be appropriate, but if you want to assess knowledge, a quiz game might be best. The key to games is to make sure that everyone has fun and everyone wins in some way.

Competitions challenge skill and knowledge and can be a great motivator for people to excel. How-

ever, they also can make people feel dejected if they don't win (we've all seen the crying and depression evident in the sport team that just lost a big game). Set up the competition so that the stakes are not too high and so that everyone will have fun even if they don't win. For example, in a class on the geology of the area we are traveling in, I often review with a quiz competition, challenging the students with questions related to what we explored earlier. The incentive for active participation and winning is the prize of a small geology guidebook written by a local author. Everyone is involved, has fun, and pays close attention.

Games and competitions are useful as parts of a lesson, but rarely are they adequate as the entire lesson. Games and competitions are excellent introductions to a lesson and are effective in the middle of a lesson. They can also be used to evaluate students or to conclude a lesson. The timing and placement of the method within a lesson will be determined by your planning. How will the method best contribute to your students' learning?

A word about risk management is necessary. Games and competitions often involve movement, including running and chasing. You must know your site well before you begin, including where all the hazards are. Twisted ankles from stepping in a hole in the ground or poked eyes from tree branches are unacceptable. Establish ground rules for movement and action so that people don't get tackled or tripped. Boundaries are also important. Make sure students know where they can and cannot go. Losing members is not a good thing—keep track of your students.

Theatrics

Theatrics involves portraying a character from another time period or context. By simply dressing, talking, and acting like a person in another period

Stories From Real Life: Game for Assessing Skills

All the members of the group were leaders in outdoor education, but we needed to assess their skill and ability in canoeing. To do this, we set up a canoe basketball competition on the local pond. We divided the students into two groups, set the playing area, established rules, and created goals. Once play began, we were able to see who could maneuver their canoe into position to receive, pass, or score with the ball. The students had great fun participating, even though there were no prizes other than the pride of winning. And the best part was that we were able to assess skills without the students even knowing it.

Stories From Real Life: Buffalo Soldier

There's a group of school children waiting for me in Yosemite National Park's Pioneer Cemetery. I can see them staring up at granite cliffs and at the ponderosas and cedars that surround them. They're moved by what they see, but try to mask their wonder behind bravado and laughter. I walk up in my turn-of-the-century cavalry uniform. They look at me and smile, and a few are giggling, but once I start talking their faces become more serious. I begin to tell them about my experiences as a soldier, as a *Colored* boy growing up in South Carolina in the early 1870s. These stories pull them out of the *now,* away from the cars, tourists, and noise of the twenty-first century. Within a short time they're with me back in 1903. Because I believe in who I say I am, they begin to believe it too. They also begin to believe in the Yosemite, and the America, of 1903.

Photo courtesy of Ray Santos/NPS

This would not be possible if I were wearing my ranger uniform and simply talked about this story. Now, I am this story, I am the life that I'm speaking about. Because it's real for me, it's real for them. Pain and sorrow, joy and laughter, are best expressed in the first person because it's harder to discount the authenticity of someone simply saying "This is my story!"

—Shelton Johnson (park ranger, Yosemite National Park) as a Buffalo soldier

your students will learn about the history and values of the time. It is an interesting methodology that keeps students engaged and motivated.

Theatrics is an effective educational method because it teaches our emotions as well as our brains. Theatrics presents an overall picture of the character or time period and captures students' interest and imagination. It takes more work to teach through a character rather than simply teaching about a character, but the nuances that influence the depth of learning and recall in your students are often worth the extra work.

Developing a Theatrical Character

When you decide the most effective method for teaching your topic is theatrics, begin by thoroughly researching the topic. Learn all you can about the time period, such as what the political climate was, what historical events recently happened or were about to happen, what the weather was like, and what the language sounded like. The more thorough your research, the more accurate your representation will be. Your students will learn from your every word and nuance and assume your characterization is accurate, so plan well.

If you are teaching about another culture, learn directly from that culture if possible. It is best to have a member of the culture teach about it but that may not be possible. Get permission from cultural leaders or spiritual leaders to teach about and to use artifacts. Artifacts are tools, ornaments, or weapons created by humans living in earlier cultures. Learn which artifacts are appropriate for public use and handling and which may have religious or spiritual overtones and should be avoided. Don't get creative here—if you don't know something, tell your audience you don't know. Avoid making up information about another culture, even if it's based on a solid background of experience and information.

Once you are thoroughly grounded in the setting for your character, begin to develop the character. Give your character a name and age. Describe the character's family setting. Even though your audience may never hear these details, they are what make the character come alive.

Costume and Props

After developing your character, assemble a costume and props that will convey the character's time period and situation. Clothe your character as accurately as possible, and pay attention to details. What kind of clothing fasteners did they use at the time? What kind of shoes would your character wear?

Choose a few props to help embellish the setting. Sometimes props can be reproductions of houses or workplaces or schools from the time period. But even a few simple props convey a tone and setting. For example, a rug, rocking chair, and broom can create an effective setting for a pioneer woman to inhabit.

Being in Character

Once you have developed a character and you have made that character real through costumes and props, you now become that character. Taking on the role of the character is called being in character. Once you are in character and meet your audience, you must stay in character. Respond to problems that arise as your character would. Answer questions in the first person, as your character. Breaking character is greatly discouraged.

Involving the Audience

While it's effective for your students to observe you in your role, you can also let the students share part of the experience. Can they feel or try on the silk top hat you're wearing? Can they smell the mush you're stirring up for dinner? Can you pass around the animal skin you've traded for?

Initiatives and Ropes Courses

Two popular activities in outdoor education programs are initiatives and **ropes courses.** Initiative activities go by a number of names including icebreakers, new games, or challenge activities and usually take place early in a course. Initiatives are one or more short activities that require the group or individual to solve real or created problems. Karl Rohnke, considered a master of new games and initiatives, sees them as a means to break down hierarchies, aid in decision making, build morale, and develop a sense of camaraderie (Rohnke 1989).

Ropes courses, while similar in intent to initiative activities, are different in the sense that they involve ropes or high-tensile cable stretched between trees or other support systems that are at various heights. These ropes or cables are placed in different configurations with the object being to move from location to location using these ropes or cables. As with initiative activities, individuals must often work as a team in order to move between the stations.

A ropes course is an experiential activity.

Photo courtesy of Wolf Ridge ELC, 6282 Cranberry Road, Finland, MN. www.wolf-ridge.org.

Initiatives and ropes courses have become an increasingly important part of many outdoor education programs (Rohnke 1989). These activities can be effective in achieving beneficial outcomes both for individuals and groups (Fluegelman 1976). However, this effectiveness depends on how well the instructor sets up the activity and processes the outcomes of the activity.

Ropes courses and initiatives are generally conducted in the following venues:

- High ropes-course events (usually more than 10 feet or 3 meters off the ground)
- Low ropes-course events
- Permanent initiative activity sites
- Undeveloped open space

Ropes courses first appeared as a technique to facilitate physical training in the French Navy in the late 1800s (Rohnke 1999), while initiative activities began to receive attention during the 1960s (Fluegelman 1976). Both initiative activities and ropes courses can be used in the developmental phase of an outdoor education program or as a stand-alone activity. In the developmental phase of a program, initiatives and ropes courses are used early on to achieve the following:

- Observation of the students to determine their communication skills, flexibility and physical fitness, creativity, ability to follow instructions, and ability to work as a team.
- Begin the process of group identity and role making. At this phase, instructors can establish their role of evaluator.
- Physicality. These events provide opportunities for the group to experience movement, physical touching through holding, and guiding one another.

Increasingly, ropes courses and initiative activities are used as stand-alone activities. That is, the program, often a half- or single-day event, is built around the initiative activities or ropes course. Typically, after the activity is completed, instructors conduct a debriefing to determine what happened during the activity, what meaning the students got from the activity, and how they will use that meaning in the future (see Luckner and Nadler 1997).

Teaching Through Initiatives

Initiatives typically have a clearly defined physical or mental task that the group is required to accomplish. Considerable communication and problem-solving skills are often necessary for the group or individual to be successful. Initiatives are designed to challenge the participants and usually require the joint effort of group members to be successful. Groups must be persistent, experiment with different ways to solve the problem, employ effective teamwork, and plan out the solution.

Common initiative activities include immersion walks, trust falls, and trust dives. In addition, a number of books and other sources provide more complete descriptions of initiative activities and ropes courses. A sampling of books can be found in the bibliography (Resources for Initiative Activities and Ropes Courses, p. 204).

In using initiatives, don't forget the following factors:

- Use a convenient site and ensure that all materials necessary to complete the initiative are present.
- Frontload the initiative by clearly describing the situation, goals, and rules of the activity (which means pointing out or identifying the main learning points in advance of the activity rather than after it).
- Select initiatives that match the capabilities of the group and provide each group with a chance for success.
- Consider factors such as weather, physical condition of the participants, and characteristics of the activities. For example, many programs now avoid initiatives such as the Electric Fence because of the relatively high frequency of ankle and knee injuries incurred by hitting the ground after going over the "wire."
- Avoid overcoaching the activity. Many instructors fall into the trap of thinking they are helping the group by coaching them on how to complete the activity. For most initiative activities, it's more important *how* the group got to where they are (i.e., the process they decided on and used) rather than *where* they got to (whether they completed the activity or not).
- Backload the initiative by helping the group discuss what happened, how it happened, why it happened that way, what the implications are from the experience, and how the lessons learned from this experience can be used at a different time and in a different format. Asking students to reflect on their experience and what they learned from it is one form of backloading.

Teaching Through Ropes Courses

While similar in intent to initiative activities, ropes courses are often defined in terms of obstacle-course activities that typically occur off the ground, from several inches to many feet. Particularly for high ropes courses, the participants are exposed to both real and apparent risk as they attempt to complete the course either individually or in a pair. Participants often have to use their balance, strength, agility, problem-solving, and commitment abilities. Participants are normally expected to participate in all the activities, but they should not be coerced or forced into participation (e.g., challenge by choice). In addition, participants who decide to come down or not participate should not be demeaned or disparaged (e.g., no-discount programming—no one is discounted or devalued by deciding not to continue). Emphasize to the participants that there are many ways to complete the activities. It is best to have a continuous series of activities in order to keep the participants off the ground from start to finish.

Typical objectives of using ropes courses are

- to increase the participant's sense of confidence;

- to develop a support system within a group and make it accessible to all members;

- to increase the participant's agility and physical coordination;

- to increase joy in one's physical self and simply being with other people; and

- to focus on specific program outcomes such as team building, group communication, leadership, risk taking, and decision making.

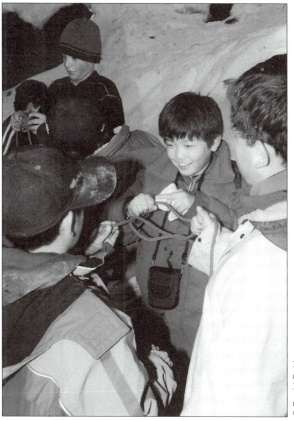

© David Dahler

Initiatives help with team building.

Summary

You have now learned some methods for teaching about the outdoors through physical activity. As you have seen, there are many physical methods to use when teaching skills outdoors. In addition, you have learned that teaching a physical skill in sequence helps students learn with less frustration, and using physical manipulation to help muscle memory further enhances their learning. You learned when and how to use activities, games, and competitions, and you learned that theatrics and characterization are highly effective methods for drawing students into the topic. Finally, you learned about the purpose of initiatives and ropes courses for learning in, about, and for the outdoors.

Explore Your World

1. Explain how physical methods pertain to outdoor education, including interpretation, environmental education, and adventure education.

2. Choose a skill topic and demonstrate how you could use physical manipulation to teach the skill.

3. Present a lesson using theatrics or characterization for outdoor learning.

4. Discuss the role of ropes courses and initiatives as effective methods in outdoor education.

CHAPTER 9

Cognitive Methods

CHAPTER OBJECTIVES

By the end of the chapter, you should be able to do the following:

- Describe appropriate use of cognitive methods.

- Explain when each cognitive method is best used in a lesson.

- Come up with questions that lead students toward their own understanding of the subject.

- Guide learning through the use of video by describing how video and simulation can be effective teaching tools.

- Describe the purpose of service learning and apply it to a relevant topic.

- Present written materials to support a lesson.

- Effectively use peer teaching in a lesson.

Perhaps the most common type of method in education of any kind is cognitive. **Cognitive methods** involve building knowledge about a topic, regardless of whether the method is focused on acquiring knowledge, is physically oriented, or is rooted in emotions. Solid knowledge of any topic that you are teaching is essential. If you are teaching about landscapes, you must have an understanding of geomorphology. If you are teaching ski techniques, you must have knowledge of biomechanics, physics, and ski performance. This kind of knowledge acquisition is considered a cognitive process.

As mentioned, a lesson should use multiple methods. Just as it is best to begin and end a lesson at a control site safe from weather and distractions, it is also best to begin and end a lesson using a knowledge-based method. For example, an introduction to the lesson typically begins with a brief lecture or discussion about the topic at hand. A lesson often concludes with a summary or example of an application that makes the students' learning relevant to their life. Usually a lesson does not start or end with a stand-alone physical activity, although physical activities such as immersion walks or initiative activities can be useful introductions.

This chapter presents methods that draw on cognitive learning, including lecture and discussion, inquiry, videography, service learning, use of written materials, and peer teaching.

Lecture and Discussion

Lecturing is a method of teaching in which the instructor presents information to the student in a one-direction manner. It is often referred to as teacher-centered (Kindsvatter, Wilen, and Ishler 1996). While often associated with a college setting, lecturing can be appropriate in a variety of teaching situations. Depending on how it is used, lecturing can be highly effective or excruciating. It is fairly common for new instructors to avoid the lecture method, often because they were subjected to boring or ineffective lectures in the past. However, lecturing is very effective when used in the right context and at the right time in the lesson. It is not hard to think of instructors who were considered boring because of their incorrect use of lecture. On the other hand, instructors who used the lecture method well are remembered as dynamic, inspirational speakers.

Lectures are used in formal presentations, when factual information needs to be imparted, when a great degree of information needs to be shared, or when immediate retention of the material is not the major consideration. Gage and Berliner (1992) found that the lecture is as effective as other teaching methods when used appropriately.

In outdoor education, lecture is typically used for short durations, such as periods of 5 to 15 minutes. It is effective for introductions, conclusions, and when technical information must be shared to prepare students for practice. Some lecture examples include the following:

- Presenting equipment types and construction
- Explaining a technique—defining it, describing it, and explaining when it is best used
- Describing taxonomy or life history of a plant or animal
- Explaining a purpose, philosophy, or theory that supports why or how a topic is being presented
- Reviewing background information to reinforce understanding of a topic

For the lecture method to be successful, it is helpful to follow these simple steps:

- Prepare your material in an organized manner.
- Arrange each topic in a sequence that is logical and easy to understand.
- Know the information well.
- Present the information in your own words; avoid simply reading facts out loud.
- Practice. This will help you become comfortable with the topic.
- Vary voice inflection and volume.
- Allow discussion during the presentation, especially if the lecture is long.
- Use examples and visual aids.
- Pace yourself so students aren't overloaded with too much, too soon.

Lecturing is a vital component of any lesson. Use it appropriately and sparingly and it will strengthen your lesson. Overuse it, or expect immediate retention, and you will rapidly lose your students' interest. This can easily result in inadequate learning, which can delay correct application of the subject material.

Inquiry

Inquiry is the use of exploration and questioning to arrive at a conclusion. Kindsvatter, Wilen, and Ishler (1996) define inquiry as developing critical-thinking skills through problem solving. The teacher guides the student through a series of steps beginning with the identification of a problem. Once the problem is identified, the student then clarifies it so it is understandable. The student formulates a set of ideas to investigate the problem. (This step is often called forming a hypothesis.) The set of ideas leads to direction in collecting information to answer the problem. The student then analyzes the information so its meaning can be interpreted. Finally, the student derives a conclusion to answer the problem. The steps for using inquiry as a teaching method as recommended by Kindsvatter, Wilen, and Ishler (259) are as follows:

1. Identify and clarify the problem.
2. Form hypotheses.

Tips and Techniques

- Ask questions about something specific, such as, "What adaptations do owls have for flying silently?" or, "If you are moving fast downhill on cross-country skis, what action do you take to remain stable?"

- Ask direct questions about material that is relevant to the students.

- Briefly pause after asking a question to elicit a response.

- If appropriate, briefly pause after a student responds to allow for further insight.

- Avoid global or vague questions, such as, "Any questions?" or, "What did you learn today?"

- Link your questions and present them sequentially. For example, ask, "What happened? What caused the event to happen? What would happen if we did something else?"

- Repeat student responses to ensure that you understand the answers. In addition, it helps ensure that other students hear the response.

© David Dahler

Inquiry promotes problem solving and student involvement.

3. Collect data.

4. Analyze and interpret data to test hypotheses.

5. Draw conclusions.

Many instructors assume that inquiry means simply posing questions to the students. While questioning is important to guide student understanding, inquiry is more systematic. Thus, questioning students is a technique used in teaching while inquiry is a teaching method.

Once you understand the purpose of inquiry, you can use it to facilitate student learning. A common problem for novice instructors is failing to plan specific questions that will lead to a clear understanding of the topic. This lack of a specific questioning strategy is often manifested in lesson plans. For example, instead of writing a note in the plan to simply ask questions to see if the students learned the subject, you want to write your questions into the lesson to guide learning.

By using good questioning techniques in the inquiry teaching method, you become student-centered in your approach. This is different than the lecture method, which is necessarily more teacher-centered.

Videography

Another teaching method has evolved that uses simulation through video technology: **videogra-phy.** The heart of the simulation exercise is the video recording of a specific event or vignette (Ewert and Galloway 2002). Each vignette consists of a hypothetical group of students engaged in some form of adventure programming. After watching the vignette, you can ask students questions about what they would do in that situation. In addition, the video can present real students with problems that require them to make a series of decisions as the scenario unfolds. Thus, students develop insight into the decision-making process and their own knowledge about a situation. However, to be believable the vignette must contain certain characteristics, including the following:

- The situation must be believable. Often the vignettes are patterned after a real occurrence from an adventure program.

- The vignette must present a situation that is operational; that is, some action must be taken. The audience cannot simply allow the events to unfold without making some decisions. Each vignette is limited by equipment and time. The events can only be depicted by the equipment and time available. The scenario is obviously limited in the amount and type of information that can be used. This is similar to real-life situations where information is often contradictory or deficient.

Photo courtesy of Salish Sea Expeditions.

Video vignettes can create useful simulations.

For both the students and the instructor, video simulations present several challenges. To be effective, there needs to be a translation from the simulation to practice. Typically, these video scenarios are developed by experienced instructors and present situations that must be addressed in often emotionally charged terms.

Using Simulation for Training

Using simulation for training presents many challenges. There may be differences in the cultural or interpersonal interpretations between the students and leader, often leading to a lack of congruency between what students think needs to be done and what the leader feels would be a reasonable response. Finally, there are often differences between what a leader and what a student would think constitutes a good decision.

Whether using video simulation, field-based scenarios, or other forms of simulation, at the most elementary level these tools can provide a picture through which the students can closely observe the decision-making process and other aspects of leadership in the outdoor education setting. This is important considering the complexity of instructing a variety of students in the outdoors. For example, consider the factors that influence the ability of an individual to make decisions in the outdoor education environment. These factors include the following:

- Types of decisions that need to be made
- Number of available options
- Time available for making decisions
- Severity of the consequences of a bad decision
- Personality and background of the decision maker
- Experience of the student
- Uncertainty of the naturalistic setting
- Environmental factors such as cold, fatigue, fear, and so on

From the perspectives of teaching and programming, simulation can be effective in training outdoor teachers and leaders on three levels: individual, programmatic, and pedagogic. The individual level focuses on the actual decision-making process of the individual. At the programmatic level, administrators, directors, and other supervisors can observe how instructors and students react to different situations. At the pedagogic level, individual programs or organizations can design training with specific field requirements in mind (geography, modality, clients) based on findings from simulations.

Implications for Cognitive Learning

Simulation enhances cognitive learning in two ways. First, the participants receive feedback on the quality of their decision making, and they get to practice making critical decisions. They gain an understanding of their decision-making skills and other abilities and knowledge. Second, when used in a group, simulation provides ample opportunity for discussion among staff and students. Such sharing includes perspectives from differing levels of experience among the group. Valuable information may be gained regarding conceptions or misconceptions participants hold with respect to decision making in particular situations.

Using Videography to Develop Physical Skills

In addition to showing simulations via video, outdoor educators can also use videography to model and build physical skills that are to be learned. This, as a teaching tool, takes what is a physical skill and helps the student understand how it works cognitively.

First let's approach the proper modeling method of video use. This takes video that the instructor or a professional company has made and uses it to show the student the proper way to perform a skill. For example, in teaching a forward stroke in a sea kayak, a student will be able to observe all of the components of an effective stroke. If this video is shown after a student has been introduced to basic parts of the skill and has practiced them, the learning will be greater because the student can build or construct new understandings. It is very important that the instructor point out the nuances that are important as the video is being played. The instructor can also stop and rewind regularly to show a key point (for example, in the sea kayak video, the instructor may point out the torso rotation of the person on the screen).

Building off this, the student can then practice the skills observed. In addition, the instructor could then take video footage of the students performing the skill. This can then be shown to students so

Tips and Techniques

Guidelines for videography of individuals for skill development (Carlson 2000):

- Instructor reviews key points of a skill and demonstrates proper form or shows video of proper form.
- Students practice proper form until they can demonstrate proper form at least twice.
- Videotape students demonstrating the skill.
- Review video with students and discuss performance. Ask students to prescribe solutions for errors.
- Conduct multiple viewings. Replay frequently to allow students an opportunity to observe improvement and errors.
- Repeat skill demonstration, videography, and feedback cycle until learning criteria are met.

that they can observe and cognitively understand what they are doing right and what they need to improve. Often, students cannot understand what they are doing wrong until they can see it on a video.

Service Learning

"With true service, the question of Whose problem is this, anyway? fades away. Service involves a connection between the helper and the helped that eventually dissolves the distance between the two."

—Rahima C. Wade (1997)

Service learning is working with students on a meaningful project that has direct use and application to the land or community. When properly sequenced, it builds cognitive learning and applies that learning to real-world needs through physical projects. Without a proper learning progression preceding the project, the service learning is reduced to purely a service project.

Service learning has become a common method in many different outdoor education settings. Some examples of service learning include the following:

- Planting trees
- Restoring wetlands
- Repairing and constructing trails
- Building a garden
- Sharing an outdoor experience with people who have limited access to the experience

(such as inner-city youths, senior citizens, or members of a group home for people with developmental impairments)

Service learning is predominantly student-centered. That is, the students do most of the interaction during the lesson. It is also project-oriented. Because service learning takes the form of a project, it requires a great deal of preparation and instruction to ensure that students are ready to implement the project. For example, if a group of students are going to help a local park manager build a trail, you will need to plan for the appropriate time of year. Do you have enough tools? Are your students skilled in the safe and proper use of the tools? Do they have adequate background information to understand why they are doing the project?

If students fail to understand the purpose and outcome of the project, they may perceive the project as meaningless and a form of cheap labor. Be sure to design a project where the students and community members work side by side. Although this alone does not imply the project has purpose or meaning, it enhances a sense of community.

The primary steps to successful service learning are as follows. These guidelines have been adapted with permission from Anderson (1999).

Preparation

For any service learning to be successful, you must engage in careful preparation. Without a clearly defined purpose and strong foundation, service-learning programs have an unlikely chance for

© Ira Estin

Service learning is a student-centered approach to teaching.

survival. When preparing to implement a service-learning project there are some basic components to consider.

- Be sure to keep in mind the size and scope of your project when making preparations.

- Does the project depend on your group of students, or will more be needed?

- Can the project be accomplished in a short time, or will it require a longer period to complete? For example, building a bridge over a wet area on a trail may only require 2 to 4 hours, while conducting site rehabilitation through revegetation will likely take a couple of seasons.

Support

Any successful service-learning project must have adequate support from the school, environmental education center, or outdoor education provider. Ideally, students, parents, administrators, and instructors will believe in service learning; however, this often is not the case. Do your homework. Prepare your case for service learning so you can get support from these groups. They may not yet value service learning, but they may be willing to give it a try.

The school principal or center director needs to value the project as a learning experience as well as

a contribution to the agency. Otherwise, the project will likely be seen as a form of cheap labor, or a job that would be better accomplished by simply hiring a professional.

Goal Statement

Know what you are trying to achieve on a broader level. Why are you getting into service learning? If carefully constructed, this goal statement can serve as the foundation for service learning in your agency. It also will come in handy when you rally for financial or community support.

Your Community

Identify the factors that make the community you intend to work with a community. Are these factors socioeconomic, geographical, cultural, racial, environmental, or a combination of these? Recognize the issues that your community faces and discuss how these will affect your service-learning program and your students. Additionally, before deciding on a specific project, consider how the community will react to and work with your students.

Roles

Define the role of each member of your service-learning project. All members of the process must have clearly defined responsibilities so they know what they are accountable for. For example, the local state park may be responsible for providing the trees for erosion-control planting, but your organization is responsible for bringing the shovels to plant the trees.

Agencies

Establish a list of agencies (e.g., resource agencies, parks, nature centers) that are willing to work with your group. Again, do your homework. Know the basic goals and interests of the organizations before contacting them. At this point you are only establishing a primary contact. Do they have any needs to be met, and are they interested in collaborating with you? This contact can be a simple phone call or visit. Let them know you are in the preliminary stages of planning and you may or may not end up working with them. The longer the list of potential contacts, the better chance you have of finding a project that fits the needs of your students and the agency. Maintain friendly relations by letting all agencies know what project you end up choosing, because you may want to work with them another time.

Limitations

Take the time to identify barriers to your service-learning project. Common problems are time, money, staff training, liability, transportation, and special student needs. Recognizing these limitations will give you a realistic picture of what your class is capable of completing. Early identification of these issues will also give you a chance to take action and mobilize for change and financial support. You don't want to have to cancel a program or disappoint your students because you did not take the time to adequately investigate your limitations.

Evaluation Procedures

When all is said and done, how will you know if you've been successful? Evaluation is the step most often forgotten in service learning. Evaluation procedures are most effective if they are created and implemented at the beginning of a service-learning project. Since evaluation is based on your objectives, it drives your programming. For the best results, evaluation must take place at all phases of the project. Evaluation can range from a simple opinion survey to a complex assessment. Consistent evaluation will help you to refine and improve your program. It will also provide you with results that are essential for continued support, whether it be community approval or financial backing.

Logistics

Give yourself plenty of time to prepare for a service project. Extra time will account for roadblocks you may encounter during the planning phase. For example, you may need to order supplies early to ensure you will have them for the project day. Additionally, if you are organized you will have more time to prepare your students.

Following is a list of questions that everyone in your partnership should be able to answer (Addison-Jacobsen and Batenburg 1996):

- Has proper transportation been scheduled?

- Are all the right people involved? Have they been properly informed?
- What is the risk-management plan?
- How long will you be at your site?
- What supplies are needed?
- What do students need to bring? Food? Outdoor clothing? Special gear?
- Have accommodations been made for students with special needs?
- Is a behavior-management plan in place?
- Do you want to invite any special people to visit the project, such as media or government officials?

Student and Agency Preparation

Once your plans are in place, it is time to get the students and agency ready for the service project. This project may be a first for many of the participants, so you will want to give them the tools they need to succeed.

Here are some questions students should be able to answer:

- Do they know what they'll be doing?
- Do they need special training?
- What is appropriate behavior?
- Who should they report to while at the service site?
- Are they aware of the natural or social context of the place?
- Do they have any questions they'd like answered?

Here are some questions agency representatives should be able to answer:

- Is the agency prepared to offer an orientation for the students?
- Will the agency staff need any special training?
- Have you and the agency agreed on the number of volunteers?
- Who will supervise the students?
- Are you sure the work is appropriate for students?

Reflection

Reflection before, during, and after a service-learning project can enhance your students' academic skills and personal development. A service project becomes a service-learning project during reflection. Remember, reflection is not only for the students! Take the time to reflect with your community partners about your own experiences. It will provide you with suggestions and feedback about your program.

Celebration

At the end of your project, take the time to celebrate your success. It is a great time to acknowledge and thank those individuals who made the project successful. A celebration also provides closure for the project and gives students a chance to say goodbye to people they may not see again. (This is especially important for tutor, mentor, or intergenerational projects.) Keep your celebration consistent with your project goals. For example, it may not be appropriate to use paper plates, napkins, and cups at a party to celebrate a waste-reduction project. A celebration will leave everyone with a positive feeling about the project.

Written Materials

Written materials are handouts that support what you are teaching. They serve as guides while you are teaching. They can also serve as a future reference for more detailed information supporting your lesson. You should have appropriate materials prepared for your lesson. Avoid handing out materials that your students will consider unnecessary. Examples of written materials include the following:

- Diagrams (e.g., a diagram of snowshoe parts; a diagram of flower parts)

- Steps of a skill (e.g., photos of the key steps of the diagonal stride in Nordic skiing)

- Key parts of a concept (e.g., designing a lesson plan)

- Equipment or clothing lists

Students retain more of material that they both see and hear. Written materials, no matter what the setting, can greatly enhance student understanding.

Peer Teaching

Effective teaching often comes when you take the focus off you, the outdoor educator, and put it on the students. One way to do this is through peer teaching. Peer teaching is when students teach each other knowledge or skills. There are two effective ways to use this method.

© Ira Estin

Peer teaching can be very effective.

First, peer teaching is useful when some students are more advanced than others. Use the advanced students to help the others along. An example would be when you are teaching a skill that some of the students already know or can master quickly. Have these students assist the others. The upside of this technique is that it empowers the advanced students and gives them a sense of satisfaction through helping. In this way they don't get bored while the instructor focuses on the other students. The downside is that the advanced students may help the others in a wrong way—they may have the skill, but their level of ability to assist may create incorrect skills for the other students.

In the second way to use peer teaching, you teach half of the group one set of knowledge or skills and teach the other half a different set of knowledge or skills. Then the students teach each other what they learned. Students may be better able to speak to their peers and use language that is understandable.

Stories From Real Life: Peer Teaching

The lesson on reading the landscape through the changes of a creek over time had gone poorly in past years. It was difficult to get the whole group of college students to the various sites (beaver lodge, logging ice road, creek bed) to learn the material—there just was not enough space or time to get through it all. Then my coinstructor and I hit upon the idea of students teaching each other. We split the group in half with one half going with him to learn how beavers and other natural forces change the creek and the other half coming with me to learn how human beings have changed the creek. Then each person paired up with someone from the opposite group and they had the responsibility to teach each other what they had learned in the first half of the lesson. The result was amazing! Students enjoyed being able to teach what they learned, and the learning that took place was tremendous. We hit a home run on this one.

Summary

The predominant type of learning discussed in this chapter was cognitive learning, or learning that demands thought to gain understanding of the material. Cognitive learning occurs in any lesson, and how it is used will determine the students' interest in your lesson. Overuse of such methods typically results in boredom, while avoidance results in the loss of effective ways to transmit certain types of information such as facts. Methods that draw on cognitive learning include lecture and discussion, inquiry, videography, service learning, use of written materials, and peer teaching. Any lesson taught in the outdoors will involve some aspect of cognitive learning and will require the use of cognitive teaching methods.

Explore Your World

1. Describe where cognitive methods are most commonly used in an outdoor lesson.

2. Write a set of questions that guide student understanding of an outdoor topic.

3. Explain how videography would be used to teach a physical skill (e.g., sea kayaking).

4. Design a service learning project that will teach forest succession in your local area.

5. Write a lesson and indicate where in that lesson you will include specific written materials for handouts. Also indicate how you will utilize peer teaching in that lesson.

CHAPTER 10

Affective Methods

CHAPTER OBJECTIVES

By the end of the chapter, you should be able to do the following:

- Describe affective teaching methods and give three examples.

- Explain guided discovery and its role in outdoor education.

- Describe the role of storytelling in outdoor educational experiences.

- Describe visual imagery and relate it to effective outdoor education.

- Give two examples of how case studies can be used in outdoor education.

Emotion-based learning is referred to as **affective learning.** If learning is a combination of head, hands, and heart, affective learning is the heart element. The previous two chapters outlined physical-based (kinesthetic, or hands) and knowledge-based (cognitive, or head) methods of teaching.

Emotions influence learning. Think of the times you've heard people say, "I hate this! It's boring!" or, "This is great! It's so much fun!" The main goal of the teacher in either situation is to teach certain information, but what the students experience is the emotion involved in learning the content. Emotions actually take precedence during cerebral processing. They can either assist or impede cognitive learning.

One of the goals of outdoor education is to create an emotional link with the environment. In 1975, the United Nations Educational, Scientific, and Cultural Organization (UNESCO) sponsored a worldwide meeting in Belgrade, Yugoslavia, to discuss environmental protection strategies. The meeting resulted in a general goal statement to guide environmental education. This statement, known as the Belgrade Charter, states:

> The goal of environmental education is to develop a world population that is aware of, and concerned about, the environment and its associated problems, and which has the knowledge, skills, attitudes, motivations, and commitment to work individually and collectively toward solutions of current problems and the prevention of new ones. (UNESCO 1978)

Fostering attitudes, motivations, and commitments implies creating an emotional connection with the environment.

It is impossible to separate emotion from learning. Imagine struggling with a flint and steel to start a fire. After 20 minutes, a spark finally lands on the charcloth and you blow the spark into a flame. How would you feel after this experience?

Making a fire with flint and steel is a physical skill. Yet you also need to learn certain information first (how to scrape the steel with the flint, where to place the charcloth), so it involves knowledge. And emotion is involved, perhaps frustration when you fail, jubilation when you succeed. This chapter focuses on teaching methods that mobilize your students' emotions and help you build a personal connection with your students. It also addresses situations when emotions inhibit engagement.

Photo courtesy of Salish Sea Expeditions.

Direct experience is affective learning.

Stories From Real Life: An Emotional Connection

The birds class at Wolf Ridge Environmental Learning Center is an effective blending of cognitive, kinesthetic, and affective learning. After learning about bird adaptations (cognitive learning) and using binoculars and field guides (kinesthetic learning), students visit Chickadee Landing. At Chickadee Landing, wooden cutouts of people are attached to chairs underneath a set of bird feeders. The birds quickly adapt to the human silhouette and simply go about their business. When students sit in the chairs under the feeders, the birds don't seem to notice the difference. The birds, most often black-capped chickadees, will land on the students looking for seed.

Following an experience at Chickadee Landing, a teacher commented, "I can tell when a bird lands on a student, not because I see the bird, but by looking at the expression on the student's face." This experience emotionally connects students with their environment.

Guided Discovery

Closely associated with problem solving is a teaching method called **guided discovery.** With this method, the instructor establishes a problem or task that the students must accomplish. The instructor also provides general parameters to guide the students, and from that point on the students work on their own to complete the task. Some people might call this experimentation. The difference, though, is that in guided discovery the instructor steps in occasionally to help the students so they are successful. Without guidance, students are at risk of learning incorrect information or skills.

A tree identification key is a good example of guided discovery. You might start by giving students a basic understanding of how an identification key works and defining common terms that may be used in tree identification. Then turn the students loose in an area with defined boundaries and have them work through the key to identify marked trees. It is important to move around the group so you can assist students when they have questions about the key. You do not do the work for the students, you guide them toward the proper process. Once a guided-discovery activity is complete, you must process and review what happened and how the students went about accomplishing their tasks. Input from the students at this point is essential.

In guided discovery, students are actively engaged in their own learning. They have more ownership in the process and the outcome, which usually is great motivation. Guided discovery is most often useful in situations where groups are small enough that the instructor can access all the students during the activity. This method is also effective in helping students apply ideas and concepts to real-world situations.

One of the major drawbacks to this method is that it is slow. If you want to accomplish many tasks in a short period of time, this probably isn't the method to use. In addition, not all students can learn through this method. They may not be at a developmental level where they can work through tasks toward a goal. Thus, it is necessary to match this method with the needs and motivations of the group.

Keys to Guided Discovery

- Explain basic concepts that will help students understand the task.

- Be clear on what behavior is expected of the students. Set physical boundaries (if necessary) and ground rules.

- Use with smaller groups (fewer than 20).

- Use with groups that are capable of working on their own as individuals or in small groups.

- Move around among the students to help guide their success.

- Review and process the learning that occurred.

Visual Imagery

Visual imagery (VI) allows for mental rehearsal of an event, program, or action before its actual occurrence (Edwards, Honeycutt, and Zagacki 1988). VI can be useful in training students in program design, problem solving, and the learning of cognitive and physical skills. VI can also be useful in training students to anticipate the outcomes of particular behaviors or actions.

Stories From Real Life: Guided Discovery Works!

The small group of students in the college-level class called Teaching Outdoor Skills had little experience in maintaining and repairing camping equipment, so we decided to add that lesson in place of another. We set up two stations for the first part of class: sharpening (knives and axes) and stove repair. At each station we gave a brief overview of the concepts. At the sharpening station, we told students the proper angle to hold the blades on the sharpening stone, and at the stove station we described how the stove functioned and included a parts diagram. Then students worked individually or in pairs to sharpen tools or dismantle the stove to determine its problem. We moved between the groups and gave advice when the students asked for help or when a student's technique was going far astray. At the end of the session, success was determined by the students' product: sharp knives and functioning stoves. The lesson worked well and the students learned by doing through guided discovery.

For example, VI can help instructors design an environmental education program by allowing them to visualize the ways they might present a lesson to their students as well as the different methods they can use to teach the underlying principles. Suppose an instructor wants to expose a class to the concept of the water cycle and is waiting for a rainstorm so she can present the lesson. Using VI, the instructor can visualize where to place the students as the storm approaches, what questions to ask them in introducing the topic, and what examples to use as the rain arrives, dissipates, and is followed by sunshine. Finally, the instructor can visualize what specific locations would be useful to further demonstrate the components of the water cycle and what student reactions might be expected.

Like all tools, VI can be made more effective by employing specific techniques. Schlatter and Rossman (2003) describe a number of these techniques, including the following:

- Frequency—How often have you used or do you plan to use VI techniques?

- Congruency—How well does the VI match up with the actual event? The more accurate the match, the more useful VI is in designing programs, making decisions, and anticipating problems.

- Timing—Was VI used before the event as a planning and anticipatory tool or after the event as a reflective and evaluative tool? In either case, VI can be effective in reducing problems and increasing effective learning opportunities.

- Perspectives—To maximize effectiveness, VI should employ several perspectives. Consider how a particular situation looks from the perspective of the student, the teacher, or the program administrator. Each perspective will have a different opinion about what needs to be learned, how it is learned, and how useful that particular approach is.

Using a multidimensional VI approach can strengthen VI by resulting in more diverse visualization.

Storytelling

Storytelling weaves cognitive and affective learning into a cohesive, engaging whole. It is an unusually captivating medium. In a story you can convey a lot of information in a memorable manner, and you also create an emotional link between your listener and the story. Think about this text, for example. Why did we include so many real-life stories?

Stories evoke emotion in the listeners. However, other methods we covered earlier have strong emotional components as well. For example, theatrics and characterization in chapter 8 could be categorized under affective methods as well as under physical-based methods because they involve emotion. No technique is strictly cognitive, physical, or emotional.

Stories teach holistically, meaning they reach our emotions as they teach cognitive information. There are many levels to a well-told story. The listeners involve their whole brain when listening to a story. Because of their holistic nature, stories can animate and drive home the key points of your class. Stories can also help you set the tone in your class. The words "I want to tell a story" focus the energy and attention of students.

What Stories Do

Stories teach us in many ways. Because stories have many levels of meaning, they bridge developmental level and experience. For this reason stories can be used to teach audiences with different backgrounds and maturity levels.

Stories hone the language skills of the storyteller as well as the listener. By encouraging children to tell stories you help them develop the ability to

---

Explore Your World

Think of a story that is meaningful to you. It may be a legend or a story from your family or a historical story. Identify some reasons why you like the story and why it has meaning for you. What do you connect with and care about in the story?

"A good story can warm you like a fire, direct you like a map and teach better than any professor."

—Kevin Strauss, storyteller (www.naturestory.com)

Photo courtesy of Salish Sea Expeditions.

Students share a crab hat to take turns speaking while storytelling.

sequence ideas as well as determine which points are salient and which are unimportant details.

Stories involve imagination. As a listener you are able to mentally create characters' appearance and clothing and fill in the landscape in which the story takes place. When students write or tell stories they are called upon to use information in innovative ways, to move beyond the known and into the unknown. Imagination and creativity are valuable components of problem-solving skills.

"I am enough of an artist to draw freely upon my imagination. Imagination is more important than knowledge. Knowledge is limited. Imagination encircles the world."

—Albert Einstein

Stories help students practice effective listening. Listening is more than sitting quietly; it is an active mental pursuit to make meaning of and connection with the information. Listening can be assessed by the listener's behavior. The listener should be alert and attentive and respond (laughter, silence, and so on) at appropriate times. Upon completion of the story an effective listener would be able to recap the story.

Storytelling helps students progress developmentally. Concrete thinkers must move to abstract thinking to make meaning of symbols and metaphors in the story. Listeners must also use higher-order thinking skills, such as evaluation or judgment, to anticipate a story resolution.

Stories help English language learners learn cultural norms and social conventions of speech in the culture the story is from. Telling stories gives ELL students practice using English in creative ways.

Because stories involve the whole brain, storytelling helps create an open atmosphere for trust. Telling a story, whether a real-life experience or a fiction, can work well to begin a reflection and wrap-up session.

Stories and Culture

To teach students effectively, you must understand and affirm their cultural background. Stories bridge cultural gaps and can teach class members about different cultures. Because stories connect the listener emotionally to the content, they build cultural understanding. You honor a culture by respectfully telling stories about it and trying to understand it. Avoid the "holiday and hero" syndrome—don't just tell stories about special occasions or exceptional people. Tell stories about normal, daily life, stories that reveal some of the complexities of a culture. Check the list of references on page 204 in the bibliography for books on stories from different cultures.

Be careful to ask cultural representatives, such as elders or elected representatives, for permission to tell stories from cultures other than your own. Ask permission to use a story so you can learn about any special meanings the stories may have or whether there are times and conditions under which the story shouldn't be told. Some stories may have religious or symbolic meaning and need to be told accurately and respectfully. Find out when and how the stories should be told. You should also invite your students to share stories from their own culture. In this way they become cultural ambassadors to the class.

How to Tell Stories

While telling stories is an effective, holistic method of teaching, outdoor educators are often intimidated by it. However, you don't have to be a professional storyteller for your students to benefit from your stories.

To begin storytelling, start with stories that are meaningful to you. Find stories in your own life that are meaningful and share those with students. Once you begin to feel comfortable with the medium of storytelling, seek out other sources for stories.

Once you have chosen a story, familiarize yourself with it. Read the story over and over until you have mastered the plot and sequence. Don't memorize stories; the story will change each time you tell it. The best way to practice is to tell the story, and tell the story, and tell the story again. Practice in front of a mirror at home. Ask a close friend to listen to your story. This helps you master telling the story, and your friend can provide feedback on your techniques.

Once you've mastered the story out loud, start filling in the details, building the characters, plot,

and setting. Details add life to a story. Was it a fox that walked down the path or a lively brown fox? Use words to create the setting and animate the characters in the story. However, don't get carried away. Details are like salt—a little adds flavor, but too much ruins the story.

A basic tenet of constructivism is to build on what the student already knows and understands. Stories are a wonderful means for assessing what your students know and who they are. Ask your students to tell their personal stories, and respectfully honor what they share.

Story Ideas

- Star stories during night hikes, such as how the stars got into the sky
- Animal adaptation stories, such as how the beaver got its tail
- Cultural history stories
- Interconnections and systems stories, such as the story of a rock (from igneous to metamorphic to sedimentary)
- People stories, such as stories about scientists, explorers, pioneers, and native people

Scenarios and Case Studies

Finding outdoor teachers who have good judgment and decision-making skills has always been a challenge for many outdoor education programs. Pro-

---

Stories From Real Life: Power of Real-Life Stories

Our hiking group had struggled up the 3-mile (4.8-kilometer) trail with 1,000 feet (305 meters) of elevation gain to our first vantage point. We had originally planned to continue on to a waterfall. However, we had a lovely view of the valley below, and the students were questioning their choice of final destination. They were ready to turn back.

The outdoor educator had us get in a circle and then he began a discussion about reevaluating our final goal. He wanted us to push ourselves, but he wanted it to be our decision. We shared our thoughts around the circle. The chaperone told a poignant story:

Every morning I get up and do a workout video. During the stomach workout the video instructor cheers me on! Just about when I don't think I can do any more crunches, he says, "Here's the best one of the workout! Concentrate! Make it your finest effort!" What he's saying is that I have to spend all that effort to get exhausted before I do the last crunch, the one that really strengthens my muscles.

The chaperone passed the talking stick to the next person, but the change in the group was palpable. When we had our final vote the entire group decided to push on for the waterfall. I am certain it was the chaperone's real-life story that turned the tide.

---

grams have often relied on hiring teachers and leaders who already possess a great deal of experience. The underlying assumption is that an individual with a great deal of personal experience must have also acquired good decision-making skills and judgment. Thus, personal experience is considered one way to determine an individual's ability to make sound decisions and practice good judgment.

This approach has evolved into one of the two major approaches to handling risk management and decision making: the **instructor judgment approach** and the **policy guidelines approach.**

In the instructor judgment approach, programs rely on the instructors to make effective decisions based on their personal judgment, which is formulated from their personal experience. While this approach allows for a great deal of flexibility, it doesn't work very well when a program does not have access to instructors with high levels of training and experience.

Due to the growing difficulty in hiring instructors with substantial personal experience, some programs have moved toward using extensive policy statements, checklists, and manuals. This policy guidelines approach allows programs to substitute extensive instructor experience in part with written policies covering many, though not all, situations. It is this last point that is the Achilles' heel of this approach—no manual or checklist can anticipate every situation that the outdoor instructor may face. Thus, the question arises of how to account for the gaps. Some programs use a combination of policy guidelines and instructor judgment in training their staff. They encourage instructors to adhere to the guidelines until circumstances arise that are beyond the guidelines, at which point the instructors should use their experience-based judgment. This approach relies on the instructor knowing the policies, procedures, and guidelines of the program as well as having good judgment. Two very effective methods for creating a base of knowledge that supports the development of good judgment are scenarios and case studies.

Using Scenarios

Whether using instructor judgment, policy guidelines, or some combination of the two, organizations are increasingly using field-based scenarios to train instructors in decision-making skills and judgment. Originally used in medical training under the rubric of problem-based learning, field-based scenarios use elaborate play-acting as examples that can effectively demonstrate actions and decisions for specific situations. One common scenario is the lost hiker, where students are told that a hiker is lost and their job is to set up a search-and-rescue operation to find the missing person. Often the hiker has one or more medical problems that also must be dealt with, thereby complicating the situation.

To be effective, the field-based scenario must represent a real-life situation in the following ways:

- The scenario must be believable. Could it really happen? Has it happened in the past? Are the scenario's resources, setting, and possible outcomes similar to what might actually occur?

- While the scenario must be believable, it must not be too realistic. Effective scenarios walk a fine line between believability and being too realistic. If your participants could get injured or face substantial risk, you've crossed the line and need to reconfigure the scenario.

- Effective scenarios emulate real-life examples in both the speed of events and feel. Thus, participants need to be willing and able to play roles. For example, someone may need to be a patient, someone else the team leader, and so on.

© David Dahler

Students play out an injury scenario.

Given these requirements it is not surprising that the field-based scenario is not without its challenges as a teaching method.

Because of these limitations, field-based training scenarios should not be considered the only way to train outdoor educators or students.

Using Case Studies

The case study differs from the field-based scenario in that instead of playing roles that emulate a real-life example, the case study allows the participants an opportunity to examine a past real-life event, discuss the options of the teacher or students in the situation, and evaluate the options. Vogt (1993) defines case-study methodology as gathering and analyzing information about an individual example as a way of studying a broader phenomenon (30). As a method for training outdoor educators and students, case studies are particularly valuable in helping people understand the what and how of a specific situation (Yin 1984). The underlying assumption is that knowing how something happened in a specific case helps an individual understand the broader picture.

For example, on May 10, 1996, 11 climbers were caught in a sudden storm while climbing Mt. Everest, and 8 of the climbers were killed. Because of the complexity, human drama, multiple decision-making processes, and widespread publicity of this situation, it provides an excellent case study for several training issues such as how hostile weather and other outdoor conditions affect the decision making of the outdoor leader and what seemingly innocent factors may lead to tragedy and loss of life.

Along with providing useful "what if" discussion points, case studies also offer the training organization or individual a chance to understand the comprehension, decision-making processes,

and anticipated behaviors of the outdoor educator or student. There are many useful tools that can help the trainer select and develop case studies for a particular program or situation. A sampling of these tools include *Incidents in Challenge Education* (Smith 1994), *Lessons Learned: A Guide to Accident Prevention and Crisis Response* (Ajango 2000), and *Adventure Program Risk Management Report: Volume III* (Leemon and Merrill 2002). Each source details actual events involving accidents, close calls, medical problems, or poor judgment and provides a wealth of topics for discussion.

Case studies provide the outdoor educator with examples of events that have occurred in outdoor settings and programs. As such, they can provide an opportunity to discuss what happened, what should have been done, what the outdoor teacher or leader would do in that situation, what the organization would expect a teacher or leader to do in that situation, and what options a leader or teacher might have in resolving or dealing with the issue or event.

Summary

Emotions are a powerful tool for learning in the outdoors. You may have noticed that the methods in this chapter all require imagination. Storytelling helps us imagine a different place, time, or situation. Case studies and scenarios are similar in that they put the learner in the role of the imagined situation—it is recreated. These methods influence learning through emotions by using problem solving in a realistic situation. On the other hand, storytelling may not involve problem solving, yet it fosters learning through imagination. Engaging your students emotionally can be highly effective in helping students learn, appreciate, or become aware of an issue or topic.

Explore Your World

1. Define the meaning of *affective.*

2. Give three examples of affective teaching methods.

3. Describe the positive use of storytelling in outdoor education.

4. What is visual imagery? Give three examples of how it can be used effectively in outdoor education.

5. Explain how a case study can be a useful method in outdoor education. Give an example in each area: interpretation, environmental education, and adventure education.

CHAPTER 11

Sample Lessons

CHAPTER OBJECTIVES

By the end of the chapter, you should be able to do the following:

- Identify how to apply teaching methods in a lesson.

- Explain how you could use each lesson in your outdoor education setting.

- Describe how the lessons apply to differences in students (age, skill, interest).

This chapter presents sample lesson plans that illustrate how to build outdoor education teaching methods into a lesson. As we have indicated throughout this book, several methods are typically used in a single lesson. For this reason, we present six sample lessons that incorporate the methods discussed in this book. Pay close attention to what method is used and where it is used in the lesson.

The lessons address topics that are typically taught in outdoor education. We have strived to cover all areas of outdoor education discussed in this book. The lessons include night hikes, map and compass use, maple sugar bushes, weather, fishing ethics, and paddling for sea kayakers. These lessons have been gathered from a variety of outdoor educational agencies. Each lesson has been slightly altered to minimize confusion and to ensure consistency in format, but because of the diverse agencies represented, you will notice some slightly different formats.

NIGHT HIKE

This lesson is extensive and has an unusual amount of detail. The realities of outdoor education may preclude the amount of time needed to develop lesson plans as detailed as this one. However, it is a level of quality to aim for.

Eagle Bluff Environmental Learning Center, 2004.

Goals

1. Explore the use of all five senses.
2. Discover adaptations of nocturnal animals.
3. Develop an appreciation for night creatures.

Objectives

Students will be able to do the following:

1. Define the term *nocturnal,* give examples of local nocturnal animals, and describe adaptations of nocturnal animals for life in low-light conditions.
2. Describe interactions and interdependencies among nocturnal animals and their ecosystem.
3. Demonstrate the use of all five senses for observations at night rather than relying solely on sight.
4. Demonstrate an awareness and appreciation of the nocturnal animals and their environment.

Methods

Lecture; inquiry; guided discovery; storytelling; games

Time

3 hours

Audience

5th grade to adult

Content

    I. Lesson Preparation (30 minutes)

   II. Introduction (15 minutes)

      A. Greeting and Purpose

      B. Names and Introductions

      C. Activity Description

      D. Behavior Guidelines

      E. Task Analysis and Learner Assessment

  III. Sensory Observation (50 minutes)

      A. Feel Your Way Around

      B. Don't You See It?

      C. Natural and Unnatural Sounds

      D. Are You "Scent"sible?

  IV. Individual Exploration (30 minutes)

      A. Solo Sit

      B. Storytelling

(continued)

V. Nocturnal Animals and Other Creatures (40 minutes)

   A. Eyes That Glow in the Night

   B. Animals of the Night

   C. Adaptation Games

VI. Conclusion (10 minutes)

VII. Cleanup (15 minutes)

VIII. Fact Sheet

IX. Standards Met

   A. Minnesota Profile of Learning areas (This lesson was designed and taught in the state of Minnesota; thus, we are indicating the state education standards that this lesson meets. Not all states require standards to be indicated within a lesson.)

   B. Major emphasis: applied scientific methods, living systems; Minor emphasis: inquiry

X. Appendix

   A. Equipment

   B. Glossary

   C. Activity and Safety Management

I. Lesson Preparation

Before you begin the lesson, prepare in the following ways:

- Plan the route ahead of time and hike it during the day to look for potential problem areas (e.g., low branches, extremely uneven trails, roots, stumps) and interesting features.

- Choose and plan your activities to make your night hike unique. (There are more activities than you will have time to do.) Because you will be stopping often to do activities, a short loop that ends where it begins is usually sufficient. You will also want to gather all materials for the chosen activities.

- Decide whether or not students will have flashlights. Some of the activities require flashlights. When students bring their own flashlights, instead of focusing on the night hike they usually end up focusing on the flashlights by losing them, arguing about them, or shining them in each other's eyes. You, however, should have a flashlight in case of emergency.

- Because of seasonal daylight variation, you may have to do some of your night hike during daylight hours. For many of the activities, total darkness can be simulated by blindfolding students. However, the three sensory observation activities under Don't You See It? (III.B) should be done without blindfolds and in conditions that are as dark as possible. Save these activities until the end of the hike if daylight is an issue.

Here are a few tricks of the trade for leading hikes in the dark:

- Watch the sky. Wide trails have a slot opening in the treetops that can help you along the trail.

- Pay attention to the feel of the trail beneath your feet. Grass, leaves, dirt, twigs, and gravel all have their own feel.

- Appoint a sweep person, an adult stationed at the back of the group. This person makes sure that no one drops behind or gets lost. This also helps you know when everyone has caught up at a stopping point.

- Trail intersections are good places to stop for activities.

II. Introduction

A. **Greeting and Purpose** (Methods: lecture, discussion, inquiry). Introduce the Night Fears Brainstorming and Poetry activity by discussing common fears about the night and how

You can listen for the call of a great horned owl, but you won't hear its flight.

they might have come to be (i.e., some students may be afraid of the dark because they hear strange noises that they aren't aware of during the day). Have the students write down one or two words or phrases on a piece of paper describing their feelings about the night. Read the words in random order as a poem. Students may come up with words or phrases like spooky, scary, quiet, dark, can't see, scurrying creatures, vampires, peaceful, and so on. At the end of the hike, write all the thoughts and words on the board and have students write a poem or a short story incorporating everything on the board.

B. **Names and Introductions** (Methods: inquiry, lecture). Tell the class a little bit about yourself and then go around the group to become familiar with each student. Use a method that suits your style. Explain that you will be teaching the class and that the other adult chaperones may be assisting at times.

C. **Activity Description** (Method: lecture). Explain to the class that they will be going on a hike on the trails at night. There will be times when they stop along the way to do activities that will help them better understand and appreciate nighttime, darkness, and the creatures that are active during the night.

D. **Behavior Guidelines** (Method: lecture). Discuss clearly and specifically the behaviors you expect from your students during the class. Explain the necessity of respect for you, for each other, for the equipment, and for the site itself. Mention the importance of keeping quiet so all students can hear directions and so that they can hear evidence of nocturnal animals. You might decide to use whisper voices during the hike. Reinforce the idea that in low-light situations, and especially when a student is blindfolded, actions and behaviors that may be appropriate during the day can be dangerous. Instruct students to stop, stay where they are, and call out to be found if they become separated from the group. The best way to keep the group together is to have adult chaperones in the front and back of the group and not allow students to get ahead of or fall behind the adults.

E. **Task Analysis and Learner Assessment** (Method: inquiry). Ask students to list reasons why they or others are afraid of the dark.

(continued)

III. Sensory Observations

When one of our senses is diminished or taken away, the other senses compensate for the loss. During a night hike, when sight (the sense we rely most heavily on to orient ourselves) is reduced, we must use our other senses to help us feel more comfortable. The following activities help students to use all of their senses to explore the night environment and can enhance their appreciation of the natural world around them.

A. **Feel Your Way Around** (Method: guided discovery). Without our sense of sight, we often feel disoriented and have difficulty keeping our bearings, or knowing where we are. One way to compensate for the absence of sight is by using our sense of touch. If we can feel something with our hands or beneath our feet, it can be reassuring and provide us with a sense of where we are. Also, using our sense of touch can enhance our appreciation of the natural things around us. By feeling the texture of tree bark or a mossy rock, we can experience these natural objects in a way that is more intimate and insightful than simply looking at the object.

   1. **Featured Tonight** (10 minutes) (Methods: activity, initiative, guided discovery). Find a geological or biological feature such as a tree bending around another tree, a rock, or a rotting log. Have the students approach it, touch it, and see if they can figure out what it is or why it is as it is. This is a quick activity to get students to realize that they can not always trust their eyesight, especially at night when they must use as many of their senses as possible for investigating the world around them.

   2. **Night Sensory Trail** (15-20 minutes). Before the hike, set up a length of rope that travels along a tree, across a log on the ground, around a stump, and so on. Have students pair off and instruct one student in each pair to put on a blindfold. This student grasps the rope and follows it along its path. The student's partner follows closely along to prevent the blindfolded student from injury. They need to use their sense of touch to discern where they are and how to get through the course. Be sure to follow all safety guidelines. Then have students switch roles on another section of the rope trail.

   3. **Blindfold Hike** (20 minutes) (Methods: activity, initiative, inquiry, guided discovery). Have the students pair off. The first student is blindfolded (to explore and discover things in a new manner) and the second is the guide (responsible for the safety of the blindfolded student). Lead the paired students over different types of terrain asking students to guess where they are going. Have them study a tree and tell all they can about it by using all their other senses, or ask them which direction they are traveling. Have the students switch roles.

B. **Don't You See It?** The human eye can see colors remarkably well during the day. Although our night vision is not as good as that of most nocturnal animals, our eyes are still able to adjust amazingly well to changes in light levels. These activities demonstrate some of the differences in how our vision works in light and dark conditions.

   1. **Light and Color** (10 minutes) (Methods: inquiry, guided discovery, lecture). Give each student a small scrap of paper and a crayon. Have them examine the crayon and determine its color (stick to dark, basic colors like blue, orange, red, and brown, and remove the wrappers). Tell students to write their answer on the piece of paper. Nine times out of 10 they will be wrong. Have them keep their paper for the duration of the hike, but collect the crayons. You can check to see who was right and who was wrong at the end of the hike when you get back to the building (the guess will be written in the color of the crayon).

      Explanation: Colors are nearly impossible for human beings to see at night. We have two types of cells in our eyes, rods and cones. Rods are light-sensitive cells that help us see at night and cones are cells that allow us to see in color. Humans have many more cone cells than rod cells; therefore, our color vision is great (during the day) and our night vision is poor. The only other animals that can see colors nearly as well as humans are diurnal (active during the day) birds. How do we know this? Many female birds choose their mates by the bright coloration of the males. Owls, on the other hand, have mostly rods in their eyes so their low-light vision is very good. (See table 11.1 on page 145).

2. **The Brightest Match in the Universe** (5 minutes) (Methods: guided discovery, lecture, discussion). Tell the students that they are going to see the brightest match in the universe. Have them stand in a circle and cover one eye. Tell them to cover it well so that no matter what, no light will enter that eye. Students should leave the other eye open. Explain that you are going to light a match (or candle) and you want them to stare at the flame until you blow it out (10-15 seconds). Light the match, and after you blow it out, have the students open and close each eye, switching from side to side. Ask students to describe any differences between what they can see with the eye that was covered and with the eye that was uncovered.

   Explanation: Looking with your eye that was covered, things should appear clearer and brighter. This is due to a chemical called rhodopsin. Our eyes produce this chemical in low-light situations to improve our night vision. In fact, within 5 minutes of being in the dark, we can see 1,000 times better than when we first went into the dark. When our eyes are exposed to light, all of the rhodopsin we have been producing is instantly destroyed, making our night vision poor again. Our eyes are not able to produce the rhodopsin again until we are out of the light.

3. **LifeSavers** (5 minutes) (Methods: activity, guided discovery, lecture). Have the students form a circle. Pass one (only one per student) wintergreen LifeSaver candy to each student. Tell them to put the lifesaver in their mouth and chew with their mouths open (something they aren't allowed to do at home). They should look in each other's mouths and observe what is happening.

   Explanation: The LifeSavers will spark. Why? According to *Discover Magazine*, December 1988, the sparks, which are essentially bolts of lightning in your mouth, have been studied by Linda M. Sweeting, a chemist at Towson State University in Baltimore. Plenty of other substances (most you wouldn't want to put in your mouth) also give off light when they are rubbed, crushed, or broken. This is called triboluminescence (try-bo-loom-in-es-cents; *tribein* means "to rub" in Greek). Some crystals of quartz and mica triboluminesce. So does adhesive tape when torn from certain surfaces.

   When sugar is fractured, as in the case of chewed LifeSavers, separate patches of charge, either positive or negative, form on the new surfaces or on opposite sides of cracks. The difference in charge compels electrons to leap back and forth across the gap and neutralize the patches. When these jumping electrons come into contact with nitrogen in the air (the atmosphere is 78% nitrogen), they cause the nitrogen to emit tiny blue-white bolts of light at the same wavelength as natural lightning. This is why we see tiny flashes of light when the LifeSavers are chewed.

   Sweeting discovered that when candies containing both sugar and wintergreen are crushed, an additional wavelength is emitted. Wintergreen, however, is not triboluminescent. It is fluorescent, like the paint on a black-light poster. It absorbs ultraviolet light and reemits it as light our eyes can see. When the candies are cracked, some of the light emanating from the sugar is ultraviolet, which gets absorbed by the wintergreen and reemitted as bright, blue-green light. A more simple way to explain this phenomenon is when the sugar crystals break, they release a weak burst of ultraviolet energy. This energy excites the molecules of the wintergreen oil in the LifeSavers and causes the oil to glow, or fluoresce. A similar effect can be seen when two pieces of quartz are struck together.

C. **Natural and Unnatural Sounds** (5 minutes) (Methods: guided discovery, discussion, inquiry). For many animals, keen hearing is essential to their survival. Nocturnal animals especially tend to have a highly developed sense of hearing to help them locate prey or to hear approaching predators. In the dark, humans also depend more heavily on sound. We are able to hear many things around us at night that we are not able to see. For example, it is common to hear the hooting of an owl in the woods, but it is a rare treat to actually see one.

   On the side of the trail is a parabolic listening ear (like a satellite dish) that has been set up previously, which allows us to hear even quiet sounds from a far distance (the location is marked on the night-hike map). Allow students to listen through the ear for a short while,

(continued)

one at a time. The rest of the group should be on the trail quietly listening. After identifying sounds, have the students decide whether the sounds are natural (made by animals or plants) or unnatural (made by people). Next, point out sounds the students may have missed. Listen for natural sounds like owls hooting, trees squeaking, wind blowing through trees or grass, water gurgling, ice cracking, falling objects, and so on. Some unnatural sounds might be radios, cars, people talking, airplanes, and so on. Another option is to define boundaries in a safe area that you selected in the daytime and then have students determine where the sounds are coming from and follow them.

Explanation: Sound travels more easily through the cool, calm, moist night air. Also, we are more acutely aware of sounds as we become comfortable with the darkness.

D. **Are You "Scent"sible?** (5 minutes) (Methods: lecture, guided discovery). Many animals, especially predators, have an acute sense of smell to help them locate food or prey. Predators that are active during the night such as wolves and coyotes depend heavily on smell to locate prey that may be too far away to see. At night, we may be able to recognize the smells of familiar natural features, which will help give us a sense of where we are. The refreshing smell of pine or the infamous odor of a skunk are just a few of the familiar scents you may encounter on your night hike.

Encourage students to smell the night air and see if they can identify any scents. Be alert for the scent of animals such as skunk or even deer musk. Have them find and describe smells around them such as soil, a rotting log, or different plants.

Explanation: The following explanation is from Gibbons and Psihoyos (1986):

> Odors are volatile molecules. They float in the air. When you sniff, they rush through your nostrils, over spongy tissue that warms and humidifies the air, and up two narrow chambers where, just beneath the brain and behind the bridge of the nose, they land on a pair of mucus-bathed patches of skin the size of collar buttons. Here, in a process that's still a mystery, the molecules bind to receptors on tiny hair-like cilia at the ends of the olfactory nerves, or neurons, which fire the message to the brain. The signal crosses a single neural connection, or synapse, at the olfactory bulbs. (Sensations of sight, sound, and touch reach the limbic lobe less directly, across more synapses.) The amount of brain tissue in humans devoted to smell is still very great.

Assessment

Take a moment to assess students' understanding of the lesson so far. Concept to assess: Humans are not physically adapted for life in the total dark and must use all of their senses when investigating in low-light situations.

- Listen to student comments as the group first goes out into the dark. Are students afraid? Disoriented? Uncomfortable?
- During sensory activities, do the students rely on senses other than sight to explore and learn about their surroundings?

IV. Individual Exploration

Methods: guided discovery, self-discovery, storytelling.

Many times the most profound and meaningful experiences are due to the time we spend alone. We all know the satisfaction of solving a problem or discovering something on our own. In addition, solitude in nature provides a more intimate connection with the environment around us. These activities encourage individual discovery and introspection.

1. **Solo Sit** (10-15 minutes). Have the students spread out along the trail, sitting alone in a place away from others, and have a chaperone at the beginning of the group and at the end. Have students sit quietly for 5 to 10 minutes. Gather the students in a circle and ask each one to share what they saw and heard and how they felt.

2. **Storytelling** (5-20 minutes). Storytelling is one of the oldest and most sacred human traditions. People of all ages love stories. Be creative. There are many Native American legends dealing with stars, the moon, owls, night, and so on. Use props and involve listeners for a more complete sensory experience. Tell a story that you know. You can tell a story along the hike or at the beginning or end. If you have time during the day, select a spot along the route that could serve as a natural theater or backdrop for the story.

Perhaps you have a favorite story of your own to share. Or, have students make up a story by going around in a circle and allowing each student to add a few sentences as you go. Start the story with an introduction such as, "It was a dark and stormy night. . .," "It was a long time ago, in a place not unlike this. . .," or even the famous, "Once upon a time. . . ." If some students are very uncomfortable in the dark, you might want to remind students that the night hike is not a time for ghost stories and scaring people.

V. Nocturnal Animals and Other Creatures

Methods: lecture, guided discovery, inquiry, games.

Spending time outside at night can make many people nervous, uncomfortable, or even afraid. This may be due to the fact that human beings are not physically adapted to dark environments. Nocturnal animals, however, have developed specific physical and behavioral adaptations that allow them to be successful in the dark.

A. **Eyes That Glow in the Night.** Throughout the hike, periodically use a flashlight to try and catch the eyeshine of different animals. (Be aware that the flashlight will affect the night vision of the whole group.) Eyeshine is the ability of the tapetum lucidum (a part of the retina) to reflect light (see table 11.1). The light reflects off of the back of the eye and passes back through the retina to increase the eye's efficiency in low light. Eyeshine is stronger in nocturnal animals than in diurnal ones. Table 11.1 is a chart of relative eyeshine strength.

B. **Animals of the Night.** Nocturnal animals have adaptations that help them to survive in low-light conditions. These adaptations may allow them to find prey, avoid a predator, find a mate, or succeed by avoiding competition with an animal that is active during the daytime (for example, owls and hawks).

1. **Owls.** Owls localize sound in an amazing but fairly simple manner. Of all land animals, owls are the best at locating a moving target in three-dimensional space. While a human is as good as an owl at identifying the source of a sound in one plane (e.g., to the right or

Table 11.1   Relative Eyeshine Strength

Iris color	Animal	Eyeshine color	Relative strength
Yellow	Screech owl	Red	Weak
Yellow	Great horned owl	Red	Medium
Yellow	Long-eared owl	Slightly red	Strong
Yellow	Snowy owl	Slightly red	Medium
Brown	Barred owl	Red	Strong
Brown	Barn owl	Red	Weak
Various	White-tailed deer	Silver-white	Strong
Various	Fox	Red	Medium
Various	Rabbit	Red	Medium
Various	Cat	Red	Strong

(continued)

left while standing on the ground), owls are far better at localizing sounds that come from above or below. This superior ability is due to the asymmetrical positions of the owl's outer ears. A person can tell if the sound comes from the right, left, or straight ahead because a sound from the left strikes the left ear first and the brain interprets this as direction. Owls can do the same, but can also localize sounds above or below their head because the left ear is much higher on the head than the right. Sounds from above will thus strike the left ear first while sounds from below will strike the right ear first. The owl's brain compares the difference and interprets the source of the sound as above or below the owl.

2. **Bats.** Some bat species employ the technique of echolocation to determine where things are in relation to themselves. They emit a steady stream of clicking noises, approximately 10 per second, called ultrasounds. Bats hear extremely faint echoes of ultrasounds as the echoes return from distant objects. When the bat hears a pattern of echoes from an airborne insect, it increases the ultrasounds to as many as 200 per second. There are only a few milliseconds of silence between clicks, but in that blip of silence the bat's receptors detect the echoes. The signals are sent to the brain where they are processed and decoded. The brain creates a sound map that the bat uses to maneuver and capture the insect without even seeing it.

3. **Pythons.** The python and other pit snakes use thermoreceptors to help them hunt at night. The thermoreceptors are located in pit areas around the snake's mouth. The receptors are sensitive to the body heat (infrared energy) of the prey, which is much warmer than the night air. The thermoreceptors notify the brain, which assesses the signals and determines the location of the prey. The snake can then strike with accuracy without even seeing the prey. The same snake, however, may slither past a motionless but edible frog because the frog's skin is cool and blends in with the background colors.

4. **Frogs.** Certain species of frogs use sound frequency to communicate with local populations, even in the dark. The ears of the female cricket frog are sensitive only to a narrow band of frequencies specific to the frog's locality. The calls of the males also vary geographically. This variance is similar to different groups of human beings having different dialects. A female's lack of response to a distant male's "dialect" may be due to a mismatch between her ears and his call: She may be deaf to the frequency of his calls. Thus, the males and females of the same locality are able to locate one another and communicate without disturbance or interference from frogs in a different locality even if they are the same species.

C. **Adaptation Games.** The adaptations of nocturnal animals are sometimes difficult to understand because they are so different from what we are used to experiencing as humans. Several of the unique strategies animals use to survive in the dark can be modeled through games. These games can provide a break for students who have been quietly experiencing the nighttime world.

1. **Owl and Prey.** Discuss how owls use sound to locate prey. Designate two people as owls. They stand blindfolded, facing each other on opposite sides of the trail, with flashlights. The other students are mice and try to sneak past the owls. When the owls hear a mouse, they flash their light on the sound. If mice are hit by the flashlight beam, they are caught. (You may have to act as the official for any decisions.) This activity can also be done in the daylight by having students point rather than use a flashlight. Discuss how different environmental conditions (e.g., rain, wind, snow) would affect the catch rate. Also, discuss the influence of noises from different ground cover (e.g., dry leaves versus hard-packed trail).

2. **Bat and Moth.** Choose a flat, open area free of obstructions. Designate three or four students as bats and the rest as moths. Bats and moths have to make some sort of sound (pick one of the following sounds: clicking, hand clapping, finger snapping). Have the moths scatter over the area. The bats, who are blindfolded, make the sound and then the moths return the sound to simulate the sonar effect. After returning a sound, the moths can take one step. The bats can move freely and must close in on the moths for the capture. Touching the moth completes the capture.

3. **Firefly Tag.** Choose an open area for play. One player with a flashlight is the firefly and everyone else tries to catch the firefly. The firefly must occasionally reveal its position by flashing the light. Whoever catches the firefly becomes the firefly in the next round.

Assessment

Concept to assess: Nocturnal animals have special adaptations allowing them to succeed in the dark.

- Does the group search for nocturnal animals? Are they especially quiet? Do they search for eyeshine?
- Ask the group to compare and contrast the senses and adaptations of nocturnal and diurnal predators.

VI. Conclusion

Share the following concepts with your students to guide the conclusion.

One of nature's most spectacular events takes place as day turns into night. When the sun sinks below the horizon, the familiar becomes something mysterious. A large number of seemingly strange and unfamiliar animals awaken and begin their preparations for the night's activities of gathering food, hunting, mating, and calling to one another. These nocturnal animals live in a world that may seem frightening or unusual to us, but they are superbly adapted to life in the dark. Their bodies and habits are perfectly suited to survival at night.

Human exploration and observation of the nocturnal world can lead to insight into and appreciation of nature. However, it can be a challenging task as we find ourselves in a dark and uncomfortable world that we are not used to. Our sight is diminished and we must use all of our other senses to simply walk, let alone observe the creatures of the night and their habits.

Review the activities in class. Ask the group how they feel about the night. Did their feelings change? Encourage students by telling them that it is natural to feel uneasy when you are in an environment that you are not accustomed to. However, understanding the nighttime and nocturnal animals can open the door to a new world full of wonder, mystery, and enjoyment that most people do not take the time or effort to understand and appreciate.

Assessment

Concept to assess: The dark and its creatures are unappreciated and misunderstood by many people.

- Does the group's comfort level seem to increase as the hike progresses?
- After the last activity, tell the group to search for as many signs of nocturnal animals as they can find. Do the students look in different places than before the night hike? Do they listen quietly without moving?

VII. Cleanup

Make sure all materials are accounted for and haven't been left on the trail. This may involve walking the trail the next day if anything is missing. Return all the materials to their proper storage place. Inform the equipment manager of any supplies that are low (i.e., wintergreen LifeSavers, paper scraps, matches). If you've used classroom space, be sure to stack chairs, erase the board, and so on.

VIII. Fact Sheet

Method: written materials.

Use this information to guide your lesson. Use it as supplementary knowledge to the lesson, depending on the knowledge level of your students.

- Although we cannot hear bat cries, the sound waves they produce are not weak. The cries have been measured at 100 decibels (about the same intensity as thunder booming overhead or a freight train rumbling past).

(continued)

- Unlike brain neurons, which last a lifetime, olfactory neurons are replaced every 1 or 2 months.
- How we hear: Sound waves vibrate the eardrum, then three small inner ear bones, and finally, fluid in the coiled cochlea. Stereocilia on the hair cells of the cochlea move in response to sound, and the hair cells convert this mechanical movement into an electrical signal that crosses a synapse and triggers a sensory neuron. This neuron sends a message to the brain that a sound has been received.
- You might suspect that the owl's large eyes are responsible for its hunting prowess (the great gray owl in particular). However, the owl's night vision is no better than that of some people with particularly good night vision. A simple experiment disproves the primacy of vision in the owl: If an experimenter ties a dry leaf to a mouse's tail and places the rodent in a dimly lit room with an owl, the rodent will scurry about and the bird will pounce—not on the prey but on the rattling leaf. Thus, the owl relies more on sound than sight.
- People tend to recall the visual details of a given painting with almost 100% accuracy but will forget the details within 3 months. The same subject will recall a series of odors with only 80% accuracy but the accuracy remains at that level for a year or more. An odor once remembered is rarely forgotten!
- Different senses and different behaviors can be localized in specific regions or groups of regions in the brain. The human brain is the most intricately organized entity in the world, and it is this structural organization that allows the brain to work.
- Sense organs contain bare nerve cell endings modified in ways that increase their sensitivity to one physical aspect of the environment.
- Sensory reception and the brain: Brain regions that play key roles in memory include sensory reception areas. Sensory input is processed by the cerebral cortex and sent to parts of the limbic system and the forebrain. The limbic system, or "emotional brain," includes regions called the thalamus, hypothalamus, amygdala, and hippocampus.
- Rods and cones are the photoreceptors of the vertebrate eye.
- Sense of smell can be defined as the sensory pathway leading from olfactory receptors in the nasal cavity to primary receiving centers in the brain.

IX. Standards Met

A. Minnesota Profile of Learning areas (This lesson was designed and taught in the state of Minnesota; thus, we are indicating the state education standards that this lesson meets. Not all states require standards to be indicated within a lesson.)

B. Major emphasis: applied scientific methods, living systems; Minor emphasis: inquiry

X. Appendix

A. Equipment
- Flashlight for leader
- Night Fears Brainstorming and Poetry—paper and pencils
- Blindfold Hike—blindfolds for half the group (at least 10)
- Light and Color—scraps of paper and crayons
- The Brightest Match in the Universe—matches and emergency candle
- LifeSavers—wintergreen LifeSavers
- Natural and Unnatural Sounds—parabolic listening ear
- Are You "Scent"sible?—numbered scent containers
- Storytelling
- Eyes That Glow in the Night, Owl and Prey, and Firefly Tag—flashlights (1, 2, and 1)

B. Glossary (use these terms for your own reference or hand them out to your students)

- cones—Light-receiving cells found in mammalian eyes that respond to bright light and contribute to sharp daytime vision and color reception.
- diurnal—Relating to the day; refers to animals that are active during the daytime.
- echolocation—Process of sending out signals and receiving their echoes to determine the location of an object.
- electron—Particle associated with the charge of negative electricity; part of an atom.
- eyeshine—Ability of an animal's eyes to reflect light frequency (the number of vibrations or cycles in a unit of time).
- olfactory—Of, pertinent to, or connected with the sense of smell.
- neuron—Nerve cell, the basic unit of communication in the nervous system.
- nocturnal—Relating to the night; refers to animals that are active at night.
- retina—Membrane of the eye that receives the image formed by the lens and is connected with the brain by the optic nerve.
- rhodopsin—Chemical created in the eye to increase the clarity of night vision.
- rods—Long, rod-shaped sensory cells in the retina, sensitive to faint light. They respond to coarse reception of movements by detecting changes in light intensity across the field of vision.
- synapse—Point at which a nervous impulse passes from one neuron to another.
- tapetum lucidum—Clear membranous layer at the back of the eye that reflects light back over the retina to improve night vision (responsible for the reflection of light that we see as eyeshine).
- thermoreceptor—Sensory cell that can detect radiant energy associated with temperature.
- triboluminescense—Luminescence resulting from friction.
- ultrasounds—Sounds emitted by bats at a higher frequency than humans can hear.

C. Activity and Safety Management

- Check students for proper clothing before leaving for the hike.
- Bring at least two bottles of water.
- Bring at least one functioning flashlight.
- Set clear boundaries.
- Encourage students to remain within sight of you while exploring.
- Choose a route within your group's abilities.
- Have adults or coinstructors in front and back of the group.
- Instruct students to stay where they are if they become lost and to call out so that people can find them.
- Periodically count the students to make sure that all are present.
- Emphasize the need for safety precautions in the dark.
- If students are blindfolded, they should always have a partner to keep them away from danger.
- Keep track of equipment you are using during the hike and make sure it is returned to the liaison when you are finished.

MAP AND COMPASS

Here is a common layout and level of detail for a lesson plan. The techniques and content are common to many outdoor educational settings.

Purpose

This lesson plan is designed for 8th graders to adults. It is necessary to learn the current knowledge of the participants to adapt the lesson to meet their needs. Greater or lesser content can be presented based on the audience skill level.

Goals

1. Learn how to read a topographic map.
2. Explore the compass and using it to take and follow a bearing.
3. Discover ways to deal with getting lost in the woods.

Objectives

Students will be able to do the following:

- Define components of a map and their use (including topographic lines, symbols, colors, scale, and direction).
- Describe how a compass relates to the map and the real landscape.
- Practice compass use, including taking a bearing, following a bearing, dealing with declination, and causes for error.

Time

2 hours

Audience

20 or fewer members; 8th grade to adult; beginner level

Materials

- At least one compass for every two students
- Demonstration compass
- 100-foot (30.5-meter) tape measure
- Topographical maps of the area (7.5-minute series) for every two or three people
- Highway maps that everyone can see
- Maps of the site where lesson is taught
- Copies of the Silva System handout (one per student)
- Basic course laid out beforehand

I. Lesson Preparation

Organizing materials and a course beforehand is crucial. Make sure there are enough compasses, handouts, and maps for everyone. The classroom and orienteering course need to be near each other to minimize travel time.

II. Introduction

Methods: lecture, inquiry.

Here is where your quality lesson gets its start. Welcome everyone, explain who you are, and go around the group to find out student names, knowledge level of map and compass work, and what they hope to learn today. Finish with your expectations as an instructor and the plan for the workshop.

III. Content: General Navigation Concept

Method: lecture.

Navigation means knowing where you are, where you have been, and where you are going. How do you learn these things? By using a map and compass to ensure that you always know where you are. Both are aids to help you to see on paper (the map) where you are actually on the ground. The compass is a tool to show you where you are in relation to direction (i.e., north, south, east, west). Being able to travel efficiently in unfamiliar terrain using a map and compass is called navigation.

Students can work in pairs to practice skills.

IV. Using the Map

Methods: lecture, guided discovery, problem solving, inquiry, games, storytelling, scenarios.

If you become an effective map reader, you may not need your compass—maps are the primary tool for finding your way. There are different kinds of maps. One of the most common is a highway map. Think about a time when you have used a highway map. This will help us determine what we learn from a map and how we use it:

- What can you find on a map? Some things include way points and control points, roads, directions, where to turn, or where landmarks such as a park or museum are located.

- How do you use a road map? When you come to a known intersection (or town or lake or other noted feature), you know where you are.

- People use road maps all the time. Ask your students to share stories of their navigation using a road map, including stories where people get lost. (Ask them to explain why they got lost so you can gain an understanding of their knowledge of maps.)

- How is a topographic map different from a road map? Explain the following symbols and terms: contour lines, contour intervals, cultural features, latitude, longitude, cultural and natural symbols, true north versus magnetic north, and scale.

- Practice map reading by asking students to find various features on the map (hills, rivers, cliffs, trails, forests, swamps, and so on).

(continued)

- More practice reading the map—Quiz students on different scenarios (for example, What would you see if you were standing at the edge of _____?).

- If available, use a different map and quiz students on contour intervals, land features, directions, distances, and so on.

V. Using the Compass

Methods: lecture, physical skills development, physical manipulation, games, guided discovery, inquiry.

The compass is actually a simple tool with a magnetized needle that responds to the magnetic field of the earth. The red end of the compass is polarized so that it points to magnetic north, which means the compass is showing which way you are facing in relation to north. This is called direction. For total navigation ability, you need to be able to use a map and compass together.

Use a demonstration compass to go over the parts of a compass, including base plate, needle ("red"), dial and degree markings, orienting (north) arrow ("shed"), orienting lines, and direction-of-travel arrow ("fred"). Red, fred, and shed are catch phrases or mnemonics to help the students remember the function of the parts of the compass. They also help students learn how to set a bearing.

Next, teach students how to use the compass. Using the big compass, set a bearing of 120°. Have your students place the magnetic needle (red) in the orienting arrow (shed) by holding the compass at their navel, with the direction-of-travel arrow pointing away from them. They should turn until the magnetic needle is directly over the shed. This is called setting a bearing. Here are the steps for setting a bearing of 120°:

- Hold the compass in the palm of your hand at the level of your navel. Be sure that the direction-of-travel arrow is pointing away from you.

- Turn the dial until your bearing (120°) is positioned at the direction of travel arrow.

- Put red in the shed and follow fred. As explained previously, this means turning your body with the compass in hand until the magnetic needle lies over the orienting arrow.

VI. Pacing

Methods: physical skills development, activity.

Pacing is a valuable tool to help you determine how much distance you have traveled. To determine each student's pace, do the following:

- Lay out a 100-foot (30.5-meter) straight line.

- Have everyone determine how many paces it takes them to cover the 100 feet. (A pace is every other step, or every time your right foot touches the ground.)

- Explain that their pace will tend to shorten when traveling over different types of terrain (thick forest, swamp, fields, hills, and so on). Estimate the difference accordingly such as reducing your pace length by 1 foot. Practice pacing in different terrain to allow students to become familiar with their average pace. Have them verify their pace distances with distances on the map.

Do a bearing activity for practice following a bearing.

Bearing Activity

1. Spread students out in a field in groups of three. Be sure they are not too crowded.

2. Have everyone set a bearing of 360°. (They should all be facing north.)

3. Set a bearing of 90°. Have the person who is holding the compass stay in one spot. Set an object such as a pencil at their feet. A second person should walk 10 paces at 90° and stop at 10 paces, with all three group members now joining them.

4. Set a bearing of 180°. Repeat step 3 (second member walks 10 paces and stops).

5. Set a bearing of 270°. Repeat step 4.

6. Set a bearing of 360°. Repeat step 5.

7. Each group should now be standing at the object they left on the ground at the start. The group has now navigated 40 paces in a square.

8. Repeat the same exercise using bearings of 120°, 240°, and 360°.

Your class has now learned how to set and follow a bearing and how to use pacing for a simple navigation.

VII. Using the Map and Compass Together

Methods: physical skill development, guided discovery, problem solving, scenarios.

Follow these steps to demonstrate how to take a bearing and distance off the map.

1. Align the edge of the baseplate with the current location of the class and your predetermined destination. Be sure that everyone is using the same points. Also be sure that everyone has the direction-of-travel arrow (fred) pointing to the destination.

2. Turn the dial until orienting lines are parallel with north–south lines on the map (north portion of dial needs to point north). This is called setting, or taking, a bearing.

3. Remove the compass and follow the bearing.

Distances can be measured in many ways. One common technique is to use the ruler on the edge of the compass and use scrap paper to mark the distance. Then compare the space marked on the scrap paper to determine the distance by placing it along the map's scale. Remember that straight-line distances, or as the crow flies, as read off a map are often different than in the field because of terrain such as hills, valleys, and wetlands.

Practice taking bearings and distances off the map by giving scenarios of where students are located and their destination. Make sure some scenarios have destinations other than north. Also, choose some southerly routes to ensure students are watching the correct end of the magnetic needle (red end points north).

VIII. Basic Course in Pairs

Methods: Activity, games, problem solving.

Set up a course in a site that has three or four control stations where students need to answer a question about what they see at the location. If you have many students, space groups out and have them start at different control sites.

IX. Conclusion

Comment on skills the students need to further their understanding. For example, introduce them to the concept of declination. Ask them how they would navigate around a lake or a wetland. What would they do to maintain their line of travel if they came upon a cliff?

Explain that practice is the key to understanding navigation because the same principles are used in many different terrains. Also, with each successful practice, students' confidence to travel in unfamiliar terrain will grow.

Future Lessons

If your group will be able to do a further sequence of learning from this basic lesson (for example, if they will be with you for multiple days), the following concepts are the next steps to teach:

- Magnetic declination—Learning how to adjust from true north to magnetic north.
- Getting lost—How to triangulate and take multiple bearings to confirm your location on the ground.
- Navigating a more complicated course.
- On-water navigation.
- GPS navigation—Using global positioning system (GPS) electronics as a navigational aid.

MAPLE SUGAR BUSH

This lesson is taught during the late winter or early spring when daytime temperatures are above freezing and nighttime temperatures are below freezing. The lack of detail is deliberate, allowing instructors to be creative within a base set of guidelines. This allows instructors to make the lesson their own.

Purpose

This lesson plan is designed for students in the 4th grade. When working with older or younger participants, you will need to change the approach a bit. With younger children, talk even less and do more. Older participants can handle broader concepts and relationships and will have more in-depth questions.

School groups typically include parents and teachers. Use them to your advantage when conducting this lesson. Invite them to help with discipline, and get them involved in the lesson.

Goals

1. Gain an understanding of identification and natural history of maple trees.
2. Explore what happens in the forest during spring.
3. Discover the components of traditional collection and processing of maple sap, including customs and cultural significance.
4. Participate in the process of collecting sap.

Objectives

Students will be able to do the following:

- Find a sugar maple tree using identification techniques.
- Demonstrate the process for tapping and collecting sap using a brace, hammer, spile, and sap sack.
- Describe the process of sap flowing from roots to buds and why it is associated with spring.
- Describe the procedure for turning sap into syrup.
- Hear and see historical methods for collecting and processing sap.

Time

1 hour

Audience

16 or fewer 4th-grade children

Materials

- 1 or 2 brace and bit combinations (drill and bit)
- 1 or 2 hammers
- 2 spiles (devices put into the tree to allow the sap to drain into a bucket)
- 2 sap sacks or buckets with lids (make sure spiles and collecting devices are compatible)
- Enlarged, laminated historical photos of sap collecting and processing (obtain from the online resources of the Minnesota Historical Society, www.mnhs.org)
- Naniboujou story (Caduto and Bruchac 1988)
- Chief Woksis story (Nearing and Nearing 1970)
- Small paper cups for all participants
- Garbage bag to collect the paper cups in

- Bottle of real maple syrup for tasting
- Bottle of imitation syrup for demonstration
- Laminated visual aid for demonstrating 32:1 ratio

Lesson Preparation

Organize all equipment in an easily accessible location. If you are teaching immediately after another instructor, coordinate the equipment switch-over.

Have student groups meet at a well-defined place that is located near the sugar-bush lesson area. Instructors need to be ready and waiting at least 10 minutes before the group is scheduled to arrive. If the group is large, one person needs to meet the bus and work with the teacher to divide the group quickly and efficiently. The sooner you divide the class into groups, the less likely chaos becomes a problem.

Have each group come up with a name for themselves that relates to nature. This adds some fun and later on may help with some friendly competition. Name examples include Maple Leaf, Melting Snow, and Spring Sun.

When multiple instructors are leading groups at the same time, have a plan for using different teaching sites (i.e., don't have all instructors start off at the same meeting spot).

Introduction

Methods: lecture, inquiry, theatrics, guided imagery.

This is where the quality of your lesson gets its start. Explain who you are and establish behavioral ground rules. For example, the presenter is always in front, and students who want to speak must raise their hand and wait to be called on. Enlist specific assistance from the adults (e.g., "Mrs. Brown, will you help by ensuring that everyone stays together and listens when others are talking?"). If you don't set rules early, you will end up creating them as you go and you will lose control.

Try to learn names, if you can. This helps greatly with discipline. Most groups will come already wearing name tags.

Explain to the group what will be happening and why they are outside. Involve the students in finding out what they will learn by using questions or a game. Before moving on, finish with a brief discussion of how the group should act toward the forest. An example might be, "We will be visitors to the forest today and it is important for us to show respect for the inhabitants. How can we show respect for the forest? Yes, by not breaking branches or injuring any of the wildlife."

Identification

Methods: guided discovery, inquiry, experimentation, storytelling, peer teaching.

Here is one way to introduce the identification lesson: "We're here to learn about maple syrup. Where does maple syrup come from?" (Pull out a bottle of imitation maple syrup.) "Where does this syrup come from? Corn! Corn syrup is very sweet. It is used as a sweetener in many processed foods. Because it's easy and cheap to make, it is actually the primary sweetener in many maple

Students tap a sugar maple to produce sap.

Photo courtesy of Wolf Ridge ELC, 6282 Cranberry Road, Finland, MN. www.wolf-ridge.org.

(continued)

syrup brands, with artificial maple flavoring added to make it taste like maple syrup. Real maple syrup comes from maple trees. We need to learn how to find a maple tree."

Another option for starting out is to use the Chief Woksis story to discuss how maple syrup came to be. After telling the story, you might say, "Chief Woksis found his tree by accident. But we need to learn how to find a maple tree. How do we do this?" Then lead the students through the identification process:

- Find a tree to identify.
- Explore the skills of identifying a tree without any leaves. Ask, "How can we identify trees without any leaves?" Students will come up with many different responses.
- Start with branching pattern, then go to bud shape and color (opposite branching; pointed buds; brown, syrup-colored buds). Make sure everyone can get a view of the branching patterns and how the buds look. Tell the students, "We are looking for a sugar maple."
- Use the kids' body parts to demonstrate the difference between opposite and alternate. Stick both arms out—this is opposite. One arm sticking out on one side and the leg sticking out on the other side is an alternate pattern.
- Check for understanding by calling out, "Everyone do opposite branching," or, "Everyone do alternate branching."

Move to a small sugar maple. Work together to identify it using branching, buds, and color. Have everyone touch the tree and describe color, shape, and texture. Repeat key terms like *opposite branching*. Once they see it is a maple, ask them if it is big enough to tap (no). When the answer is established, ask them why (need to make sure a tree is big enough and healthy enough).

Select two people to find a sugar maple bigger than 10 inches (25 centimeters) in diameter. As a group, confirm the identification: "Does it have opposite branching?" and "Are the buds small and pointy or big and fat?" If the tree is wrong, help the students along and do not embarrass them for being wrong. Move on to another tree. Some students may need additional help, in which case you can let other children help in the hunt.

How Sugar Maples Make Sap

Methods: guided discovery, discussion, inquiry, peer teaching.

Once you've found a large enough tree, gather everyone close in a semicircle. Discuss the process of leaves making sugar water (food) in the summer, sending it down to the roots in the fall, and bringing the sugar water back up the trunk to nourish the buds in the spring. Days above freezing and nights below freezing are when this flow of sap happens. With younger kids you can act this out: Fingers (sap) are stored in the feet (roots), then slowly move up the body until fingers are outstretched, feeding the buds. Quiz the students on what happens in the tree in the fall and spring.

Tree Wounds

The sap is somewhat like the blood of the tree. So, a good analogy to talk about is blood. For example, you might say, "When you get a cut in your arm, you bleed. If a tree gets a cut, it bleeds sap. Does it hurt the tree? Yes, just a tiny bit. Like a person who eventually gets a scab over a cut, a tree also scabs over. Look for healed wounds on the tree."

Tapping

Now it is time to tap into the tree. Show the tools that people use today (brace and bit). Ask, "Is this how it was always done?" Show a laminated picture of native person and the slices in the tree, and discuss how they tapped into the tree.

Get input on the proper angle to put on the bit: "Remember, the hole must act like a faucet for sap to flow out. What direction do faucets in your house flow?" Show them how to use the brace (round handle in belly, crank clockwise).

Take half the group and line them up (i.e., "I want these 4th graders to line up behind Johnny"). Get the bit started. Everyone gets five cranks on the brace (or whatever number of cranks might be appropriate). Have everyone in the group count the cranks to keep them involved. If necessary, finish up yourself.

If it is a good day and the sap is really running, let them taste the sap with their finger.

Next, show the spile and explain what it is for. You could go back to the old picture to discuss other types of spiles. You might say, "Everyone say 'spile,'" then have one student put the spile in and another hammer it in. (These are kids from the first group, who drilled the hole.) The other half of the group observes because they will be doing this process next.

Ask, "How do we collect this now?" Talk a pair of kids through putting the sap sack together. Put it on the spile. Questions you could ask might be, "Is this the only way to collect sap? What would have been used 150 years ago?" Show a picture of birch-bark buckets (makuks) or wooden buckets.

Send the other half of the students off to find a tree within a boundary area. You or another adult bring the brace and bit over, and they do the rest.

Sap to Syrup

Methods: discussion, inquiry, storytelling.

Go to a tree with sap that has collected. Distribute cups and have the children taste the sap (optional). Make sure you tell them not to crush the cup or toss it because it will be used for a special treat later on. Ask, "What does it taste like? How is this different than syrup? What needs to be added to make syrup? We need to take away water. How do we do that?"

Go to the sap-boiling area. Discuss boiling and turning sap into syrup. Explain how much sap it takes to make syrup. One good way to explain this is to ask, "How much sap would it take to fill Sarah's shoe with syrup? It would take everyone else's shoe (if there are 16 people in your group) filled with sap." Or you can use a laminated diagram to show the 32:1 ratio. A 32:1 ratio means that for every 32 gallons (121 liters) of sap, 1 gallon (3.8 liters) of syrup is made.

Story

Tell the Naniboujou story or the Chief Woksis story. If you are comfortable with the story, you can try to direct the children in acting it out while you narrate and talk the kids through it.

Tasting

Everyone gets to taste real maple syrup. If snow is clean, they can try snow cones (optional). Using the paper cup they already have, put a little syrup (about a spoonful) in each. For snow cones, put snow in first.

Students should put their cup into the instructor's garbage bag. If students don't like the syrup, they should pour it out onto the ground.

Conclusion

Method: inquiry.

While children are snacking on the syrup snow cones, review the activity. Ask questions that assess whether they learned the concepts. Examples might be, "What kind of branching do maple trees have? How much sap does it take to make a gallon of syrup?"

Thank the children and walk them back to the parking area. Finish by thanking the teacher. Do not leave until the children are loaded in the bus. If the bus is late, do some activities to keep the students together, such as a cleanup competition.

Wrap-Up

- Return all equipment to its proper place.
- Meet with your supervisor to discuss how the lesson went. This ensures quality and consistency in lesson delivery, especially when multiple instructors are teaching the same topic.

WEATHER

This lesson emphasizes the use of experiments and inquiry for gaining an understanding of weather. It is a hands-on approach to teaching weather.

Goal

Students will become familiar with basic weather components and how they interact to create weather, and they will understand how weather affects their daily life.

Objectives

Students will be able to do the following:

- List the four basic components of weather (earth, water, air, sun) and explain one role of each component in the creation of daily weather.
- Define climate, front, differential heating, and atmosphere.
- As a class, design a weather data collection sheet.
- In assigned cooperative groups, collect accurate weather data and make logical weather predictions based on the data.
- Compare and contrast weather during their outdoor education experience to their home climate (if different).

Audience

Sixth grade; multicultural and mixed-gender appropriate

Lesson Preparation

The instructor should be familiar with the trail and any safety concerns. Students are checked for proper clothing, gear, and water. The instructor is made aware of any special needs (medical, physical, mental, or emotional) of students and adjusts the activities according to student needs. Adequate rest, drink, and snack breaks will be taken throughout the day.

Choose a circular route that is relatively easy and provides ample comfortable gathering spaces. Most locations will suffice, although you need to make sure at least two of your stopping places have a view of the sky. Do a few activities and then walk to a new site and do a few more activities.

Background Information

The instructor should consult the books listed in the reference section of this lesson plan to understand the following information:

- The four basic components of weather are earth, water, air, and sun.
- Each component influences basic daily weather patterns.

Vocabulary

- climate—Average weather prevalent in an area.
- front—Interface between air masses at different temperatures.
- differential heating—Heating and cooling of substances at different rates depending on their mass and clarity.
- atmosphere—Gaseous envelope surrounding the earth and other celestial bodies.

Materials

- Cloud kit (glass jar with rubber stopper, bottle with water, wooden match, bike pump)
- Cloud charts (1 per student), readily available online (see an example at http://asd-www. larc.nasa.gov/SCOOL/cldchart.html) in printable formats or from teaching supply stores

- Thermometers (1 per pair of students)
- Compass
- Sunprint paper, readily available from teacher supply stores
- Beaufort wind gauge (1 per pair of students)—developed by Sir Francis Beaufort in the 1800s, a Beaufort wind gauge is a method of estimating wind speeds by noticing natural occurrences, such as flags and tree branches moving
- White board and colored markers
- Journals for students

Introduction

Methods: inquiry, discussion, storytelling.

Welcome students and gather them in a comfortable area with minimal distractions. Introduce the topic: "Today we're going to study something that will help you understand and become aware of this area as well as your home. We're going to explore the wild world of weather."

Ask students to share stories about when they've been caught in unexpected weather. Ask them to describe the climate, or average weather in their hometown, if it is different from your current location. What do students know about what makes the weather or how to predict the weather?

Weather Poem

Methods: written materials, storytelling.

To help students recall the four important words (major weather components), tell them you've written a poem with the words in it.

> It's raining on mice in the mountains
>
> And pouring on frogs up there, too.
>
> It's hailing if you go up higher
>
> And it's clobbered a cricket or two.
>
> But down in the valley it's balmy.
>
> They're definitely having some fun.
>
> What makes all this crazy old weather?
>
> Just the earth, water, air, and sun!

Now, certainly, the students can do better than that! Challenge the students to write a short poem about weather that contains the four key words (earth, water, air, and sun). Gather together and share poems if students are willing.

Application

Methods: discussion, written materials.

Have students get journals out. Using the white board, prompt students to identify the four main components of weather from their poems (earth, water, air, and sun). Have students write down the four components in their journal. Tell students they're going to play a game all day. Whenever you ask, "So, what makes all this crazy old weather?", students respond, "Just the earth, water, air, and sun." Practice the call and response a couple of times.

Make a Cloud

Methods: activity, experimentation, inquiry.

Tell students they're going to do something unusual that they may never get to do again—make a cloud! Instruct them to watch carefully because you're going to ask them what they've learned about clouds during the activity. Tell students clouds need some basic ingredients before they can happen. Have a student add a few drops of water from the water bottle to the cloud jar. Have

(continued)

another student light a match and drop it in (the match should go out immediately; all you want is the smoke). Attach the rubber stopper with bike pump and pump air into the bottle until there is significant pressure inside. Gather students in close and make sure they're watching, because this will happen fast. With a flourish, unstopper the bottle and voila! A cloud forms inside! Ask students what they noticed and have them list cloud "ingredients." Under what condition, high or low pressure, did clouds form?

Depending on the conditions, different kinds of clouds form. Ask students what they've already noticed about clouds. What are they interested in learning? Show them the cloud chart and have partners discuss what kinds of clouds they've seen. Gather the class and ask students to continue reflecting on clouds by asking them the following questions. Do students remember conditions when they saw particular kinds of clouds? Look at the clouds in the sky. What kinds of clouds are up there now? Describe why those clouds are there (water; nucleus, like dust, for droplet to condense on; low pressure).

Have students lie on their back for a few minutes either with a partner or as an entire group and watch the clouds. What are they doing? What can they tell us? Can they see special shapes in the clouds today? How much of the sky is covered by clouds right now?

Weather Fronts

Methods: activity, discussion.

Present the following material to the students.

Because different clouds form at different heights in the sky, the clouds can tell us what weather's coming. For example, high clouds, like cirrus clouds or "mare's tails," are the first trace of a warm front meeting a cold front. Because warm air rises and cold air sinks, the warm front slides up over the cold front at a gradual angle. As the front moves over us, the clouds slowly drop lower and lower and eventually it will start to rain.

Put your hands together, fingertip to fingertip. Slowly slide the left hand up and over the right until your fingertips reach your knuckles. This represents a warm front displacing a cold front and gradually sliding over it. High cirrus clouds today (the fingertips on your left hand) mean rain tomorrow (when the palm of your left hand moves over the knuckles on your right hand).

On the other hand, when a cold front displaces a warm front, it tries to slide underneath it. The cold front tries to sink underneath the warm front, so the two fronts meet like bulldozers. Make fists out of your hands and place the knuckles together. This represents the abrupt, vertical nature of a cold front trying to displace a warm front. When this happens, the thunderhead clouds quickly build and you may be caught by surprise in the rain!

Explain fronts (cold, high-pressure front meeting warm, low-pressure front and vice versa) and what the first lines of clouds look like with each kind of front. A front is the interface between air masses at different temperatures. Discuss this with students using your white board until they understand. Help them think about the clouds they've seen today and figure out if there is a front moving over you.

Cloud Assessment and Transference

Method: inquiry.

Ask students what they've already learned about clouds, thinking of all the activities they've done today. Does this new information make sense with what they already knew about clouds and weather? How can they use this new cloud learning at home? Ask, "So, what makes all this crazy old weather?" When students respond, ask them which of the four weather components clouds need.

Differential Heating

Methods: guided discovery, experimentation, inquiry.

Clouds are moved by wind and wind is a result of differential heating. Differential heating is how different things (rocks, water, soil) heat up at different rates because of their density and transparency. How can they create an experiment to measure differential heating?

Guide students into a thoughtful experiment measuring the temperature of different objects. One idea is to fill up one container with dirt and another (the same kind) with water, put them in the sun, and take the temperature in the beginning and after 15 minutes. But let students design their own experiment. Guide them through the steps of effective data collection.

Once students understand that density and transparency affect how materials gather and retain heat, relate that concept to wind. If something in nature, a big rock for example, heats up quickly in the sun, the warm air created by the rock will rise. This creates an empty area, or vacuum, where the warm air just left, so cooler air moves in to fill the space. This process is repeated, creating thermals or vertical wind.

Measuring Wind

Present the following material to the students.

One reason there is wind is because of differential heating and the atmosphere. Some weather scientists use tools called anemometers to measure wind. We don't have one today (they're too expensive and too fragile), but we have something close: the Beaufort Wind Gauge, which estimates wind speed based on common occurrences in nature.

Pass out the wind gauges and spend a few moments familiarizing students with them. Ask them, "So, what makes all this crazy old weather? How does that relate to clouds and weather?"

Energy From the Sun

Method: activity.

Present the following material to the students.

Describe why the sun is so important to the weather. What evidence can you think of that the sun provides the earth's energy? How does most of the sun's energy get to the earth? Today we're going to capture some of the sun's radiant energy by making sun prints.

Have students collect natural objects that they would like to create artwork out of. The objects should be nonliving or dead and lying on the ground. Following collection of materials, have students spend some time arranging the objects into a small shape they find attractive. Don't give students Sunprint paper until they are done creating their masterpiece or they may accidentally expose the paper. Pass out one piece of paper to each student. The students move their artwork onto the paper and carefully set it in a sunny place. In 15 minutes collect the artwork. The sun's energy will have changed the paper, turning it blue where it touched the paper. Where the students' artwork blocked the sun, the paper will remain a lighter color. Students will have a permanent record of their natural artwork, recorded by the sun on their paper.

Energy Flow

Method: game.

Plants and animals rely on the sun's radiant energy to survive. Tell the students you're going to play a game to show that relationship, and then play Race for the Sun or another energy-flow running game.

Race for the Sun

Select a large, flat area that is safe for running.

Appoint the chaperone, co-leader, or a student as the "Sun." Have the Sun stand at one end of the playing field. When you instruct the Sun to face the group, it is daytime. When you instruct the Sun to turn its back on the group, it is night.

Select two students to be converters of energy: Chlora and Phil.

Divide the remaining students into three groups: soil, water, and carbon dioxide. Spread the three groups along the side of the playing field, opposite the Sun. Each group is challenged to create a short chant to sing while the Sun is facing the group, or during the day.

Set out two markers indicating the starting points of the game: the roots of the tree.

(continued)

To play the game: Chlora and Phil must go to each of the three groups—soil, water, and carbon dioxide—in order. Chlora and Phil select one student from the soil group, take that student by the hand, and lead the student to the starting point: the roots. Then they run back to the next group, water, and select another student, joining the second student to the first student's hand. Slowly in this fashion, they build a tree out of soil, water, and carbon dioxide, with the energy from the sun. After the tree becomes three students large, additional students must be added by weaving under the arms of the existing tree members and joining on the end of the line. The line is stretching, trying to reach the Sun. The first group to reach the Sun wins.

Periodically interrupt the running part of the game by having the Sun go down (turn its back to the game). During the night, the new trees must face challenges. You become a challenge for the tree: fire. Try to push through the arms of the students joined to make a tree. Challenge them, but be reasonable with your effort. If you succeed in breaking the chain, all the students on the end closest to the Sun must go back to their original groups. Direct the Sun to rise again. The running part of the game begins again.

Become different challenges, such as a flood, insect infestation, and so on throughout the game.

After the game, gather the students and ask them to compare what is realistic about this game and real tree growth, and what is unrealistic.

Props can enhance Race for the Sun.

Predicting the Weather

Methods: inquiry, guided discovery, discussion.

Have students list all the things they've done so far. Then ask, "So, what makes all this crazy old weather?" Question students about aspects of the four basic weather components, then discuss how they can use their new knowledge to predict tomorrow's weather based on what they notice today. Have students pull out a blank page in their journal. With student prompts, create a chart on your white board, called Today's Weather Data Collection. When complete, have students copy it down in their journal. Here is an example:

Today's date:

Location:

Estimated elevation (from map):

Cloud type:

Percent sky cover:

Temperature:

Wind direction:

Estimated wind speed:

Assign partners and allow students to collect data. Circulate and assist students in collecting accurate data. When finished, gather the group and ask, "This is what's happening *today*.

What does all this data tell us about *tomorrow?* What kind of logical prediction can we base on this data?" Have partners make a logical prediction of tomorrow's data. Then have them act out a local weather station report, similar to the evening news. After all the reports are acted out, ask students to notice how similar or different the predictions were and to think about what affects that. Have students tuck their data sheet with a brief written prediction of tomorrow's weather into their journal. Students can check the next day to see how accurate their prediction was.

Ask students what they think the weather is doing back at home. Have they ever looked at any of the weather components at home? How can they use this new information once they get back to school?

Reflection

Send students out for a solo write in their journal with the following prompts: What were some of the most important things I learned today? How does this support what I already knew? How can I use this at home? How did I contribute to the group today? How can I improve my contribution to class in the future?

Closure

Gather students in a compelling area with good view of the sky as you hike back to your starting point. Have them spread out, lie on their back, relax, and watch the clouds and weather for a few minutes. Direct students to write a haiku about the weather. A haiku is a traditional Japanese poem comprised of 17 syllables. The first line is 5 syllables, the second line is 7 syllables, and the third line is 5 syllables. Here is an example:

> The trees are swaying
>
> Branches clatter together
>
> Gentle wind blowing

If students finish early, they can look at the clouds and relax.

Relevance

This course relates to the students' lives because they interact daily with weather no matter where they live. Everyone has had good and bad experiences because of the weather. Understanding weather and weather patterns can help students be prepared for changes in the weather.

Integrated Curriculum

This course integrates a number of curricular areas:

- Art—writing poetry at beginning and end of course
- Math—predicting, estimating percent of sky covered by clouds
- Language arts—discussions, writing, weather-prediction presentations
- Science—accurate data collection and interpretation, experiment design, observation skills, data-sheet design, critical thinking

Diversity

This course provides for participation of diverse student groups by considering the following:

- Assigned partners—peer tutoring of special needs students or ELL students
- Multisensory activities—drawing, writing, chants, oral discussions and presentations, white-board supplement, hands-on experiments, visual support
- Cultural awareness—weather connects to agrarian cultures as well as urban cultures

(continued)

Assessment

The instructor will know that the students have accomplished the objectives by the following:

- Choral response to "So, what makes all this crazy old weather?", contribution to discussion and journaling. Instructors should look for students' responses in discussions and read several, if not all, journals.

- Group discussion and journaling. Instructors should watch carefully for a variety of students to participate in discussions. If students are reticent to speak in front of the group, the instructor should have a private conversation with those students for assessment and engagement.

- Creation of the group data sheet. Instructors should watch for involvement of a variety of students during data-sheet construction.

- Accurate data collection and logical weather prediction during presentation. Instructors should observe every group during data collection and assess data accuracy. Instructors should check each group's prediction for logic as well as for participation by every group member.

- Final discussion. Instructors should collect responses from a variety of students during the final discussion about home climate and weather.

FISHING ETHICS

Here is a lesson based on a game where the participants respond to situations (scenarios) that help them understand appropriate actions toward the aquatic ecosystem.

This lesson is adapted from: Liukkonen, B. 1991. *The lake game (youth)*. Minnesota Extension Service. University of Minnesota, Duluth. Author: Ken Gilbertson. 1999 (March). University of Minnesota Duluth. Center for Environmental Education. Duluth, MN.

Purpose

The purpose of this game is to teach young anglers ethics for fishing on lakes or streams. While it is written for use in Minnesota, it can easily be adapted to any place where fishing occurs.

Need

The need for this program is not promoting fishing. That would result in even more pressure on the fish population. Rather, this program is intended to teach existing, learning, and likely anglers how to ease pressure on the fish population. This will be accomplished through teaching ethical behaviors that also include healthy land-management practices.

Audience

Five to 14-year-olds. Geared toward northern Minnesota, but not limited to this location. It is designed for a class range of 1 to 25 students.

Outcomes (Objectives)

Students will be able to do the following:

1. Describe five different aspects of a watershed involved with a fishery.
   - A. Watershed
   - B. Shoreline
   - C. Lake
   - D. Riparian zone
   - E. Inlet and outlet (streams)
   - F. Shallow areas (weed beds)

2. Explain what *fishing ethics* means. (It means behavior that is respectful of the land, the water, and other anglers.)

3. Describe responsible behaviors in the following situations. Responsible behaviors may differ slightly from state to state. Use your state's fishing regulations to learn what are considered appropriate behaviors by the department of natural resources.
   - A. Catch and release
   - B. Slot limits
   - C. How to play a fish
   - D. How to remove a hook (to protect the gills and viscera)
   - E. Litter
   - F. Loose monofilament line
   - G. Loon nests (getting too close)
   - H. Moving in on other anglers (hot-holing)
   - I. Fishing in closed zones (e.g., spawn, weed beds)
   - J. Transporting exotic species (Eurasian milfoil, zebra mussels, other fish)
   - K. What to do with rough fish
   - L. What to do with fish guts

(continued)

Time

15 to 30 minutes

Location

This lesson is designed to be taught in any large area such as outdoors or in a gymnasium.

Equipment

- 1 20-by-25-foot (6-by-7.5-meter) map of a local or imaginary lake written on a sheet of plastic with a waterproof marker
- 1 10-gallon (38-liter) aquarium (half full of water)
- 1 package of green plastic grass to represent milfoil
- 1 ice-fishing reel with line (no hook!)
- 2 buckets to haul water
- 1 bottle of red food color
- 1 business envelope full of dirt
- Several fishing lures with lead weights
- 100 scenarios (can be duplicated; see pages 167-170)

Procedures

Methods: games, scenarios, role-playing.

1. Get students together on the map.
2. Introduce yourself and have the students introduce themselves.
3. Explain the purpose of the activity and why it is important to practice proper ethical behavior.
4. Explain the map and how the game works.
   a. Each person will take a card off the pile in the middle of the map.
   b. The card will have a situation with two choices. Whichever choice the student makes, they will either get a reward (small piece of candy) or add debris to the water in the aquarium.
   c. Discuss with the group the appropriate behavior for each situation.
5. At the end, assess objectives by asking each student to say one ethical behavior that they learned.

Evaluation

Have students get in a circle. Go around in the circle and have each student name one ethic they learned today. Ask them to explain why the action is considered ethical. Ask what they can do if they find themselves in that situation again.

Anglers should strive to fish ethically.

Game Scenarios

The following scenarios can be cut out and laminated as separate cards. You can either hand these cards to the students to read aloud or you can read them to the students.

Card 1

I go fishing with a friend. When we clean our fish, we should

dump the guts in the lake,

or

take them back 150 feet (46 meters) into the woods and bury them.

Why?

Card 2

My family has a large wooded plot of land along a stream. We want to log (cut) the trees off the land. We should

cut them right down to the stream edge,

or

leave a buffer zone at least 150 feet from the stream edge.

Why?

Card 3

I am eating lunch in the boat while we fish. I don't like to have a messy boat. I should

throw my lunch wrappers overboard,

or

pack them away to be sure nothing blows into the lake.

Why?

Card 4

My friend and I are fishing for bass. My friend catches a carp. She should

throw it on the shoreline to make sure it dies because it is an ugly fish and it competes with bass,

or

return it to the water.

Why?

From Ken Gilbertson, Timothy Bates, Terry McLaughlin, and Alan Ewert, 2006, *Outdoor Education: Methods and Strategies,* Champaign,IL: Human Kinetics.

(continued)

Card 5

I have caught a brook trout that is 20 inches long. The rule book says that I can only keep brookies that are 10 to 18 inches (25 to 46 centimeters) long. I should

keep the fish,

or

throw it back.

What should I do?

Card 6

I have caught a nice-sized fish, yet I know I don't want to keep it. I should

play it until it is totally exhausted,

or

reel it in as soon as I can so I don't tire it out.

Why?

Card 7

With my fishing license, I can catch a certain number of fish every day. I'm with a friend who has a license but doesn't want to fish. I should

catch and keep as many as I can so that I have the maximum number of fish for both of us,

or

enjoy catching fish, but release all except those that will make a meal.

Why?

Card 8

I have been fishing all morning and haven't even gotten a bite! I notice a friend fishing in a small bay catching a lot of fish. I should

move over next to them so I can have some fun too,

or

find another spot to fish and leave my friend alone.

Why?

From Ken Gilbertson, Timothy Bates, Terry McLaughlin, and Alan Ewert, 2006, *Outdoor Education: Methods and Strategies*, Champaign,IL: Human Kinetics.

Card 9

While trolling along the shoreline, I notice a loon sitting on a nest. I should

get closer to take a picture,

or

move away quietly so I don't disturb the loon and its nest.

Why?

Card 10

It's the first day of fishing and I know a great spot to fish. However, because it's a spawning bed, the area is closed. I should

go fishing really early so nobody else finds out,

or

find a different spot to fish.

Why?

Card 11

After my family has been fishing all day, we pull our boat out of the lake. I should

jump in the car and go—I'm hungry!

or

thoroughly check the boat and trailer to make sure there are no mussels or weeds attached.

Why?

Card 12

My little brother has just been learning how to cast. He is constantly getting his line all snarled up on the reel. I should

cut the mess of line off and throw it in the water,

or

be sure that any line we've cut gets packed away so it won't blow into the lake.

Why?

From Ken Gilbertson, Timothy Bates, Terry McLaughlin, and Alan Ewert, 2006, *Outdoor Education: Methods and Strategies,* Champaign, IL: Human Kinetics.

(continued)

Card 13

We have a fishing boat with a 30-horse motor on it. When we need to refill the tank, we should

not worry about spilling a little gas in the lake,

or

make sure we don't spill any gas in the lake by refilling the tank out of the water.

Why?

Card 14

I'm 14 years old and am young enough that I don't need a license. Because I don't need a license

other fishing laws don't apply to me so I can catch as many fish as I want,

or

I need to abide by the same laws that apply to everyone who fishes.

Why?

Card 15

My friend and I are catching fish as fast as we can hook 'em! One fish swallows the hook. I should

just rip it out of the fish,

or

cut the line and return the fish to the water.

Why?

Card 16

I have caught a trout and the hook is really stuck. I should

squeeze very hard and pull the hook, even if the fish's gills bleed a little,

or

handle the fish as little as possible and cut the line if I can't get the hook out even with pliers.

Why?

From Ken Gilbertson, Timothy Bates, Terry McLaughlin, and Alan Ewert, 2006, *Outdoor Education: Methods and Strategies,* Champaign,IL: Human Kinetics.

CONCEPTS FOR SEA KAYAKERS

This lesson presents a difficult topic for many instructors in a manner that progresses well and incorporates effective teaching methods.

Goals

This lesson provides students an opportunity to understand the basic principles of physics and body movement that make for efficient paddling.

Objectives

Students will be able to do the following:

1. Describe the value of a boat that fits properly.
2. Demonstrate how to adjust foot braces and outfit a boat for proper fit.
3. Practice proper use of body movement to control the boat (J-lean).
4. Exhibit proper torso rotation to control the paddle.
5. Observe examples of bow deflection and stern eddies as a kayak moves through the water.

Audience

Adults in a sea kayaking fundamentals course, with no more than five participants to one instructor

Time

30 minutes (this lesson is part of an entire 2-day course)

Location

Calm, shallow-water beach area with sandy shoreline

Content and Methods

1. Introduction to the topic (1 minute) (Methods: lecture, discussion)

   Explain that this topic is important because the concepts facilitate efficient paddling, which saves energy, which we all want to do when we are paddling. There are two categories that you will address: the body's movement in relation to the boat and how the boat moves through the water.

2. The body's movement in relation to the boat

   a. **Stabilization** (2 minutes) (Methods: visualization and inquiry)

      i. Instructor (you may embellish this story): "Visualize yourself in a small rowboat. As a large wake rocks your boat from side to side, what do you do to stabilize yourself?"

      ii. Answer: Grab onto the sides with your hands.

      iii. Instructor: "You're holding a paddle with your hands while in a kayak, so how do you stabilize yourself?"

      iv. Answer: With knees, feet, hips, and butt—the lower body keeps you in the boat.

      v. Instructor: "Fitting in your boat should be like fitting in a pair of shoes. You want a fit that is just right—not too tight and not too loose."

   b. **Proper Fit** (5 minutes) (Method: guided discovery)

      i. Students pair up. One gets into the boat and the other stands in the water. No paddles.

(continued)

A kayaker rocks back and forth while doing the boat-boogie-wiggle.

ii. Before students begin, the instructor should demonstrate. The kayakers hold their hands outward and their partners rock the boat roughly. Kayakers try to stabilize the boat. If the kayakers are loose in their boat, they need to check their foot braces for a snug fit of the paddler. Coach the kayakers in proper fit and adjusting the foot braces.

iii. Students switch positions. After this segment, everyone should fit their boat properly.

c. **J-Lean** (8 minutes) (Method: guided discovery)

i. Boat-boogie-wiggle—Kayakers practice rocking their boat side to side as much as possible without flipping over. If they flip over, they need to reach down to the bottom of the lake to stabilize. (Only do this exercise in shallow water.)

ii. Have students try to stop at one end of their "rocking" and stay there as long as possible.

iii. Ask, "If we were to draw a line from your head down through your spine and out your hip, what letter would we get? This shape is important to maneuvering the boat." (Answer: The letter *J*)

d. **Torso Rotation** (5 minutes) (Method: physical skills instruction)

i. Instructor: "The strength of our strokes is a result of the strength of our upper body, not just our arms. If we were to use just our arms, we would fatigue quickly." Demonstrate the catch, propulsion, and recovery phase of the stroke with a full torso rotation. The chest swings side to side around a pivot point (the spine).

ii. Students practice the sweep stroke with coaching.

iii. Instructor: "What's the difference when your paddle blade is close to the boat versus far away?" (Answer: You turn better when it is farther away from the boat.)

e. **How the Boat Moves Through the Water** (10 minutes) (Method: guided discovery)

    i. Instructor: "The practice with the sweeps is an example of the pivot point—the farther you are away from the pivot point, the more efficient your turn. Conversely, the closer you are, the less you are going to turn."

    ii. Students practice getting some forward momentum, then J-lean toward their most comfortable side. What happens?

    iii. The boat will turn away from the side that is lower in the water. This is called bow deflection and can help in turning more quickly.

f. **Conclusion** (Methods: lecture, inquiry)

    i. Review the key point of the material presented.

    ii. Students answer or demonstrate the following: Show a J-lean. What are the elements of stability? Describe good torso rotation. Which way does the boat turn if you J-lean to the right?

CHAPTER 12

Your Future in Outdoor Education

CHAPTER OBJECTIVES

By the end of the chapter, you should be able to do the following:

- Describe at least three major issues in the field of outdoor education.

- Explain how state learning standards and testing affect outdoor education.

- Describe how an outdoor education experience can enhance and support classroom learning and test scores.

- Explain the current status of certification for adventure education, interpretation, and environmental education.

- Describe the difference between education and advocacy and outline a method for including issues education in your curriculum.

- Develop a strategic plan for your own professional development, including leadership development and membership in professional organizations.

You are participating in the field of outdoor education in an exciting time of discovery and refinement. Outdoor education is moving from being intuition-based to being research-based. As an organization of professionals, we are beginning to build a knowledge foundation as well as a philosophical focus that will give us much more influence as educators. We are exploring stronger links with the formal education system to integrate the methods, strategies, and benefits of outdoor education that are difficult for a classroom teacher to achieve alone. While new research is providing knowledge, insight, and models on how to be effective, practitioners are struggling to stay abreast of new information. Our challenge is to incorporate new information into the practice of outdoor education.

Throughout this book, we have introduced you to the field of outdoor education. The history, definitions, and theories that help form the field have been described. Basic skills in assessing an audience, creating an effective setting, writing a lesson plan, and using basic teaching methods have been outlined. All are important for the effective outdoor educator today. But what will be expected from an effective outdoor educator tomorrow?

Outdoor education is growing every day. One change is the extent that teachers are incorporating outdoor education in a formal classroom setting or bringing their students to nonformal outdoor education settings. Some states require classroom teachers to do coursework in environmental education as part of their licensing process (Kirk, Wilke, and Ruskey 2001). You can meet outdoor educators who work in nature centers, outdoor schools, museums, national parks, colleges, businesses, and many other settings.

Where is this growing field headed? What are the major influences in outdoor education today? How will this affect you now and in the future? How can you influence the state of the field? What responsibility do you have for the advancement of the profession?

This chapter will give an overview of current key issues that promise to shape the future of outdoor education, including the following:

- The pressures of state learning standards and high-stakes testing and the challenges and opportunities they create for outdoor education
- The current discussion regarding a national standardized certification protocol for outdoor educators

- Education, advocacy, and relating issues analysis to the environment
- Developing a strategic plan for professional development

Working With Mainstream Education

Outdoor education contributes to dynamic education in all settings. We teach across disciplines, using constructivist, student-directed philosophies. We teach cooperatively and thematically. Students learn information in a context that helps them understand, recall, and apply their learning to new situations. The environment lends itself naturally to issues-based education. Students become aware of their values and learn the skills and responsibilities of an active citizen. Yet, instead of being welcomed into mainstream education, outdoor education is viewed as optional, an extra in the school day.

What can we do about this? First, we must not talk past classroom teachers. We must find a common language, be aware of each other's worldview, and share the desire for similar outcomes for our students. Outdoor education is interdisciplinary and contextual. Learning about something in a context and having an opportunity to apply that learning immediately builds understanding and retention. If you view outdoor education as an extension of classroom learning, the effect on the student can be dramatic. We must understand the strengths and challenges of our field and use them to the students' advantage. We must recognize that we are part of a bigger educational system. No single educator helps a person develop environmental literacy. This chapter discusses the larger educational context in which outdoor education takes place, focusing on the current challenges facing the field.

Throughout this chapter references are made to standards, organizations, curricula, and research conducted in outdoor education including adventure education, interpretation, and environmental education. These terms—outdoor education, adventure education, environmental education, and interpretation—are related, but not interchangeable (see chapter 1). Care has been taken to use the precise term as required. Read this chapter cautiously, noting to what part of the field references are made.

State Standards and High-Stakes Testing

Classroom teachers teach content mandated by state standards. The students' mastery of this content is measured by tests. Many of us are nonformal and informal educators. You may wonder what standards and tests have to do with outdoor education, but if you are working with schools, supporting and reinforcing their work is crucial.

Teachers and school administrators are under more and more pressure to teach to the standards. They are compelled to improve school test scores as reported by school report cards and adequate yearly progress (AYP) reports (U.S. Department of Education 2003). Administrators respond to this pressure in many ways. One response is to cancel all field trips to provide students with more desk time. Or schools may continue field trips but ask you, "How does what you're teaching relate to the standards?" In addition to pressure from standards and testing, the educational system feels the effect of the recent economic slump in the United States. As school administrators evaluate possible field-trip destinations, they are looking to get the most out of the experience.

Let's take a brief look at the history of standards, testing, and high-stakes testing so we can relate it to the current state of education and outdoor education.

Testing and Standards: A Brief History

In 1965 the U.S. government became a presence in state educational systems when it passed the Elementary and Secondary Education Act (ESEA). For the first time in the United States, this act allocated federal funds to state educational systems. Minorities and economically underprivileged students were two of the main targets of the legislation. Federal monies remain available to states today as allocated by this legislation. The legislation must be reauthorized every few years, so there is usually some policy change when the ESEA is renewed.

In 1983 the National Commission on Excellence in Education published *A Nation at Risk*. This report saw U.S. education in a recession. It compared U.S. schools with schools worldwide and reported that U.S. schools were performing poorly. The report called for an initiation of high-stakes testing intended to raise the nation's academic standards of achievement (U.S. Department of Education 1983). While the report is not scholarly and its accuracy was questioned, it was still an influential document. As a result of the report, states began developing learning standards and implementing testing policy to assess the achievement of these standards.

High-stakes testing refers to a single test having serious consequences for students or schools. For example, the consequences of a high-stakes test may involve moving on to a higher grade level or receiving a diploma. A high-stakes test implies that the student has one chance to take the test.

The debate rages as to whether standards and testing have the effect on learning originally intended. Are high test scores becoming the goal of the educational system rather than education and learning? Are teachers focusing on test-taking skills and teaching to the test? Is high-stakes testing an accurate means of assessment? Can tests written to assess student learning also be used to evaluate the effectiveness of a teacher or a school? Clearly this is a complicated issue, and answering these questions is not the intent of this chapter. However, standards and testing are an integral part of formal education today and are becoming more important each year. The question we hope to address in this chapter is, "What do tests and standards have to do with outdoor education?"

Some states, such as Kentucky, have developed standards specifically for environmental education. Other states are in the process of developing such standards. Still other states, such as Florida, have embedded environmental education in their science standards. The rigor of environmental education standards varies from state to state.

Other efforts have linked national standards, such as the National Science Standards, with environmental education standards. *Excellence in Environmental Education: Guidelines for Learning* was published by the North American Association for Environmental Education (NAAEE) in 2000. This document suggests 4th-, 8th-, and 12th-grade guidelines and performance measures for environmental education.

Reinforcing Core Standards

In addition to meeting environmental education standards, your outdoor education curriculum can reinforce other core content standards. For example, imagine you and your group are assisting with a scientific research project measuring the growth rate

Students measure the circumference of a sequoia as part of state science standards.

of sequoia trees. You measure the diameter of the sequoia at chest height. Then you trudge through the undergrowth to find a spot where you can see the entire sequoia from top to bottom. Using a clinometer you measure the height of the tree. Comparing your data to previously collected data, you can estimate the rate of growth of the tree. Through this experience you reinforce the core standards of radius, diameter, and volume the math teacher is working on, as well as the core standards of field research techniques, accuracy, and precision the science teacher is working on.

Adventure education is also being incorporated into physical education programs. The physical education teacher implements standards related to teamwork and cardiovascular exercise. With the growing dilemma of increased obesity and diminished fitness, physical skills leading to life skills development will quite possibly lead to increased standards in fitness testing for youth. The use of adventure education to help meet this need is increasing.

The students could learn these core standards at a desk or in an outdoor setting, but the outcome of the learning and their retention would be dramatically different (Lieberman and Hoody 1998). At a desk, little social interaction takes place, so no interper-

sonal growth occurs. The practicality of the project is lost because it is abstract rather than concrete. You never learn what a sequoia feels like or smells like or what kinds of animals live in the grove. The outdoor experience is more memorable, and students may make an attachment to sequoias that sparks an interest in future learning. Because active, outdoor projects are interdisciplinary and experiential (feet time rather than seat time), they enhance learning and retention. Research is beginning to show that participation in a rigorous environmental education program can increase state test scores by several points (NEETF 2004).

It can be daunting to think about reinforcing state standards in your outdoor education courses. However, it's easier than you may think. Start by requesting a copy of state standards from the managing agency in your state. These are often free and available online. Familiarize yourself with these standards. Begin with the grade levels you will be working with and read through the standards. While science standards are a favorite among environmental educators and physical education standards are a favorite among adventure educators, don't overlook language arts, social studies, art, and physical education. Outdoor education is interdisciplinary, so look through all the discipline areas.

Once you are familiar with the standards by grade level, begin your curriculum development. Some activities will align well with standards and some won't. You, your client, and your employer decide how much your curriculum needs to align with the standards. Keep in mind that outdoor education is a powerful medium for education. Be very deliberate about changing your approach simply to meet standards. Much of what you already do will reinforce standards. Familiarize yourself with the language of standards but don't compromise how you teach simply to meet standards. Providing a context for the standards the teacher is covering in the classroom can reinforce student learning and help make the outdoor experience more relevant to your students' daily lives.

Professional Certification

Certification has long been a topic of controversy in outdoor education. Many professions require certification. Classroom teachers, for example, must hold a teaching license to teach in a public school. Almost since it came into existence, the field of outdoor education has debated whether professional certification should be a requirement for outdoor educators.

Like other questions facing the field, this is a complex issue. Should certification exist at all? Should it be mandatory or voluntary? If it exists, how are the competencies defined? Should certification need to be refreshed every few years? Who will the certifying agency be? Should certification be managed at the national, state, or local level? Will it exclude qualified people from the field? How will it improve the profession?

Join in this formative discussion as you enter the field of outdoor education. When you assess certification programs, ask yourself how the program improves the field:

- How does this certification make the field of outdoor education better?
- Is it flexible enough to accommodate local knowledge?
- Can this certification evolve as the field changes?
- Is it a rigorous professional development program or simply "jumping through hoops"?

Each branch of outdoor education—interpretation, adventure education, and environmental education—has taken a different approach to this topic.

Interpretation

There are two main branches for certification in interpretation: the National Association for Interpretation (NAI) and the National Park Service (NPS).

Following nearly 25 years of debate, the NAI designed a national certification program. It is a voluntary program offered and managed by the NAI. Currently there are five categories of certification:

- Certified Heritage Interpreter
- Certified Interpretive Manager
- Certified Interpretive Planner
- Certified Interpretive Trainer
- Certified Interpretive Guide

The NAI is beginning to conduct empirical research to examine the effects of the certification program. The outcome of this research will influence further development of the program.

The NPS offers a voluntary certification program called the Interpretive Development Program (IDP). It is a customized program intended to be designed by employees and their supervisor. It focuses on outcomes through benchmark competencies of knowledge, skills, and abilities. Currently the IDP requirement is at the supervisor's discretion.

The U.S. Office of Personnel Management is conducting a validation study to determine whether the NPS certifications can legally be grounds for promotion or withholding promotion. If it is found legal, the NPS will have to decide whether or not to mandate the program for all interpretive employees, interns, and volunteers.

There is some competition between NAI and NPS certification programs. Currently, the IDP is accepted by NAI, but the NAI certification is not accepted by NPS. Even though NPS doesn't accept NAI certification for professional advancement, some NPS interpreters find value in the training. In the words of Tom Medema, NPS interpretive ranger and branch chief of interpretive field operations at Yosemite National Park: "NAI has a solid program which I value and participate in. All of these certification programs help grow the profession and raise the bar for work performance" (2005).

Reprinted, by permission, from Tom Medema, 2005, Branch Chief, Interpretive Field Operation, Yosemite National Park. Personal conversation.

To learn more about the specifics of each program and to stay abreast of changes, see appendix A for NAI and NPS contact information.

Adventure Education

Similar to interpretation, adventure education has wrestled with the concept of certification for several years. Currently adventure education does not require certification. While there is no certification process available or required for adventure education, other specific certifications, such as wilderness first aid or basic kayaking instructor, may be required by an employer.

Environmental Education

Environmental education currently has no national certification process, but the issue is under debate. Several states, including North Carolina, Florida, Kentucky, and Utah, offer state certification programs. Program rigor varies by state.

The debate over national certification is hottest in the field of environmental education: "NAAEE and the Environmental Education and Training Partnership (EETAP) are collaborating on an initiative that is exploring issues related to the development, implementation and evaluation of a national certification program for environmental educators" (Osorio 2002).

At this point it's anyone's guess whether a national certification will be developed for environmental education. However, the issue hasn't gone away in environmental education, and a great deal of discussion about it continues at conferences and among professional organizations.

Education or Advocacy?

Outdoor education is often described as a pathway to the heart. We are drawn to working outdoors, driven by a strong desire to teach, and feel a moral responsibility to protect the earth through outdoor education. Because we believe in what we do, it becomes easy to advocate for our beliefs rather than help our students develop their own.

As teachers we have a moral responsibility to educate, not advocate. In addition, it's simply ineffective to tell others what to do. Telling students what to do or think doesn't help the student build issue-analysis, problem-solving, or decision-making skills.

The line between education and advocacy can be unclear. There are times when it is clear we are educating. Teaching students about watersheds is an example of education. Other times we are advocating. Having students write a letter to protest the existence of a dam in a national park is an example of advocacy, as is selecting a service project that is based on your personal agenda instead of the learning outcomes for the students (for example, building a bridge along your favorite route). However, it is the gray area in between that wreaks havoc with our teaching. Our own passion and interest in the outcomes of issues complicate matters even more.

Education versus advocacy has been an issue in education since its inception. A watershed event occurred in 1996 when Michael Sanera and Jane Shaw wrote a book entitled *Facts Not Fear* (1996) teaching children about the environment. In this book, Sanera alleges that environmental education teaches biased information and is full of soft science. Sanera's book has been accused of being inaccurate and full of anecdotal and contradictory information itself. However, the die had been cast and environmental education was under attack.

This particular attack was effective because Sanera succeeded in influencing politicians to rewrite Arizona's statewide environmental education mandate to make it more industry-friendly. He has worked at state and national levels to politically intervene with effective environmental education.

Whether Sanera will continue to be politically successful at altering environmental education mandates remains to be seen. However, at the very least, Sanera has succeeded in redirecting limited environmental education resources from effective education to political self-defense.

Today the discussion continues. The world faces many contentious challenges today. They are critical issues that need to be understood, discussed, acted on, and resolved. Advocating for a specific action when you are in the role of teacher is unethical and ineffective, yet teaching about those issues is critical. How do you tell the difference?

Issues education is a technique for introducing students to fundamental problems and the processes leading to their resolution. Environmental issues have many sides. After introducing an issue to students, help them derive a plan to learn about the issues from many perspectives. Ideally students research the perspectives of and the information about an issue. To facilitate this, you need to have

© University of Minnesota Duluth Outdoor Program

Beach sweep: education or advocacy?

contact with students over a period of weeks or months. If your contact is a shorter period of time, you will need to do the background research and distill it for the students. Make sure you are collecting several points of view on the same issue and representing each one fairly and accurately.

Throughout the course of study, introduce and reinforce a character-, values-, or moral-development activity to help students discern the values they hold that govern their daily actions and decisions.

Information collection and values clarification is followed by introducing students to various decision-making models. For example, the Diamond method (see appendix B, p. 195) leads students through a step-by-step process toward making a thoughtful decision. First the problem is clearly identified. Then alternatives are generated. Following information collection, the pros and cons of each alternative are weighed and a decision is made. Elevating decision making to a conscious level like this helps students develop patterns of thought and problem-solving skills.

This sequence is best implemented over several weeks. However, it can be adapted into a 2-hour activity if you prepare background information

and have moral-development and decision-making models ready. The shorter time period has less potential to influence students. The more involved students are in selecting the issue and doing the background research, the more thoroughly they will learn the issues-analysis skills. This is where formal, nonformal, and informal educators can work together. The classroom teacher can help students choose an issue and research it. The outdoor educator can give the students direct experience with the issue and facilitate an exploration of student values.

As with all learning, students will not assimilate this process through one exposure. It needs to be repeated several times in several settings to help students master the techniques sufficiently to use them on a daily basis. These are life skills, and they are essential for the development of environmentally literate citizens.

Steps of Issues Education

- Identify an issue.
- Break the issue into its resolute parts.
- Examine the issue from many perspectives.
- Clarify student values that influence their response to the issue.
- Make a decision on a course of action.

Education versus advocacy will continue to be controversial. Research is pointing toward effective ways to help people develop environmental literacy. Develop your own self-awareness. You are educating students about *how* to think, not *what* to think. Become critical of curricula. Assess the value-fairness of a curriculum and use it appropriately.

Strategic Planning for Professional Growth

You prepare for teaching by developing a lesson plan because you know a well-crafted lesson plan is essential to guide your students' learning. You should treat your own professional growth and learning similarly. Develop a plan so you have a structure for what you want to accomplish. A professional development plan will help you measure your own growth and progress. These are the blaze marks on the path of your professional career.

Begin by choosing a time of year when you will create and subsequently revisit your professional development plan. Perhaps your place of employment has a yearly review process that will naturally trigger the professional reflection necessary to create and update your plan. If not, choose a time of year and mark it on your calendar; otherwise your professional development plan may get lost in the paperwork and details of the day-to-day grind.

As you begin your professional development plan, start by thinking big. Dream about where you would like to be in 10 years. What kind of work setting will you be in? What kinds of responsibilities will you have? Create the dream job you'd like to have in 10 years.

Once you have your dream, it's time to come back to earth and start making the dream happen. Identify key steps that you need to take to reach your dream job. For example, if you want to start your own nature center in 10 years, you'll need to develop business and administration skills. You'll also need to learn how to hire and manage staff, raise money, and manage a budget. Sketch out a rough time line and plan how you will take steps toward your goal. Fill in as much detail as you can for the next 3, 5, and 10 years.

In addition to the cognitive aspects of planning your career, remember to include the affective, or emotional, aspects of planning. Your own values and attitudes are as important as your time line. Effective educators have an understanding that goes beyond facts to feelings, beyond the product to the process. Take the time to clearly address attitudes and values that can lead you to success. You can cultivate these attitudes in your professional life through intention and practice.

Now you've got the big picture in place. You should feel comfortable with your 3-year, 5-year, and 10-year plan. The next year is critical for implementing your plan—it's where the rubber meets the road. So spend some time developing the details for the upcoming year. Copy the sample professional strategic planning sheet in appendix B and begin to complete it. You will find it reads like a lesson plan. Think of it as your lesson plan for the next year of your professional life.

- Goal—Write a single sentence that captures your overarching goal for the year. Goals should be positively stated, indicating what you will do, not what you won't do. Consider writing separate goals for learning content, pedagogy, management, and so on.

- Objectives—Write two or three objectives, or objects of your course of action, that support your goal. Objectives should be measurable and clear.

- Steps—List the essential steps you must take to achieve your objectives.

- Time frame—Link each step with a specific time frame. This is one way you will measure your progress and the reasonableness of your goals.

- Assessment—How will you know you've accomplished your objectives? How will you measure progress toward your objectives? Clear assessments for each objective and time frame will help you measure your progress.

- Values and attitudes—What values and attitudes must you manifest to achieve your goal?

Make sure your professional development plan has flexibility and responsiveness built in. You don't want to pass by opportunities because they don't fit perfectly into your plan. However, having a well-written, thorough professional development plan will actually make you more responsive to opportunities as they arise. Knowing where you want to go will help you recognize unexpected opportunities that will take you there.

A professional outdoor educator has many obligations to participants and other outdoor educators. As part of your professional development, you should stay abreast of current issues in outdoor education by attending state and national conferences, reading journals, and continuing to learn throughout your career. Achieving a high quality of delivery and contribution is a never-ending process, which is what makes this profession so enjoyable.

Professional Organizations

Professional organizations are an important part of your professional development. As you gain experience and build your skills and knowledge, you can share your experience through professional organizations and conferences. In outdoor education, there are a number of local, regional, and national professional organizations. These organizations range from broad umbrella groups that support general outdoor education to organizations that focus on specific skill or knowledge areas. A list of national organizations is included in appendix A. Keep in mind, this list is not inclusive. Look for state and local organizations as well as organizations representing disciplines related to but distinct from outdoor education such as the National Science Teachers Association (NSTA) or the American Psychological Association (APA).

© Dave Lee

Professional foresters attend a continuing education conference in the Santa Fe National Forest.

These groups strive to advance the profession through conferences, training, publications, and networking. Consider how you would like to participate in professional organizations. Do you simply want to attend conferences? Once you are comfortable with that level of participation, you can volunteer to help organize or present at future conferences. Attend board meetings, which are usually open to all members. Join a committee as a member or volunteer to chair a committee. When you find a professional organization you really connect with, consider running for the board. The field of outdoor education has been built by the hard work and dedication of people just like you. Exercise your professional responsibility to the field and be an active participant. You can direct the growth of outdoor education through your efforts.

When choosing a professional organization to join or conference to attend, consider the following questions:

- How much professional time and money do you have?

- How much personal time and money are you willing to spend?
- What do you hope to gain?
- How will you share what you've learned with others?
- What kind of organization are you interested in?
  - Local, national, or international
  - Highly professional or casual
  - Umbrella or focused
  - Narrow or broad member base
- How will you participate?
  - Attend conferences.
  - Make presentations at conferences.
  - Volunteer to help organize conferences.
  - Join a committee as a member or chairperson.
  - Run for the board.
  - Write for the newsletter or other publications.

Stories From Real Life: Participation in Professional Organizations

Following are examples of participation in professional organizations from two successful professionals in the field of outdoor education. As you contrast these two professionals' choices, notice that there is no right way to participate in organizations. Throughout your career, expect the organizations you participate in to change.

Professional 1:

1. Current organization membership
   - California Science Teachers Association (CSTA)
   - Association for Environmental and Outdoor Education (AEOE, a state affiliate of NAAEE; northern section chair, state chair, advisory council member, secretary)
   - National Center for Science Education
   - Golden State Environmental Education Consortium (GSEEC)

2. Former organization membership
   - National Association for Interpretation (NAI)
   - Association for Supervision and Curriculum Development (ASCD)
   - North American Association for Environmental Education (NAAEE)
   - California Alliance for Environmental Education
   - California Outdoor School Administrators

Professional 2:

1. Current organization membership
   - Golden State Environmental Education Consortium (GSEEC)
   - North American Association for Environmental Education (NAAEE)
   - Association for Environmental and Outdoor Education (AEOE, a state affiliate of NAAEE)
   - California Association of Bilingual Educators (CABE)

2. Former organization membership
   - Minnesota Naturalists' Association (MNA; past president and vice president)
   - Minnesota Association for Environmental Education (MAEE; committee member)
   - Center for Environmental Education (CEED)
   - National Association for Interpretation (NAI)

Regardless of which organizations you join, you will gain many benefits with membership. You will gain inspiration from other successful professionals. You will build your network of colleagues, which facilitates job searches and builds partnerships. You will reconnect with the reasons why you joined this profession to begin with.

Professional Journals and Periodicals

Staying in touch with current research is critical yet challenging for effective practitioners. One criticism of outdoor education is the gap between current research and applied field practice. Research reveals insights into effective practices in outdoor education, but it can be years before research influences practice:

> We know what the [educational] problems are! We have the tools needed to solve those problems at our disposal! The only thing we need to do is to begin doing things differently than we have done them in the past. (Hungerford 2001)

Peer-reviewed journals and periodicals are essential for effective practitioners. Peer-reviewed journals report research findings. The writing style is scholarly, meaning it demands systematic inquiry with unbiased analysis and conclusions. It can be daunting for nonresearchers to read these journals, but you get a firsthand report of the information because the articles are written by the researchers. The articles are approved through a process called blind peer review. That means the reviewer is an acknowledged professional in that field and does not know who wrote the article they are reviewing. This review process strengthens the quality of the accepted articles because subjective favoritism is removed. Periodicals, on the other hand, are written for field practitioners. They are easier to understand but they are interpretations of research rather than direct reports from researchers. Periodicals contain a broader spectrum of articles than journals. They may include curricula or case studies of specific outdoor programs, for example.

Reading a blend of journal articles and periodicals will give you breadth and depth as an outdoor educator. Appendix A lists several outdoor education journals and periodicals. This list is not inclusive, but it will provide a strong foundation from which to begin building your library.

Moving Forward in Outdoor Education

This is a bright time for the field of outdoor education. The need for educating people about their relationship to the world has never been greater. Opportunities exist for outdoor educators in many different employment areas. Through research we are beginning to understand effective ways to help people develop environmental literacy, and through assessment we are measuring the direct effects of our programs. There is much work to be done, but the road we are traveling is becoming clear.

State standards and high-stakes testing are an issue in formal education. Outdoor education can provide a valuable context for learning standards. Students will achieve greater success on tests because of the inherent qualities of learning outdoors as well as the experiential teaching techniques commonly used in outdoor education. Be aware of how your curriculum reinforces standards without compromising the experience of learning outdoors. Environmental education standards have been or are being developed by many states in the United States.

As the field of outdoor education becomes more refined, the question of certification continues to resurface. Outdoor educators should be able to provide a certain level of skill, knowledge, and professionalism to their clients. Certification is one approach to managing those competencies, but it is a complex topic with ramifications beyond simply increasing effectiveness in the field.

The line between education and advocacy has never been completely clear. But as pressures mount to solve environmental or societal crises, it is imperative that outdoor educators honor the second half of their title: educators. The Latin root of education is *educere*, which means to draw forth or to lead out. Education is a process of drawing forth from students, not telling them what to think or what to do. Issues analysis provides an effective means to draw students out to explore contentious and vital environmental issues from a truly educational perspective.

As you gain experience, pilot your professional trajectory with a personal strategic plan for your career. Through this regular, thoughtful, reflective process you can guide your growth and learning to build the life you want.

> *For the whole earth is the sepulcher of famous men; and their story is not graven only on stone over their native earth but lives on far away, without visible symbol, woven into the stuff of other men's lives.*
>
> —Pericles (ca. 500 b.c.e.)

The desire to have a positive influence on the lives of others is the desire for immortality. As educators and scholars, we may never be the authors of the next revolution in human thinking. We may, however, plant a seed in a fertile mind. That seed may blossom into a notion, which grows into an idea. The ideas endure. You can maximize your influence by continuing your journey as a student of outdoor education throughout your career and by practicing your craft deliberately and carefully.

Explore Your World

1. Discuss your plans to stay professionally current.

2. What two professional organizations most pertain to your interests in outdoor education?

3. Describe how they help to keep you informed.

4. Write your goals for how you want to be as a professional 5 years from now.

5. Describe how you will know you have achieved your goals. Write them down.

Appendix A

PROFESSIONAL ORGANIZATIONS IN THE UNITED STATES

The following is a list of organizations that guide the practices and standards of outdoor education. We have included the national organizations to direct you to the parent agencies. From there you can easily find information on organizations in your area.

- Association for Experiential Education
  www.aee.org
- National Association for Interpretation
  www.interpnet.org
- North American Association for Environmental Education
  www.naaee.org
- Association of Outdoor Recreation and Education
  www.aore.org
- National Recreation and Park Association
  www.nrpa.org
- American Alliance for Health, Physical Education, Recreation and Dance
  www.aahperd.org
- National Science Teachers Association
  www.nsta.org
- National Intramural and Recreational Sports Association
  www.nirsa.org

Organizations Determining Industry Standards

- American Camp Association
  www.acacamps.org
- American Canoe Association
  www.acanet.org
- Professional Ski Instructors of America
  www.psia.org
- Association for Experiential Education
  www.aee.org
- American Mountain Guides Association
  www.amga.com
- American Red Cross
  www.redcross.org

- National Association for Interpretation
  www.interpnet.org
- Wilderness Medical Associates
  www.wildmed.com
- Wilderness Medicine Institute
  www.nols.edu/wmi
- Stonehearth Open Learning Opportunities
  www.soloschools.com
- National Outdoor Leadership School
  www.nols.edu
- Outward Bound USA
  www.outwardbound.com
- Boy Scouts of America
  www.scouting.org
- Girl Scouts of the USA
  www.girlscouts.org
- Association for Challenge Course Technology
  www.acctinfo.org
- Project Adventure
  www.pa.org
- YMCA
  www.ymca.net
- Professional Association of Diving Instructors
  www.padi.com
- US Sailing
  www.sailingcourse.com
- Leave No Trace Center for Outdoor Ethics
  www.lnt.org

Additional Resources

- OutdoorEd.com
  www.outdoored.com
- Outdoor Education Research and Evaluation Center
  www.wilderdom.com/research.html
- Environmental Education and Training Partnership
  http://eetap.org

Journals and Magazines

- *Applied Environmental Education and Communication*
- *Canadian Journal of Environmental Education*
- *Environmental Education Research*
- *GreenTeacher Magazine*
- *Journal of Adventure Education and Outdoor Learning*
- *Journal of Interpretive Research*
- *Journal of Environmental Education*
- *Journal of Experiential Education*
- *Journal of Physical Education and Recreation*
- *Journal of Science Education*
- *Research Connections*

SAMPLE FORMS

The forms in this appendix are presented as examples. Adapt them as needed for your specific situation.

Pretrip Questionnaire

Adapted from Yosemite Institute, Yosemite, CA.

We're delighted you've chosen us for your outdoor education experience. Please help our teaching and programming staff prepare the highest quality program for your group by thoughtfully completing this form and returning it at least 4 weeks prior to arrival.

Demographic Information

Group coordinator or lead teacher _____

Address _____

Day phone (_____) _____

Total youths attending: _____ (Female) _____ (Male) _____ # of returning youths

Total adults attending: _____ (Female) _____ (Male) _____ # of returning adults

Grade in school: _____

Please describe the demographics of your group (by percentage).

_____% African American _____% American Indian _____% Asian-Pacific Islander

_____% Caucasian _____% Hispanic/Latino _____% Other _____

What percent of your group speaks English as a second language? _____

Describe any pertinent cultural, ethnic, or religious identities of your group. _____

_____

Academic Information

Educational philosophy: Describe the educational philosophy of your school or group. _____

_____

_____

Home community: Briefly describe your group's home community environment. _____

_____

Learning outcomes: Describe the most important learning outcomes for your group during their experience with us. Include any state educational standards.

Academic: _____

_____

Social: _____

_____

Physical: _____

_____

Other: _____

_____

 From Ken Gilbertson, Timothy Bates, Terry McLaughlin, and Alan Ewert, 2006, *Outdoor Education: Methods and Strategies*, Champaign, IL: Human Kinetics.

Pretrip work: Outline the topics your students have been studying in preparation for their experience. Have you used the pretrip curriculum on our Web site? Include physical and social preparedness.

Science: _____

_____

Language arts: _____

_____

Social studies: _____

_____

Other: _____

_____

In what ways can our educators support your assignments? _____

_____

_____

_____

_____

Is there any reason why your group might be unable to participate in a service-learning project? _____

_____

_____

_____

_____

Is there anything else we should know about your group to prepare for your experience with us? _____

_____

_____

_____

_____

Behavioral expectations: What disciplinary actions do you have planned for student misbehavior? Should a problem arise, how can we best support you in implementing your disciplinary actions? _____

_____

_____

_____

_____

"When we try to pick out anything by itself, we find it hitched to everything in the Universe."

—John Muir

Confidential Health Form

This form is essential for your safety and enjoyment of your program. Please take time to fill it out completely and accurately. Please return promptly to the address above.

Course name: _____ Course date(s): _____

Name: _____ Male/Female Date of birth: _____

Address: _____
                Street   City   State   Zip

Phone: Home (_____)_____ Work (_____)_____

In case of emergency, notify: _____

Relationship: _____ Phone: (_____)_____

Health insurance company: _____ Policy #: _____

Medical History

Allergies

Are you allergic to any of the following? (Indicate if yes)

Insects _____

Foods _____

Medication (e.g., penicillin, aspirin, sulfa drugs) _____

Environmental _____

Other _____

If yes to any of the above, please describe your allergic reaction and how you treat it._____

_____

_____

Diet

Do you require a special diet? If yes, please explain._____

_____

_____

Tetanus

Date of your last tetanus shot: _____

Habits

Are you a regular user of caffeine, tobacco, alcohol, or recreational drugs? Please explain. _____

_____

_____

History

Do you have a history of any of the following (indicate if yes):

___ heart conditions	___ breathing conditions (including asthma)
___ seizures	___ diabetes
___ abnormal blood pressure	___ back problems
___ stomach problems	___ vision problems (including glasses or contacts)
___ knee or other joint problems	___ corrective brace or device
___ hearing problems	___ are you pregnant?
___ arthritis	___ migraines
___ Raynaud's Syndrome	___ dizziness
___ frostbite	___ poor circulation
___ hypothermia	___ toothaches
___ past surgery	___ periods of unconsciousness

If yes to any of the conditions, have you been treated? Explain._____

_____

Have you taken or do you presently take any medications on a regular basis? If yes, describe. _____

_____

Is there anything else that we should know about you (e.g., phobias, special needs, sensitivities)?_____

_____

I have read and understand this form's contents completely and have answered the questions accurately.

I believe that I/participant am in good physical condition and that I/participant can participate fully in scheduled activities.

The staff of the UMD Recreational Sports Outdoor Program has my authorization to review and retain this form as protected health information for the purposes of the above program. The staff of the UMD Recreational Sports Outdoor Program has my permission to seek and/or administer emergency care for the participant in the event that the participant or guardian cannot respond at the time of emergency and has authorization to provide this form to health care personnel for the purposes of the participant's emergency treatment in that event. I understand that UMD Recreational Sports Outdoor Program is not responsible for any charges for such health care services provided to the participant.

I understand that I have the right to revoke, in writing, this authorization at any time; however, this authorization will automatically expire at the end of the program. I am aware that my revocation is not effective to the extent that the persons I have authorized to use and/or disclose the participant's protected health information have acted in reliance upon this authorization. Further, I understand that, if a participant's protected health information is disclosed to someone who is not required to comply with the federal privacy protection regulations, then such information may be redisclosed and would no longer be protected.

Date _____ Signature of participant _____

Date _____ Signature of parent/guardian_____
(if participant is under age 18)

Outdoor Activity Evaluation

Please provide your thoughts and feelings to help us improve and develop future programs. Your feedback is greatly appreciated.

Activity name: _____

Instructor(s): _____

Did you receive adequate information before the activity?

If not, what was missing?

What did you like about this activity?

How can we improve it?

How can the instructor(s) improve?

What would you tell someone about this course?

 From Ken Gilbertson, Timothy Bates, Terry McLaughlin, and Alan Ewert, 2006, *Outdoor Education: Methods and Strategies,* Champaign, IL: Human Kinetics.

Decision Making
Using Diamond Method

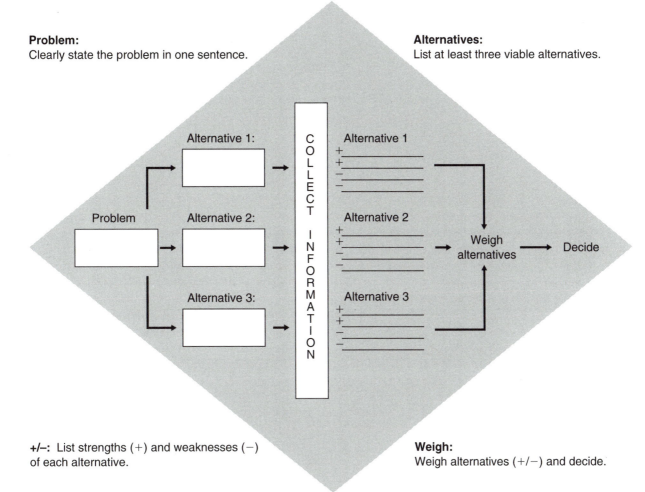

Problem:
Clearly state the problem in one sentence.

Alternatives:
List at least three viable alternatives.

+/–: List strengths (+) and weaknesses (−) of each alternative.

Weigh:
Weigh alternatives (+/−) and decide.

Once you decide, reflect on your decision-making process.
List the things you learned throughout this process that may help you make sound decisions next time.

From Ken Gilbertson, Timothy Bates, Terry McLaughlin, and Alan Ewert, 2006, *Outdoor Education: Methods and Strategies*, Champaign, IL: Human Kinetics.

Professional Strategic Planning Sheet

Date _____

Goal _____

Objectives

   1. _____

   2. _____

   3. _____

Steps

   1. _____

   2. _____

   3. _____

   4. _____

   5. _____

   6. _____

   7. _____

   8. _____

   9. _____

  10. _____

Time frame _____

Assessment (How will you know you've completed your objective?)

Objective 1.

_____

Objective 2.

_____

Objective 3.

_____

Underlying values and attitudes

_____

_____

GLOSSARY

actual risk—Real risk present in an outdoor experience.

adaptive programming—Changing programming to meet participants' physical, mental, and social levels of function.

adventure education—Education that is conducted in a wilderness-like setting or through nature and physical skills development to promote interpersonal growth or enhance physical skills in outdoor pursuits.

affective learning—Learning through emotions.

attention deficit/hyperactivity disorder (ADHD)—Condition affecting children and adults that is characterized by problems with attention, impulsiveness, and overactivity.

cognitive development theory—Cognitive thought develops in four ordered states influenced by age and experience; developed by J. Piaget.

cognitive methods—Teaching methods that focus on knowledge.

concept map—Diagram that shows relationships between a main concept and subconcepts and facts.

constructivism—Educational theory that builds upon students' prior knowledge and experience to help them to construct new learning.

control site—Site protected from weather and distractions where lessons should begin and conclude.

describe, demonstrate, do—One sequence for structuring a teaching topic.

developmental theories—Theories that explain the stages of development a person goes through. Such theories include constructivism, developmental stages of environmental learning, and personal meaning.

environmental education—Learning about the natural world and associated human influences.

environmental literacy—Ability to move comfortably in the outdoors and understand natural as well as human interactions.

environmentally responsible citizenry—People who have developed environmental literacy and as a result are environmentally responsible.

experiential connection—Learning connection in which students further their understanding of a real-life example by living it.

experiential education—Education through direct experience. For example, in outdoor education, experiential education involves learning about the outdoors by being directly outdoors and experiencing the topic at hand.

flow—A sense of oneness or harmony that exists when a person has become familiar with their surroundings and when their skills, knowledge, and experience are integrated with the place they are in.

formal education—Education that occurs within an organized school system.

formative assessment—Assessment conducted during a lesson while ideas are still forming.

framing—Repeating an activity at the beginning and at the end of a course.

GAME FACe—Seven key variables to consider when assessing an audience, including gender, age, medical conditions, experience, familiarity of group members, abilities, and culture and ethnicity.

guided discovery—Affective teaching method where the instructor establishes guidelines for solving a problem or completing a task and then guides the students as they attempt to solve the problem or complete the task.

humanistic approach—An approach to education in which feelings and knowledge are important. Cognitive and affective impacts on the student are main considerations in humanistic education.

individualized education plan (IEP)—Program for students with special needs that guides their strategies, treatment, and progress in the classroom.

informal education—Education that is entirely determined and controlled by the student.

initiative—Short activity where participants work together to accomplish an assigned task that requires problem solving and teamwork.

inquiry—The use of exploration and questioning to arrive at a conclusion.

instructor judgment approach—Approach to risk management and decision making where a program relies on the instructors to make effective decisions based on their personal judgment.

interpersonal growth—An increase in one's understanding of how one interacts with others.

interpretation—Transference of natural or cultural history through an educational presentation to the general public.

journaling—The act of recording thoughts and learning progress on paper, preferably in a small book. Journaling can be personal and reflective; be directed and structured by the outdoor educator; and include words, drawings, poetry, and general impressions.

kinesthetic method—Teaching method that focuses on physical learning and body movement.

learning disorder (LD)—Umbrella term covering a vast range of conditions involving learning ability, such as language processing difficulties, difficulties in social interactions, and lack of physical coordination.

learning styles—Manner in which a person learns something.

learning theory—Theory of how an individual or group of people learn. Learning theories include experiential education, multiple intelligences, and learning styles.

lesson plan—An organized outline of a day's teaching plan, including goal, objectives, assessment strategy related to objectives, materials needed, activity description, and relation to state learning standards.

motivation—A student's intent to learn.

narrative connection—Learning connection that consists of stories about a place.

nonformal education—Structured education that takes place outside of a formal school building, usually in a nature-based area.

numinous connection—Learning connection that links students with a particular place through a spiritual bond.

objective hazards—Aspects of the learning environment that can't be controlled, such as the weather, remoteness, popularity, and physical structure of a site.

outdoor education—Learning in and through the natural world.

perceived risk—Risk or harm participants believe is present.

performance triad—Model for helping students perform and learn in the outdoors that is based on hydration, nutrition, and pacing.

physical learning—Learning through physical development, such as the skills of rock climbing. In outdoor education, physical learning is associated with or in the natural environment.

physical manipulation—Moving a student's body into the proper position so that the muscles can begin to memorize a new motion.

policy guidelines approach—Approach to risk management and decision making where programs rely on written policies.

professionalism—The conduct, aims, or qualities that characterize a profession, such as outdoor education, or a professional person, such as an outdoor educator.

progression—Definition to be added by authors at pages. Definition to be added by authors at pages. Definition to be added by authors at pages.

rapport—Harmonious relationship with students.

reflection—Quiet thoughtfulness following activities and experiences. The goal of reflection is to allow the individual to distill meaning from the activity. That meaning can then be applied to new learning situations.

risk management—The process before, during, and after a program that strives to reduce the likelihood of accidents and health-related incidents.

ropes courses—A set or series of obstacles that create a challenge to help develop personal growth, teamwork, or group cohesiveness. Often referred to as low ropes or high ropes courses.

rubric—Grid of essential behaviors, knowledge, and skills necessary for mastery of a topic or skill.

scaffolding—Constructivist concept of adjusting curriculum as students develop.

sequencing—Definition to be added by authors at pages. Definition to be added by authors at pages. Definition to be added by authors at pages.

service learning—Doing a meaningful project that has direct use and application to the land or community.

social development theory—The theory that social interaction profoundly influences cognitive development; developed by L.S. Vygotsky.

subjective hazards—Aspects of the learning environment that can be controlled, such as leader and student behavior, gear, and training.

summative assessment—Assessment conducted at the end of a lesson.

theory—An explanation of a pattern of behavior that is consistent and reliable.

theory of multiple intelligences—Theory that there are eight different types of intelligence; developed by H. Gardner.

theory of personal meaning—Theory that learning must derive from the learner making meaning of what is being taught.

toponymic connections—Learning connections that involve the names of places and topographical features.

videography—The use of video to develop skills or demonstrate simulations.

visual imagery (VI)—Mental rehearsal of an event, program, or action.

whole–part–whole—A sequence of teaching complex skills.

wilderness setting—A remote outdoor setting that has minimal human influences such as roads, shelters, or services.

zone of proximal development (ZPD)—The zone between a person's ability to problem solve independently and with guidance; introduced by L.S. Vygotsky.

BIBLIOGRAPHY

Addison-Jacobson, J., and M. Batenburg. 1996. *Service learning: Transforming education.* Guidebook and video. San Francisco: Linking San Francisco.

Ajango, D. 2000. *Lessons learned: A guide to accident prevention and crisis response.* Anchorage, AK: University of Alaska.

Alexander Graham Bell Association for the Deaf and Hard of Hearing. 2003. www.agbell.org (accessed February 2005).

Anderson, A. 1999. *Service learning.* Duluth, MN: Stowe Elementary School, I.S.D. #709.

Association of Experiential Education (AEE). 2003. Definition of experiential education. www.aee.org/ndef.html (accessed February 2005).

Ausubel, D.P, J.D. Novak, and H. Hanesian. 1978. *Educational psychology: A cognitive view.* 2nd ed. New York: Holt, Rinehart, and Winston.

Beard, C., and J.P. Wilson. 2002. *The power of experiential learning: A handbook for trainers and educators.* London: Kogan Page Ltd.

Brannan, S. 2003. Outdoor programs and persons with disabilities. In *Including youth with disabilities in outdoor programs,* ed. S. Brannan, A. Fullerton, J. Arick, G.M. Robb, and M. Bender, 3-18. Champaign, IL: Sagamore.

Brannan, S., A. Fullerton, J. Arick, G.M. Robb, and M. Bender. 2003. *Including youth with disabilities in outdoor programs.* Champaign, IL: Sagamore.

Burns, B., and M. Burns. 1999. *Wilderness navigation: Finding your way using map, compass, altimeter and GPS.* Seattle, WA: The Mountaineers.

Caduto, M., and J. Bruchac. 1988. *Keepers of the earth: Native American stories and environmental activities for children.* Golden, CO: Fulcrum.

Caduto, M., and J. Bruchac. 1994a. *Keepers of life: Discovering plants through Native American stories and earth activities for children.* Golden, CO: Fulcrum.

Caduto, M., and J. Bruchac. 1994b. *Keepers of the night: Native American stories and nocturnal activities for children.* Golden, CO: Fulcrum.

Cahill, T. 2003. *Sailing the wine-dark sea.* New York: Anchor Books.

Cain, K.D., and L.H. McAvoy. 1990. Experience-based judgment. In *Adventure education,* ed. J.C. Miles and S. Priest, 241-249. State College, PA: Venture.

Carlson, R.E. 1980. Contributions of Julian W. Smith. In *Fifty years of resident outdoor education: 1930-1980,* ed. W.M. Hammerman, 29-36. Martinsville, IN: American Camping Association.

Carlson, R.S. 2000. Using a videotape feedback package to improve sea kayak skills. Thesis. University of Minnesota, Duluth.

Csikszentmihalyi, M. 1975. *Beyond boredom and anxiety.* San Francisco: Jossey-Bass.

Day, J., and V. Schaefer. 1991. *Clouds and weather.* Boston: Houghton Mifflin.

Dewey, J. 1938. *Experience and education.* New York: Touchstone.

Discover. 1988. Mouth lightning. December.

Donaldson, G.W., and L.E. Donaldson. 1968. *In outdoor education: A book of readings.* Minneapolis: Burgess.

Eagle Bluff ELC. 1997. *Night hike ideas; lesson plan.* Lanesboro, MN.

Edwards, R., J.M. Honeycutt, and K.S. Zagacki. 1988. Imagined interaction as an element of social cognition. *Western Journal of Speech Communication* 52:23-45.

Engleson, D., and D. Yockers. 1985. *A guide to curriculum planning in environmental education.* Bulletin #6094. Madison, WI: Wisconsin Department of Public Instruction.

Ewert, A. 1989. *Outdoor adventure pursuits: Foundations, models, and theories.* Scottsdale, AZ: Publishing Horizons.

Ewert, A. 1990. Wildland resource values: A struggle for balance. *Society and Natural Resources* 3:385-393.

Ewert, A.W., and S. Galloway. 2002. Using video simulation in training for decision-making. In *Proceedings of the 2002 Wilderness Risk Management Conference*, 39-44. Lander, WY: NOLS.

Fluegelman, A., ed. 1976. *The new games book.* New York: Doubleday.

Ford, P., and J. Blanchard. 1993. *Leadership and administration of outdoor pursuits.* State College, PA: Venture.

Gage, N., and D. Berliner. 1992. *Educational psychology.* 5th ed. Princeton, NJ: Houghton Mifflin.

Gair, N.P. 1997. *Outdoor education: Theory and practice.* London: Cassell.

Gardner, H. 1983. *Frames of mind: The theory of multiple intelligences.* New York: Basic Books.

Gibbons, B., and L. Psihoyos. 1986. The intimate sense of smell. *National Geographic* 170(3):324-362.

Hammerman, D.R., W.M. Hammerman, and E.L. Hammerman. 2001. *Teaching in the outdoors.* Danville, IL: Interstate.

Hammerman, W.M., ed. 1980. *Fifty years of resident outdoor education: 1930-1980.* Martinsville, IN: American Camping Association.

Hines, J., H. Hungerford, and A. Tomera. 1986/87. Analysis and synthesis of research on responsible environmental behavior: A meta-analysis. *The Journal of Environmental Education* 182:1-8.

Hungerford, H.R. 2001. The myths of environmental education, revisited. In *Essential readings in environmental education.* 2nd ed. The Center for Instruction, Staff Development and Evaluation. Champaign, IL: Stipes.

Hunter, M. 1982. *Mastery teaching.* Thousand Oaks, CA: Corwin Press.

Jensen, E. 2000. *Brain-based learning: The new science of teaching and training.* San Diego: Brainstore.

Kaplan, R., and S. Kaplan. 1989. *The experience of nature: A psychological perspective.* Cambridge: Cambridge University Press.

Kerlinger, F. 1986. *Foundations of behavioral research.* 3rd ed. New York: Holt, Rinehart and Winston.

Kindsvatter, R., W. Wilen, and M. Ishler. 1996. *Dynamics of effective teaching.* 3rd ed. White Plains, NY: Longmen.

Kirk, M., R. Wilke, and A. Ruskey. 2001. A survey of the status of state-level environmental education in the U.S. In *Essential readings in environmental educa-tion,* 2nd ed. The Center for Instruction, Staff Development and Evaluation. Champaign, IL: Stipes.

Kjellström, B. 1994. *Be expert with map and compass: The complete orienteering handbook.* New York: Collier Books.

Klein, G.A. 1989. Strategies of decision-making. *Military Review,* May, 56-64.

Knapp, D. 2001. Environmental education and environmental interpretation: The relationships. In *Essential readings in environmental education,* 2nd ed., 325-332. Champaign, IL: Stipes.

Kolb, D.A. 1984. *Experiential learning.* Englewood Cliffs, NJ: Prentice-Hall.

Leave No Trace. 2004. www.LNT.org (accessed February 2005).

Leemon, D., and K. Merrill. 2002. *Adventure program risk management report.* Vol. III. Lander, WY: NOLS.

Levine, M. 2002. *Educational care: A system for understanding and helping children with learning differences at home and in school.* 2nd ed. Cambridge: Educators Publishing Service.

Lieberman, G.A., and L.L. Hoody. 1998. *Closing the achievement gap.* Poway, CA: Science Wizards.

Luckner, J.L., and R.S. Nadler. 1997. *Processing the experience: Strategies to enhance and generalize learning.* Dubuque, IA: Kendall/Hunt.

Maslow, A. 1986. *Religions, values, and peak experiences.* New York: Penguin.

Medema, T. 2005. Personal communication.

Moran, J., and M. Morgan. 1994. *Meteorology. The atmosphere and the science of weather.* Old Tappen, NJ: Prentice Hall.

National Environmental Education and Training Foundation (NEETF). 2004. The EE-Works. www.theeeworks.org (accessed February 2005).

National Project for Excellence in Environmental Education. 2000. *Guidelines for the preparation and professional development of environmental educators.* Rock Springs, GA: North American Association for Environmental Education.

National Resource Center on AD/HD. 2003. www.chadd.org (accessed February 2005).

Nearing, H., and S. Nearing. 1970. *The maple sugar book.* New York: Schocken Books.

North American Association for Environmental Education. 2000. *Excellence in environmental education: Guidelines for learning (K-12).* Rock Springs, GA: North American Association for Environmental Education.

Novick, A. 1973. Bats aren't all bad. *National Geographic* 143(5):614-636.

Olson, S. 1984. *Reflections from the north country.* New York: Alfred Knopf.

Osorio, R.E. 2002. Establishing a national EE certification program. *NAAEE Communicator* 32(1):3.

Palmer, P. 1998. *The courage to teach.* San Francisco: Jossey-Bass.

Petzoldt, P. 1984. *The wilderness handbook.* New York: Norton.

Piaget, J. 1952. 1963. *The origins of intelligence in children.* New York: Norton.

Piaget, J. 2001. *The psychology of intelligence.* New York: Routledge.

Piaget, J., and B. Inhelder. 1969. *The psychology of the child.* New York: Basic Books.

Postlethwait, J. 1989. *The nature of life.* New York: McGraw Hill.

Priest, S. 1986. Redefining outdoor education: A matter of many relationships. *Journal of Environmental Education* 17(3):13-15.

Priest, S. 1990. The semantics of adventure education. In *Adventure education,* 113-117. State College, PA: Venture.

Priest, S., and M.A. Gass. 1999. *Effective leadership in adventure programming.* Champaign, IL: Human Kinetics.

Raffan, J. 1995. The experience of place: Exploring land as teacher. In *Experiential learning in schools and higher education,* ed. R.J. Kraft and J. Kielsmeier, 128-136. Dubuque, IA: Kendall/Hunt.

Rillo, T.J. 1980. Contributions of Lloyd B. Sharp. In *Fifty years of resident outdoor education: 1930-1980,* ed. W.M. Hammerman, 19-28. Martinsville, IN: American Camping Association.

Rohnke, K. 1989. *Cowstails and cobras II: A guide to games, initiatives, ropes courses, and adventure curriculum.* Dubuque, IA: Kendall/Hunt.

Rohnke, K. 1999. Ropes courses: A constructed adventure environment. In *Adventure programming,* ed. J.C. Miles and S. Priest, 347-352. State College, PA: Venture.

Roston, H. 1985. Valuing wildlands. *Environmental Ethics* 7(1):23-48.

Roth, R.E. 1969. Fundamental concepts for environmental management education (K-16). Doctoral dissertation. The Ohio State University, Columbus.

Rothenberg, P.S., N. Schafehausen, and C. Schneider. 2001. *Race, class and gender in the United States: An integrated study.* 5th ed. New York: Worth.

Sanera, M., and J.S. Shaw. 1996. *Facts not fear: Teaching children about the environment.* Washington, D.C.: Regnery.

Schlatter, B.L., and J.R. Rossman. 2003. Using visual imaging in recreation programming. *Journal of Physical Education, Recreation, and Dance* 743:44-47.

Sharp, L.B. 1947. Basic considerations in outdoor and camping education. *Bulletin of the National Association of Secondary School Principals* 31:43-47.

Smith, T.E. 1994. *Incidents in challenge education: A guide to leadership development.* Dubuque, IA: Kendall/Hunt.

Sousa, D.A. 2000. *How the brain learns.* 2nd ed. Thousand Oaks: Corwin Press.

Stapp, W.B. 1969. The concept of environmental education. *Environmental Education* 1(1):30-31.

Starr, C. 1992. *Biology: The unity and diversity of life.* Belmont, CA: Wadsworth.

Strauss, K. 2003. Lavinia's world. www.naturestory.com (accessed February 2005).

Tamir, P. 1990. Factors associated with the relationship between formal, informal, and non-formal science learning. *Journal of Environmental Education* 22(2):34-42.

Tatum, B.D. 1997. *Why are all the black kids sitting together in the cafeteria? And other conversations about race.* New York: Basic Books.

Tbilisi Declaration. 1947. www.epa.gov/enviroed/pdf/report.pdf (accessed February 2005).

Tilden, F. 1957. *Interpreting our heritage.* Chapel Hill, NC: University of North Carolina.

UNESCO. 1978. *Final report: Intergovernmental Conference on Environmental Education.* Tbilisi, USSR, 14-26 October 1977. Paris: United Nations.

U.S. Census Bureau. 2003. *Nearly 1 in 5 speak a foreign language at home; most also speak English very well.* Press release. Washington, D.C.: U.S. Department of Commerce.

U.S. Department of Education. 2000. *Twenty-second annual report to Congress.* Washington, D.C.: GPO.

U.S. Department of Education. National Commission on Excellence in Education. 1983. *A nation at risk.* Washington, D.C.: GPO.

U.S. Department of Education. Office of the Secretary, Office of Public Affairs. 2003. *No child left behind: A parent's guide.* Washington, D.C.: GPO.

U.S. Office of Science and Technology. 1997. *Climate change: State of knowledge.* Washington, D.C.: GPO.

Vogt, W.P. 1993. *Dictionary of statistics and methodology.* Newbury Park, CA: Sage.

Vygotsky, L.S. 1962. *Thought and language.* Cambridge, MA: MIT Press.

Vygotsky, L.S. 1980. *Mind in society.* Cambridge, MA: Harvard University Press.

Western Regional Environmental Education Council. 1992. *Project WILD.* Boulder, CO: Western Regional Environmental Education Council.

Williams, J. 1992. *The weather book.* New York: Vintage Books.

Women's College Coalition. 2003. Expect the best from a girl. www.academic.org (accessed February 2005).

Yates, F.J. 2001. Outsider: Impressions of naturalistic decision-making. In *Linking expertise and naturalistic decision-making,* ed. E. Salas and G. Klein, 9-34. Hillsdale, NJ: Erlbaum.

Yin, R.K. 1984. *Case study research: Design and methods.* Newbury Park, CA: Sage.

Cultural Literacy for Outdoor Educators

Chapelle, S., and L. Bigman. 1998. *Diversity in action: Using adventure activities to explore issues of diversity with middle and high school youth.* Hamilton, MA: Project Adventure.

Derman-Sparks, L., and C. Brunson Phillips. 1997. *Teaching/learning anti-racism: A developmental approach.* New York: Teachers College Press.

Gay, G. 2000. *Culturally responsive teaching: Theory, research, and practice.* New York: Teachers College Press.

Ladson-Billings, G. 1994. *The dreamkeepers: Successful teachers of African American children.* New York: Jossey-Bass.

Madfes, T.J. 2004. *What's fair got to do with it? Diversity cases from environmental educators.* San Francisco: West Ed.

Villegas, A.M., and T. Lucas. 2002. *Educating culturally responsive teachers: A coherent approach.* Albany, NY: State University of New York Press.

Culturally and Ethnically Representative Resources

Miller-Lachman, L., ed. 1992. *Our family, our friends, our world: An annotated guide to significant multicultural books for children and teenagers.* New Providence, NJ: R.R. Bowker.

Slapin, B., and D. Seale. 1987. *Through Indian eyes: The native experience in books for children.* Philadelphia: New Society.

Learning Disabilities and Attention Disorders

All Kinds of Minds. Understanding differences in learning. www.allkindsofminds.org (accessed February 2005).

How Difficult Can This Be? The F.A.T City Workshop. 1989. The Learning Project at WETA. Videocassette.

Resources for Initiative Activities and Ropes Courses

Cain, J., and B. Jolliff. 1998. *Teamwork and teamplay: A guide to cooperative, challenge, and adventure activities that build confidence, cooperation, teamwork, creativity, trust, decision making, conflict resolution, resource management, communication, effective feedback, and problem solving skills.* Dubuque, IA: Kendall/Hunt.

Fluegelman, A., ed. 1976. *The new games book.* San Francisco: Headlands Press.

Fluegelman, A., ed. 1981. *More new games.* San Francisco: Headlands Press.

Meier, J.F., and A.V. Mitchell. 2003. *Camp counseling: Leadership and programming for the organized camp.* 7th ed. Long Grove, IL: Waveland Press.

Rohnke, K. 1989. *Cowstails and cobras II: A guide to games, initiatives, ropes courses, and adventure curriculum.* Dubuque, IA: Kendall/Hunt.

Storytelling Resources

Web sites

www.naturestory.com—A good resource for stories; has a storytelling newsletter and other storytelling resources and links.

www.storyarts.org—Lists curriculum ideas and explanations of how stories relate to specific disciplines such as science, social studies, and so on; includes stories from diverse cultures.

www.storynet.org—Professional storytellers' Web site listing conferences, festivals, guilds, professional storytellers, and resources.

Books

Cassady, M. 1990. *Storytelling, step by step*. San Jose, CA: Resource Publications.

Lipman, D. 1995. *The storytelling coach: How to listen, praise, and bring out people's best*. Little Rock, AR: August House Publications.

INDEX

Note: Page numbers followed by an italicized *t* indicate that there is a table on that page.

ABOUT THE AUTHORS

Ken Gilbertson, PhD, is an associate professor of outdoor education in the department of health, physical education, and recreation, at the University of Minnesota Duluth (UMD), where he is also director of the Center for Environmental Education. He has 30 years of experience teaching outdoor and environmental education at the college level and has taught at nature centers, conducted wilderness education, taught at Outward Bound Schools, and educated a wide range of audiences through the UMD Outdoor Program. Gilbertson's specialty is in understanding how people learn and applying the methods that will best help them learn about the outdoors. He has designed and constructed a wilderness education curriculum, including a state-of-the-art kit applying several learning theories. Gilbertson has received two outstanding faculty awards, has a UMD leadership scholarship in his name, and is a board member of numerous outdoor education and environmental committees. He also serves as reviewer for the *Journal of Experiential Education* and of abstracts for the Symposium on Experiential Education Research.

Tim Bates, MEd, is the associate director of the Recreational Sports Outdoor Program, an adjunct faculty member, the coordinator of environmental education, and assistant director of the Center for Environmental Education at the University of Minnesota Duluth. He is certified by the American Canoe Association as an instructor trainer educator of coastal kayaking and is a wilderness first responder from Wilderness Medical Associates. Bates has more than 20 years of experience teaching outdoor, environmental, and science education to people of all ages. In addition to developing curricula for schools and other organizations, he has been involved with the creation of an elementary school focused on environmental education and serves on numerous boards and committees related to the outdoors. His specialty

is working with preservice students to help them understand the natural environment; those students then teach this knowledge to others.

Terry McLaughlin, MS, is a freelance environmental educator working in the Sierra Nevada Mountains in California. With more than 20 years of experience, she has worked in nature centers, with school districts, and in residential outdoor education programs. McLaughlin's specialty is training outdoor educators to teach. She has taught her creative and innovative methods to graduate students in environmental education. Her methods involve many of the strategies employed in this book. McLaughlin has served on state and local environmental education boards and has served in an advisory capacity for environmental education centers.

Alan Ewert, PhD, is a distinguished and titled professor at Indiana University. He holds the Patricia and Joel Meier Endowed Chair in Outdoor Leadership and serves as the editor of the *Journal of Experiential Education.* He was the 1996 recipient of the Reynold E. Carlson Award for Distinction in Outdoor Environmental Education; the

2002 recipient of the J.B. Nash Scholar Award through the American Association for Leisure and Recreation; and the 2005 recipient of the Julian W. Smith Award through the Alliance for Health, Physical Education, Recreation and Dance. A prolific scholar, Ewert has published articles in a variety of journals and books related to outdoor leadership and recreation. He continues his professional service through numerous venues, including his status as a fellow and past president of the Academy of Leisure Sciences and one of the founding editors of the *International Journal of Wilderness.* Dr. Ewert also serves as a course director and instructor for Outward Bound and the Wilderness Education Association.